WITHDRAWN

# WOOLF
# AND
# LESSING

# WOOLF
# AND
# LESSING

## Breaking the Mold

Edited by
Ruth Saxton and Jean Tobin

St. Martin's Press
New York

The lines of poetry on pp. 148 and 177 are taken from the poem "A Lesson in Floating," by Hilda Morley, in *A Blessing Outside Us* (Providence, R.I.: Pourboire, 1979) and are reprinted by permission of the author.

First published in the United States of America in 1994

Printed in the United States of America
Design by Acme Art, Inc., New York, NY

ISBN 0-312-12051-6

Library of Congress Cataloging-in-Publication Data

Woolf and Lessing : breaking the mold / edited by Ruth Saxton and Jean
    Tobin.
        p.   cm.
    Includes bibliographical references (p. ) and index.
    ISBN 0-312-12051-6
    1. English fiction—Women authors—History and criticism.
2. Women and literature—Great Britain—History—20th century.
3. English fiction—20th century—History and criticism.   4. Woolf,
Virginia, 1882-1941—Criticism and interpretation.   5. Lessing,
Doris, 1919-     —Criticism and interpretation.   I. Saxton, Ruth.
II. Tobin, Jean.
PR888.W6W66   1994
823'.91099287—dc20                                              94-15015
                                                                CIP

*For*
*Kirsten T. Saxton and Dorothy Winchester*

# CONTENTS

## Part I: Constitution of a Female Subject

## Part II: Redefining Roles and Relationships

## Part III: Creativity, Consciousness, and the Privileged Mind

# PREFACE

While scholarship on Virginia Woolf and Doris Lessing individually has grown in recent years, this is the first collection of essays to examine together these two great writers of the twentieth century. A number of contributors speak of influence, including Sprague, Sizemore, and Tobin, but most speak of affinities. In addition to the groupings suggested by our section titles, there are other resonances between essays. For example, Rubenstein and Michael both discuss Woolf and Lessing in terms of modernism and postmodernism. Michael, Sizemore, and Sprague explore the fragmentation of identity. Tobin, Chown, Rubenstein, and Saxton examine issues in creativity, consciousness, and the privileged mind. Rubenstein, Saxton, and Tyler discuss the ever-changing and vexed configuration of female development and relations. Perhaps because our subtitle is focused on rebellion and innovation, the essayists in writing their articles also focused on ways Virginia Woolf and Doris Lessing have refused to follow established patterns and have relied on their own experiences to make something new. Thus the articles have generated a good deal of excitement for all of us, and we hope that for our readers too, the collection will prove to be generative. We think of not only this preface, but our book, as a beginning.

*Ruth Saxton and Jean Tobin*
*March 21, 1994*

## ACKNOWLEDGMENTS

### Together

This collection of essays originated with Jo Glorie, and we would like especially to thank her for her practical expertise and warm encouragement. We'd like to thank Peter Coveney for his enthusiasm for the project along the way, and Wendy Williams and Jennifer Armstrong for their energy as the project came to conclusion. Our thanks to all the contributors in this volume, who met deadlines both promptly and courteously, and special thanks to Claire Sprague for helpful advice. Together we have a multitude of students to thank for enjoyable hours over the years, but special thanks go to those members of the Mills College Virginia Woolf seminar who read copy with yellow highlighting markers in hand. We consider ourselves fortunate that our editor at St. Martin's Press has been Laura Heymann and thank her for her amiable calm, patience, and ability to make problems seemingly disappear.

Additionally, we would like to thank members of the Virginia Woolf Society and of the Doris Lessing Society for the stimulation of their conversation and their pleasant collegiality.

### Ruth Saxton

Women have served for me as looking glasses for the twenty years that I have taught at Mills College, with the marvelous and delicious propensity to reflect me at natural size, questioning my assumptions, and regularly pointing out that spot the size of a shilling on the back of my head. Within that collegial conversation, I have developed courage and a sense of collaboration. Women who believed in my scholarship before I did include Imogene Walker, Libby Pope, Roussel Sargent, and Diana O Hehir. A spring 1993 sabbatical leave provided time in which to think and write. President Jan McKay, Provost Faith Gabelnick, and Dean of Letters Christian Marouby recognized the importance of this book in allowing me to extend my sabbatical throughout the summer and assume my dean responsibilities in August instead of the more customary June. David Hartmann in the campus computer center helped translate disks and demystify technology, and Yvonne Marcelis provided excellent secretarial support.

Deirdre Lashgari, Jean Tobin, and Wendy Williams all read drafts of my essay, responding honestly and with kindness, and Kirsten Saxton helped fatten the little fish of my idea with her insightful comments until I dared to haul it in.

Family and friends did more of what they always do—listening, shoring up the foundations of daily life in the final push, believing in me. Katherine Saxton was my resident computer whiz; Paul and David Saxton helped with family logistics; and Karl Garcia, Robert Saxton, and Mom and Dad always assumed the book would see print. Thanks to everyone.

## Jean Tobin

Years ago, at the University of Wisconsin in Madison, Cyrena Pondrom and Annis Pratt shared with me their interest in Virginia Woolf and Doris Lessing, and I thank them for it. My present educational institution, the University of Wisconsin Centers, has generously given me both warm personal support and the practical support of two sabbaticals, a quarter released time in spring 1993, and a professional leave of absence. MaryAnn Yodelis Smith has believed in this and other projects and has given me strong backing. My thanks also go particularly to Kathy Glynn, Lee Grugel, Art Kaplan, Kathleen O'Connor, and Phil Zweifel for their help in this specific project, and more generally to all the members of my statewide department and colleagues on my local campus.

A portion of my essay "On Creativity" was written during a National Endowment for the Humanities 1993 Summer Seminar, and I am grateful to the NEH, to Cornell University, to Daniel R. Schwarz, and to my fellow participants in the seminar for their encouragement and timely support.

Carol Green and Mary Em Kirn are friends first of all, but their friendship has entered into my professional life and made it better. Hilda Morley, who has become a friend, graciously gave permission to quote from "A Lesson in Floating." John DiGaetani shared his considerable expertise in publishing; Noah Dixon, Dick Jarosch, and Al Kaeppel shared their expertise in computers. Roberta Filicky-Peneski, Ruth Saxton, Dan Schwarz, and Jim Tobin all read my essay at various stages and gave detailed suggestions.

Further, my gratitude in large measure goes to my aunt Dorothy Winchester, not only for her interest in the progress of this book, but for a lifetime of sustaining love that has deepened with each year. Most of all, I thank Jim Tobin, whose gifts to me over the twenty-five years of our marriage have been immeasurable, but whose creation for me this year of the Tobin Fellowship—thus giving me an entire year off—in a most tangible way made my work on this collection of essays possible.

# LIST OF ABBREVIATIONS

## Works by Virginia Woolf

| | |
|---|---|
| CE | *Collected Essays* |
| Diary | *Diary of Virginia Woolf* |
| Letters | *The Letters of Virginia Woolf* |
| TL | *To the Lighthouse* |
| MB | *Moments of Being* |
| MD | *Mrs. Dalloway* |
| O | *Orlando: A Biography* |
| RF | *Roger Fry, A Biography* |
| ARO | *A Room of One's Own* |
| VO | *The Voyage Out* |
| TW | *The Waves* |
| AWD | *A Writer's Diary* |
| TY | *The Years* |

## Works by Doris Lessing

| | |
|---|---|
| AL | *African Laughter: Four Visits to Zimbabwe* |
| "AR" | "Among the Roses," *The Real Thing: Stories and Sketches* |
| BDH | *Briefing for a Descent into Hell* |
| DJS | *The Diaries of Jane Somers* |
| "DW" | "The De Wets Come to Kloof Grange," *African Stories* |
| FGC | *The Four-Gated City* |
| GN | *The Golden Notebook* |
| LL | *Landlocked* |
| MQ | *Martha Quest* |
| MS | *The Memoirs of a Survivor* |
| PM | *A Proper Marriage* |
| S | *Re: Colonised Planet 5: Shikasta* |
| SPV | *A Small Personal Voice* |
| SBD | *The Summer Before the Dark* |

# NOTES ON CONTRIBUTORS

Linda E. Chown, Assistant Professor of English at Grand Valley State University at Allendale, Michigan, is the author of *Narrative Authority and Homeostasis in The Novels of Doris Lessing and Carmen Martin Gaite* (1990).

Magali Cornier Michael, Assistant Professor of English, teaches at Duquesne University in Pittsburgh, Pennsylvania.

Roberta Rubenstein, Professor of Literature at American University, Washington, D.C., is the author of *The Novelistic Vision of Doris Lessing: Breaking the Forms of Consciousness* (1979).

Ruth Saxton, Associate Professor of English and Dean of Letters at Mills College, Oakland, California, edits the *Doris Lessing Newsletter* and is an associate editor of *Woolf Studies Annual*. She is completing work on a study of Doris Lessing called *Garments of the Mind*.

Christine W. Sizemore, Professor of English at Spelman College in Atlanta, Georgia, is the author of *A Female Vision of the City: London in the Novels of Five British Women* (1989).

Claire Sprague, Professor of English Emerita of Brooklyn College, is the author of *Virginia Woolf* (1971), coeditor of *Critical Essays on Doris Lessing* (1986), author of *Rereading Doris Lessing* (1987), and editor of *In Pursuit of Doris Lessing: Nine Nations Reading* (1990). She is a founding member of the Doris Lessing Society and a former editor of *The Doris Lessing Newsletter*.

Jean Tobin, Professor of English with the University of Wisconsin Centers, teaches in Sheboygan, Wisconsin, and currently is writing a book called *Creativity and the Poetic Mind*.

Lisa Tyler, Assistant Professor of English, teaches at Sinclare Community College, Dayton, Ohio.

PART ONE

— ◆ —

# CONSTITUTION OF A
# FEMALE SUBJECT

# 1

— ◆ —

## MULTIPERSONAL AND DIALOGIC MODES IN
## *MRS. DALLOWAY* AND *THE GOLDEN NOTEBOOK* [1]

### Claire Sprague

Like many Doris Lessing and Virginia Woolf readers, I have always imagined a deep and visible connection between Lessing and Woolf. But that connection was elusive. Was it more wishful than actual? Woolf's name never appears in Lessing's criticism, and verifiable allusions to Woolf in Lessing's work are almost nonexistent. One such allusion is Martha Quest's recollection in *The Four-Gated City* of the birds who sing in Greek to a mad young man (550). So we know that Lessing read *Mrs. Dalloway* and stored away one vivid image relating to Septimus's madness. Of course, we could have assumed without proof that Lessing's omnivorous reading habits hadn't bypassed Woolf, but we couldn't have guessed what precisely she had stored for herself or for her fictional use. So that stubborn little allusive nugget, retrieved when Martha is ready to learn from madness, does have a special resonance. It shows us something, but it cannot take us very far. More resonant interconnections did not fall into place until I heard Lessing speak in New York on January 31, 1991 at the 92nd Street Y. What a surprise and a delight to hear from her for the first time a very warm, extended, and effective appreciation of Woolf and her novels. What she said started me on a new train of recovery of and discovery about her relation to her formidable predecessor.

Lessing was particularly struck by Woolf's ability to bracket pain and depression in *To the Lighthouse,* a bracketing she likened to Woolf's literal bracketing of death in the "Time Passes" section of the novel (i.e., "[Mrs.

Ramsay died]," "[Andrew died in the war]," "[Prue died in childbirth]"). She presented Woolf's practice as a triumphant contrast to the "victim" posture of writers such as Jean Rhys and Sylvia Plath. Her remark implicitly asks for a feminist approach more critical of the "female-as-victim" posture. It also explicitly removes Woolf from the victim category by choosing to focus on narrative strategy rather than on biography. As usual, therefore, Lessing takes a wry, revisionary stance, deliberately distancing herself from what she perceives as mainstream feminist criticism.

There is, I knew unequivocally that night, a connection between Lessing and Woolf. *Influence* isn't the right word for it. *Affinity* is closer, although not wholly satisfactory, for the patterns and perceptions Woolf and Lessing share. I single out here their profound conviction that the world is best seen and shaped through what Erich Auerbach (1892–1957) called *multipersonal method* and what Mikhail Bakhtin (1895–1975) called the *dialogic imagination*. I adopt—and adapt—the rubric of multipersonal method from Auerbach's essay on "The Brown Stocking" in *Mimesis* (1946), a study of the representation of reality in Western literature from Homer to Woolf. What Auerbach says about *To the Lighthouse* applies with equal aptness to *Mrs. Dalloway*. I assume that Bakhtin's concept of the dialogic, as it is developed in *Problems of Dostoevsky's Poetics* (1984) and *The Dialogic Imagination* (1981), has enough features in common with Auerbach's multipersonal method to support a provocative dialogue between the two concepts and their application to Woolf and Lessing.[2] I take the further liberty of using Bakhtin's definition of the polyphonic novel to cover both multipersonal and dialogic modes in *Mrs. Dalloway* and *The Golden Notebook*.

My use of multipersonal method also serves to renew attention to Auerbach, a critical writer who shares many perceptions with his currently more well-known contemporary, Bakhtin, a man whose works were not available to us until recently and which are now enjoying a belated vogue. Thus, historical accident makes Bakhtin seem new and Auerbach more old-fashioned, despite their shared perceptions and actual contemporaneity.

"The distinctive characteristics of the realistic novel of the era between the two great wars," as Auerbach sums them up, are the "multipersonal representation of consciousness, time strata, disintegration of the continuity of exterior events, [and the] shifting of the narrative viewpoint" (84; see also 546). These four constantly intersecting modes have become familiar in critical discourse about Virginia Woolf and other novelists, but they have not been common in discourse about Doris Lessing, whose early reception, coinciding with the second women's movement, ignored or rejected narrative issues. We have reached a different point in time, one which assumes that narrative strategies have a politics. Woolf and Lessing always assume that narrative choices are political choices.

Consciousness is not unitary, to use a pejorative Auerbach and Bakhtin word, in either *Mrs. Dalloway* or *The Golden Notebook*. Woolf's novel is, for example, named for Clarissa Dalloway, but Clarissa's voice is only one of the many voices we hear in the novel. Clarissa's friends and family members all take center stage at one time or another. Even strangers who speak only once are permitted to come onstage as walkers and gawkers in the London streets, shops, and parks. A subplot coexists with these multiple voices, though we do not know that it is a subplot or that it will ever connect with the main plot until it does so in a most evanescent— perhaps even parodic—way at the end of the novel. Exterior events at best run parallel to interior musings; they merely punctuate the speaker's thoughts. Auerbach's rubrics omit Woolf's most radical, most crucial decision. In creating for Clarissa a male double whom she never even meets, whose name she never learns, and for whom Clarissa has not even a referential existence, Woolf breaks all the rules. That creation, a major feature of her multipersonal method, requires a fresh look and perhaps a fresh name—since *androgynous* no longer seems the right word for the Clarissa/Septimus interaction. They are only in the most superficial sense female and male. In fact, neither character is very male—or both seem more female than male. (How different from the bellicose Anna/Saul interaction!)

What goes on between Clarissa and Septimus is convincing in large part because the novel they inhabit persuades us that personality is volatile— subject to change, division, and reunification. Like Woolf, Lessing believes, to use Jeanne Schulkind's phrasing, "in the ceaseless transformation of personality" (Schulkind 12). When Schulkind goes on to describe Woolf's essays as "filtering the past through a succession of present selves" (13), her description seems to me to suit what Lessing does in the Martha, Marnie, Stella, and Maisie characters who stream through the *Martha Quest* novels, as well as what she does in *The Golden Notebook*. For in that novel, the past is filtered through a succession of its many Annas, not just in other women (like Molly, Ella, Julia, Maryrose, Marion, Muriel, and Elise), but in the many selves Anna is in her own name (e.g., "the 'Anna' of that time"[153], "that other Anna's eye is on me" [351], "the Anna who goes to the office" [362], "younger, stronger Annas" [592], "sick Anna" [602]).

These plural Annas function in both split and unified ways. Anna is a multipersonal figure only weakly united by the common name all her selves bear—or wear, as clothes are the perfect metaphor to express the changeability of personality. They can so easily be put on or taken off. Thus, there only *appears* to be a central consciousness in *The Golden Notebook*. In fact, both

*Martha Quest* and *The Golden Notebook* subvert the postulate of a central consciousness. Axiomatic to each is the proposition that there is no "same person" in fiction or in life, that people are different at different times with different people in different situations. This proposition, perhaps now degenerated to a truism, has a painful and exhilarating presence in these two works.

It has taken us a long time to begin to recognize the multiple voices in *The Golden Notebook*. That recognition has yet to run its critical course. Anna invites us to see her as a multiple, chameleon figure in the long night of dreams she has during her time with Saul. On that night, she sexchanges (compare Leopold Bloom in the "Nighttown" section of *Ulysses*) as part of a playing out of the many roles she has not played in life. She explicitly tells us that people and texts are mirrors into which she looks for guidance to her behavior, to her possible futures. She watches herself melt into her other characters in the film sequence in the novel. (The shift to film is apt, for film surpasses prose, as Auerbach recognized a half century ago, in its ability to condense and rearrange time and space. It is the perfect medium for Anna's metamorphoses [546].) Anna tells us over and over again from the opening line of the novel, "The two women were alone in the London flat," that she is not unitary. She perfectly celebrates what Bakhtin describes and Auerbach assumes is the novel's essential nature—its eternally upstart ability to catch the multiple, heteroglot, polyglot nature of life as no other form has ever done.

Both novels overturn the characteristic "doubles" novel of the nineteenth century. The doubles novel pits socially-obedient male selves against their daring, usually criminal, other male selves, such as Jekyll and Hyde or Dorian Gray and his portrait. When Woolf and Lessing imagine women doubles (Clarissa and Sally, perhaps; Mrs. Ramsay and Lily Briscoe, certainly; Anna and all her other selves) and female/male doubles such as Clarissa/Septimus and Anna/Tommy/Paul/Saul, they explode the male doubles novel of the last century. For Bakhtin, Dostoevsky's frequent use of doubles reflects his endemic dialogizing. Dostoevsky forces a character "to converse with his own double, with the devil, with his alter ego, with his own caricature" to create "out of every contradiction within a single person . . . two persons" (Bakhtin, *Problems* 28). The phenomenon of doubling in Woolf and Lessing continues to dramatize internal contradictions. It also reevaluates and extends the conception of the "other." Above all, it adds to doubling the fact of gender, for Woolf and Lessing use their single sex and mixed doubles as a means of dramatizing the ironies and the limitations of gendered behavior.

As a radical exploration of gendered behavior, the novels are wholly original, sharing nothing with the perceptions of their critical predecessors, for gender is never a feature of Bakhtin's explorations and only, as it were, accidentally of Auerbach's.[3] Clarissa has one male double; Anna has many (Tommy, Max/Willi, Paul Blackenhurst, Paul Tanner/Michael, De Silva, Saul/Milt). Both Lessing and Woolf redefine the Hyde self of the nineteenth-century double, but the striking fact about Anna's male selves is how much they share with Hyde. They are not criminal, but they are violent, aggressive, and stereotypically male. They are the male selves within Anna whom she, as a woman, finds it hard to confront. Ironically, although Virginia Woolf developed an androgynous theory of gender, her mixed double is more female than androgynous, while Lessing's multiple mixed doubles are throwbacks to older stereotypes about what is masculine and what is feminine. Madness may be Septimus's major androgynous quality, for it connects him both to the women who overcrowd institutions and to the men whose madness is war-related.[4] Clarissa, on the other hand, is not male or male-identified, despite her "coldness" and her preference for memoirs over novels, or even her moment of orgasmic illumination "when she did undoubtedly feel what men felt" (*MD* 33).

Bakhtin's interest in the phenomenon of doubling is inevitable, given his axiomatic commitment to the dialogic basis of existence. He insists that the definition of the self must occur in confrontation with another; the search for the development of individual consciousness is not a solitary pursuit: "I cannot become myself without another; I must find myself in another by finding another in myself" (*Problems* 287). The phrasing perfectly suits Clarissa's redefinition of herself through Septimus. Anna's redefinition of herself through multiple female and male selves, although more complicated and less certain, proceeds in essentially the same manner. Both novels "dialogize thought," as Dostoevsky does (*Problems* 111). That is, they are, like Dostoevsky's novels, not "ideological" in the negative sense because their ideas become "form-shaping" (*Problems* 83, 97). Doubling is at once a "form-shaping" strategy and a reflection of the dialogic basis of existence. In developing his concept of dialogized thought, Bakhtin is responding to charges that Dostoevsky is an ideologue. There have been related charges against Woolf and Lessing.

The "idea" that personality is volatile helps to make the one-sided and fragile interchange between Clarissa and Septimus convincing. We have been willing to grant that "[t]his view of the self which emphasizes simultaneously the change and continuity of the individual identity is of central importance in Virginia Woolf's fiction" (Schulkind 14), yet Schulkind's judgment might as easily have been made about Doris Lessing. For the volatility and multiplicity of Lessing's characters are exceptional. Words like *flux* and *multiplicity* (Schulkind 14), so common in Woolf criticism, can be used for Lessing.

(Compare the *Martha Quest* series, *The Golden Notebook,* and later novels like *The Making of the Representative for Planet 8* and *The Diary of a Good Neighbour,* which share certain basic assumptions about personality and external events with *Mrs. Dalloway* or *To the Lighthouse* or *The Waves.*)

Furthermore, like Woolf, Lessing has developed a unique multipersonal mode, a new time strata, a new way of disrupting narrative viewpoint and the continuity of exterior events. To say, for example, that *The Golden Notebook* is seen through Anna's consciousness is inexact and incomplete, for the Anna who speaks, as I have suggested earlier, is never the same Anna, unless we wish to say that the overriding narrative voice that constructs the entire novel is the same voice. It is certainly the most directorial or authorial; it is the present-tense voice to all the other past-tense Annas. This Anna may or may not be real. The other Annas are definitely "unreal" or fictional. Remember the shock we, as readers, experienced when we first realized that the Anna of the black notebook is a fictional Anna, according to the directorial Anna who "brackets" her revelation as Woolf brackets her reports of the Ramsay deaths. Or the shock of discovering that the whole of "Free Women" is fiction. Perhaps the notebooks and their many subsections are forms of bracketing? Lessing's bracketing (and Woolf's) creates an ironic counterterm to the unbracketed material around it. In Bakhtinian terms, bracketing is one more example of the dialogic in a novel teeming with polyphonal discourse.

The classic Proustian recall, what Auerbach calls "the layered structure of a consciousness engaged in recollection" (542), undergoes noticeable changes in both Woolf and Lessing. Woolf's title character goes back to a single summer, Septimus to the moment of Evans's death in the Great War. Clarissa's return at age fifty-two to her moment of marital decision at eighteen occurs more than once and in different ways, while she is simultaneously situated in the present time of a single day in the middle of June, five years after the war's end, a day of whose hourly movement we are emphatically reminded by the punctuating hourly bells of Big Ben. Woolf says, "thought she" (*MD* 3), or "she stiffened a little on the kerb" (*MD* 4), or "she thought, going up Bond Street" (*MD* 15), so that there is no confusion about what Clarissa is doing in present time, where she is, and what she is thinking about.

Early readers of *The Golden Notebook* showed little interest in how Lessing managed time in her now over-thirty-year-old novel. Like Woolf, Lessing is meticulous in providing her readers with precise dates. Both postwar novels are firmly anchored in historical time, firmly remembering, centering, and evaluating the war and its social-political consequences for the body politic and for the individual past in revisionary ways. At a first reading, the multiple and overlapping chronologies of *The Golden Notebook* are likely to seem confusing; but that time is important is clear from the first page, when we learn that "*Anna meets her friend Molly in the summer of 1957 after a separation*" (3). Anna's notebooks, placed after each "Free Women" section, selectively return to her past.

Time, specifically the present-past dialectic, is differently sandwiched in Lessing's novel, but as in *Mrs. Dalloway,* retrospection in *The Golden Notebook* is both crucial and highly selective. In both novels, retrospective modes can be described as richer, more adventurous, more various than present-time modes. Or, to use Auerbach, consciousness "keeps confronting" a past emancipated from "exterior temporal continuity as well as from the narrow meanings" of its occurrence in present time (542). Woolf and Lessing in effect reinterpret human memory itself, suggesting that, like art, memory also selects and fictionalizes. Neither novel takes us back to the childhood of its protagonist, for example. Lessing's novel concentrates on seven years, 1950 to 1957; Anna returns to her wartime African past only in memory and primarily in one notebook. Readers are given, however irregularly, specific years, even months and days, throughout the novel. By the end of the novel, the notebooks have caught up with the present time of 1957. Present time is both respected and undermined in both novels as it counterpoints with a past that almost overwhelms it.

The novels may differ most in the way they deploy authorial voice and in the degree to which each uses polyglot voices and genres. The authorial voice has a personality in *Mrs. Dalloway.* It comments, it muses, it creates the tone of the novel; it breaks frame to tell us which outsiders will be selected to speak, which objects it chooses to see. The hand of the author is everywhere, even, of course, in the "she thoughts" and the "[s]he had reached the Park gates" (11) interpolative guideposts. Lessing's hand is far more disguised, traditionally so in the "Free Women" sections, which are close to the kind of nineteenth-century realism that Auerbach and Bakhtin understand so well. Unsettlingly so in the many voices and genres of the notebook sections. If Lessing rather than Anna is present at all, it is in the literally bracketed sections that so often precede the notebook entries. Lessing tries to obliterate the author; Woolf does not. However, as Bakhtin insists, authorial voice never disappears; it merely deploys itself differently, allowing, in the polyphonic novel, rare freedom to its characters.

The uncertainties of authorial voice in the novels are related to the novel's historic posture as a parodic or carnival counterform to the epic, as Bakhtin might say. On one level, these novels mock their nineteenth-century predecessors. But their mockery relates to the very nature of the novel, which has always been, in Bakhtinian and Auerbachian terms, a heterogeneous hybrid form—never univocal; always mixing low and high speech, classes, tones, genres; always inviting laughter (that greatest form of irreverence); always a critique of "serious" forms, or a "destabilizing" form, to use current critical vocabulary. The parodic or carnival nature of *The Golden Notebook* is easier to see, yet a full-scale treatment of the parodic in that novel has yet to appear.

The standard definition of parody as a humorous or burlesque imitation of a serious form fits many of the forms of *The Golden Notebook* and *Mrs. Dalloway* apparently not at all. Yet, like Bakhtin, we do use the term parodic more loosely. If we can accept the novel as critique, then *Mrs. Dalloway* is also parodic, for its innovative narrative strategies, its shifting, multiple points of view, its choice of a triggering exterior event, and its deployment of time can all be considered implicit critiques of earlier novelistic practices. The parodic qualities in *Mrs. Dalloway* have a strong, although much gentler kind of tonal presence than the parodic in *The Golden Notebook*. Can we call it humor or wit or both when Clarissa's interior monologue is interrupted with information about when or where she is stepping off the curb, or hearing Big Ben strike, or seeing a motorcade pass? These minutiae surely undercut, perhaps even mock, the weight of the protagonist's musings.

All novels that depart from their predecessors cannot, of course, be called parodic. Yet such novels may be said to contain hidden allusions to the forms they are displacing. Will only readers who know essays such as "Mr. Bennett and Mrs. Brown" and "Modern Fiction" see a dialogic interchange between those essays and Woolf's fiction? Perhaps. Beyond that interchange there is *Mrs. Dalloway* itself, which refuses to privilege earlier plots and earlier heroines. Surely the more conventional novel, "the implied model" (Bakhtin, *Problems* 195), is somewhere in the reader's mind as he or she watches its shape and language being undercut, sometimes slyly, sometimes overtly, by Woolf and Lessing. We continue to need better terms and more discussion about the meaning and the place of parody in Woolf's and Lessing's novels. Even when the parodic is obviously savage, as it so often is in *The Golden Notebook,* critics have rarely confronted it.

*Hybrid* is the perfect word for *The Golden Notebook,* a novel which speaks satirically, nostalgically, angrily, self-pityingly, self-mockingly in multiple genres—diary entry, headline, film script, letter, notebook, book review, synopsis, novel in progress, short story—and tries to suggest nonverbal forms like "a changed startled writing" (56), "scattered musical symbols" (56), "a complicated design of interlocking circles" (56), gummed in and rubber-banded pages and newspaper clippings, doodlings with words and actual notations of the pound sign, asterisks, and scattered dots.[5] The novel has a vast encyclopedic quality that mocks continuity, order, and meaning and simultaneously longs for it. It is filled with parodic inserts like "Blood on the Banana Leaves" or the Soviet reviews of Anna's novel, which invite the most corrosive laughter.

These examples are obvious inserts. A less obvious example of the parodic is the third entry of the black notebook, dated "11th November 1955," whose opening line, "Today on the pavement a fat domestic London pigeon waddling among the boots and shoes of people hurrying for a bus" (410), initiates a complicated, anguished, satiric wartime recall of a pigeon-shoot episode in Africa. In this episode, the kicked and bleeding and finally dead pigeon that triggers Anna's recall performs the same function as Proust's madeleine. Lessing's covert allusion to Proust is wonderfully parodic, her London scene the perfect example of street theater.[6]

Furthermore, Lessing's street-theater episode inevitably recalls Bakhtin's conviction that the novel has its roots in carnival. In the folk origins of carnival, Bakhtin locates the essential distinctiveness of the novel form, its always upstart, inclusive, overturning nature. Carnival ritualizes the bringing together of many opposites; it collapses distinctions, hierarchies, distances. All the rules that govern ordinary life are suspended as *"free and familiar contact among people"* (*Problems* 123) becomes the rule in this earliest exemplum of street theater.

Lessing's episode functions to recall a past episode; it has no consequences. Her characteristic other street happenings are unpleasant and sporadic; in one Anna feels menaced by a man who follows her (390), in another by a man who "had exposed himself on a dark street corner" (407). Lessing's London is threatening and fractured. Her characters prefer small rooms in flats. Woolf's street events are quite different. Joyous and various, they create community. They connect social classes, however incompletely, and celebrate the continuity of England. Street events are the spine of the novel. They are its linear structure, the *topos* part, so to speak, of Bakhtin's description of the novel as *chronotope*. Clarissa, then Peter and other characters, take adventurous walks through London, never quite touching yet almost meeting—a fact and a metaphor manipulated dialogically for the reader, as Bakhtin might put it. These walks are at once celebratory and elegiac, for Clarissa and Septimus never meet, and distinctions are only broken down superficially and momentarily in space and time.

When Auerbach speaks of the "minor, unimpressive, random events" that characterize events in Woolf, he is speaking of a choice that Bakhtin might call parodic in that these events represent a deliberate refusal to privilege great personages and great happenings. Perhaps it is more precise to say that Woolf and Lessing reinterpret the ordinary and the special. Consider the single day we spend with Clarissa Dalloway, which ends with a dinner party. That party redefines "important" in witty, countervalent ways. The prime minister passes through the setting and leaves no mark. Septimus Smith, an absent background figure, and a nameless old woman undressing for bed across the street precipitate the protagonist's revelation about her relation to time and death. Two people reach across the divide of class—and age and gender and space and death—to suggest the novel's ability, as Bakhtin puts it (*Problems* 243) and Auerbach suggests, to collapse social distance. This kind of collapsing is, of course, a feature of carnival.

Great public events in Lessing never "collapse," even briefly. They literally speak another language through newspaper headlines that look and read like bullets. Even "great" events in private life often have a sharp parodic edge. Consider and compare Tommy's failed suicide attempt with Septimus's successful one; the act meant to kill only blinds Tommy. Instead of self-destructing, Tommy accomplishes his self-unification and a malevolent power to manipulate and terrorize his two mothers, Anna and Molly. Lessing, like Woolf, is confident, to use Auerbach's words, that "the more the [random moment] is exploited, the more the elementary things which our lives have in common come to light" (552) or the more we uncover "a more real reality" (540).

The choice of the apparently random ordinary moment becomes, therefore, as political, as destabilizing a formal choice as the disruptions of time or of narrative viewpoint. These choices reveal the feminist (*female-centered* may be a better word for Lessing), left, and dialogic bias that both novelists share. The most obvious analogue to Clarissa's "ordinary moment" on June 16, 1923, is Anna's effort to truthfully "fix" the events of September 15, 1954. These dates will never make headlines. They did not begin or end wars, see a coronation or a moon landing. They are not history book material.

Clearly hostile to "any sort of *conclusive conclusion*" (Bakhtin, *Problems* 165), these novels prefer instead "the fundamental openendedness" (*Problems* 39) of the polyphonic novel. The final line of *Mrs. Dalloway,* "For there she was," is less conclusion than curtain raiser. Yes, it does suggest that Clarissa's appearance caps the evening, but it also suggests that Clarissa's arrival raises the curtain and permits the festivities to begin again. At the end of her dinner party, Clarissa has inherited, incorporated, transformed, and reinterpreted Septimus's voice. She has become at least a double character in a novel that at once has and has not a conclusion.

Lessing's novel has a different kind of double ending. The line which ends "Free Women 5" and the novel, "The two women kissed and separated," is so definitive, it totally discourages even a curtain call. Of course, its conclusiveness is deceptive, for it cannot finally be seen in isolation from the preceding book, the inner golden notebook, with which it is dialogically connected. In that penultimate book, to give one example, Anna conquers her writing block, while in "Free Women 5," she forgets her writing and becomes a social worker. So we appear to have two last books and two endings—if not actually and potentially more than two. How can that be? Must the reader pick one ending? Is one true and the other false? Does the last line of "Free Women 5" end the novel because it comes last? In a novel that upends social, political, sexual, and esthetic truisms, linear positioning cannot be a persuasive reason. The Lessing and Woolf novels both display that erosion of confidence in the knowability of reality that Auerbach found so characteristic of twentieth-century fiction: the "obscuring and even obliterating the impression of an objective reality completely known to the author" (535).

Auerbach and Bakhtin, or A and B, as I have come to call them to myself, have been useful to me. They have extended and deepened and given me new words for my own long-standing musings about the volatility and multiplicity of personality in Woolf and Lessing. They bring two more voices to the already rich dialogues within and between *Mrs. Dalloway* and *The Golden Notebook* and a "counter-hegemonic" (Donovan 86) approach that is proving attractive to the larger community of feminists (see Bauer and McKinstrey). The beginning dialogue between "feminism and dialogism" (Stevenson 182) can be continuing and useful if these two outlooks do not behave like "isms." Feminism and dialogism can, for example, join forces to see how *Mrs. Dalloway* and *The Golden Notebook* catapult gender onstage to show that it is no more fixed and no less political than time, place, or narrative strategy. Wherever we look, and we have looked at many aspects of the two novels, they celebrate process over closure.

---

## NOTES

1. This chapter was presented in earlier form at the Modern Language Association conference, New York, 1992.
2. When Todorov imagines another critic of Bakhtin's stature, that is, someone who goes beyond yet absorbs "previous formalist schools," he thinks of *Mimesis*, "which puts the 'new stylistics' (of [Leo] Spitzer's vintage) in the service of a historical and social vision" (40). Later in his book, Todorov makes an exception to his "rule of avoiding comparisons between Bakhtin and later writers because a comparison seems so much

called for." He notes that Auerbach—again in *Mimesis*, when he reviews "the history of European literature in the light of the opposition of two stylistic attitudes: the separation of styles (*Stiltrennung*) and mixture of styles (*Stilmischung*)"—is, like Bakhtin, aware that a mixture of styles characterizes the modern novel. Furthermore, both critics share "an interest in the literary representation of the real" (77). Todorov also reminds us that Bakhtin's "Discourse in the Novel" was written only "some ten years earlier" than *Mimesis*, although it was published thirty years later. Bakhtin might possibly have known Auerbach's work; the reverse is unlikely.

3. Margaret Drabble's essay on Auerbach, unearthed after I completed this chapter, anticipates my connection between Auerbach and Lessing. It singles out *The Golden Notebook* as the major example of the new realities opened up by "the woman's novel." Drabble praises the richness and variety of *Mimesis*, its emphasis on mingling of styles, and its delight in particularity. She finds Auerbach's approach immensely usable, while she is simultaneously aware that he sometimes reflects traditional gender stereotyping. She wittily correlates "the old literary doctrine of separation of styles " (whose passing *Mimesis* celebrates) with "the separation of the sexes" (9).

4. Herman's *Trauma and Recovery* argues that women's hysteria is a response to trauma and equivalent to male posttraumatic stress syndrome.

5. Anna would welcome the new nonlinear computer space called hypertext (available in software like Storyspace and Intermedia), which frees the "text" from time and space. See Coover.

6. I have found only one reference to Proust (and Joyce) in Bakhtin's two major books in English. Another Soviet critic is quoted who refers "'to the degenerate decadent psychologism of Proust or Joyce'" (Bakhtin, *Problems* 37). This reference suggests one reason Bakhtin never went outside the Soviet Union for examples of the polyphonic novel in the twentieth century. The only non-Russian writer he considered at length is Rabelais. It is remarkable that Auerbach chose to end his study of European literature from Homer ("Odysseus' Scar") to the present with Woolf ("The Brown Stocking") rather than with Proust or Joyce. (Shakespeare is the only other writer in English considered in *Mimesis*.) It would have been so even in the 1970s when the Woolf revival began to take flight. Part of the reason for Auerbach's choice is his preference for Woolf's "feminine" outlook, for work "filled with good and genuine love [and] in its feminine way, with irony, amorphous sadness, and doubt of life" (552). Auerbach appreciates but does not empathize with Joyce (551) and considers Proust an example of "unipersonal subjectivism" (541).

# 2

— ◆ —

## FIXING THE PAST:
## YEARNING AND NOSTALGIA IN
## WOOLF AND LESSING

### Roberta Rubenstein

A central impulse in the work of Virginia Woolf and Doris Lessing, two otherwise quite dissimilar writers, is *nostalgia:* the expression of yearning for an earlier time or place or person from one's past, the memory and significance of which or whom contributes to the sense of the self in the present moment. The word *nostalgia* originates in the Greek *nostos* (the return home) and *algos* (pain).[1] In addition to the literal sense of homesickness, nostalgia has come to signify "a longing for what is past, a painful yearning for a time gone by" (Jacoby 5). More than simply expressing a preoccupation with the past, Virginia Woolf and Doris Lessing recurrently explore the emotionally saturated meanings of two categories of memories in particular—of place (*home*) and of person (*mother*). These memories are filtered through and inevitably revised by particular consciousnesses, including those not only of fictionalized characters but of the authors themselves as they reflect on places and people significant during earlier parts of their lives. Thus, while a number of Woolf's and Lessing's characters embody the authors' respective representations of nostalgia, each author has also written autobiographical accounts describing important figures, places, and experiences in her life that corroborate and underlie her fictional representations of "homesickness."

More than Woolf, Lessing consciously acknowledges that memory itself is an elusive, fluid, and often unreliable component of consciousness, whose manifestations depend on the shifting relationship between any present moment and an always-receding past. Anna Wulf observes with exasperation that trying to remember her experiences during her formative years in southern Africa is "like wrestling with an obstinate other-self who insists on its own kind of privacy. Yet it's all there in my brain if only I could get at it. . . . How do I know that what I 'remember' was what was important? What I remember was chosen by Anna, of twenty years ago. I don't know what this Anna of now would choose" (*GN* 137). Similarly, as Woolf phrases it in her autobiographical essay, "A Sketch of the Past," "It would be interesting to make the two people, I now, I then, come out in contrast. And further, this past is much affected by the present moment. What I write today I should not write in a year's time" (*MB* 75).

Yet elsewhere Woolf affirms a view of recollection that runs counter to this observation: her conviction that one source of her fiction-making impulse is vivid memories that are preserved as "scenes," quite unaltered by her evolving relation to them over time:

> I find that scene making is my natural way of marking the past. Always a scene has arranged itself: representative; enduring. This confirms me in my instinctive notion: . . . the sensation that we are sealed vessels afloat on what it is convenient to call reality; and at some moments, the sealing matter creaks; in floods reality; that is, these scenes—for why do they survive undamaged year after year unless they are made of something comparatively permanent? (*MB* 122)[2]

If—as Woolf so memorably declares in *A Room of One's Own*—"we think back through our mothers if we are women" (76), it is also instructive to approach her writing from the other direction: to think back through one of her "daughters," as it were. The presence of nostalgia in Doris Lessing's writing—not only as emphatically resisted by (the suggestively surnamed) Anna Wulf, but elsewhere and more ambivalently as both the domain of unreliable memories and a harmonious unitary world—ultimately casts a critical light on the ways in which nostalgia functions in Woolf's fiction and autobiography: if not as a "lie," at least as a scrim that revises and blunts the sharp edges of distant memories.

## I. HOME

Born of English parents in Persia (now Iran), Doris Lessing was reared in Southern Rhodesia (now Zimbabwe) and emigrated to England when she was thirty. Ultimately, as a result of her leftist political activities, she was listed as a "Prohibited Immigrant" (*AL* 11) and proscribed from reentering her African homeland for more than twenty-five years. Both of her autobiographical narratives, the significantly titled *Going Home* (published in 1957) and the recently published *African Laughter* (1992), record her successive returns "home" to Zimbabwe, providing unique intertexts for the expressions of nostalgia that occur throughout her fiction as well.

Lessing's first experience of literal "homesickness," if not the nostalgia that colors adult recollections, occurred when she was still a child, living away from home in a convent boarding school in Salisbury. While there, she was "always ill at school and not only with homesickness" ("My Mother's Life" 236). As early as *Martha Quest,* Lessing highlights the uneasy quality of nostalgia as sixteen-year-old Martha, isolated in a darkened room because of infectious pinkeye, awaits her matriculation exam. The narrator describes an October day, bright with light and pungent with the scent of flowers, as Martha feels "the waves of heat and perfume break across her in shock after shock of shuddering nostalgia. But nostalgia for what?" (*MQ* 32). Although described as Martha's experience, the passage transparently expresses Lessing's own yearning for features embedded in the site of her emotionally complicated childhood; Martha, who had not yet left home as Lessing had done by the time she wrote the first novel of *Children of Violence,* could not have known such homesickness. Later, when Martha does leave home to take a secretarial job in Salisbury, she falls ill with a "dubious" illness and resists acknowledging a likely source of her malaise: "One might imagine I was homesick! she said to herself drily . . ." (*MQ* 209).

When she drives across the open veld with Douglas Knowell (the man she soon marries), Martha's voice again blends with Lessing's nostalgia in her celebration of the "naked embrace of earth and sky. . . . This frank embrace between the lifting breast of the land and the deep blue warmth of the sky *is what exiles from Africa dream of; it is what they sicken for, no matter how hard they try to shut their minds against the memory of it*" (*MQ* 240, my emphasis). Once again, it is the exile from Africa who speaks, not Martha Quest.

Martha's earlier question ("nostalgia for what?") is ostensibly answered in *A Proper Marriage* when, newly pregnant, she attributes her odd confusion of anxiety and excitement to "Nostalgia for something doomed"

(*PM* 341).[3] The paradoxical expression of retrospective foreknowledge is more descriptive of the voluntarily exiled Lessing's knowledge of loss than of the still-adolescent Martha's.

The yearning for a place—and for a past—that is simultaneously real, ideal, and true becomes considerably more complex in Lessing's subsequent fiction, particularly for Anna Wulf of *The Golden Notebook,* for whom such nostalgic impulses are especially problematic. As Anna considers the experiences of her formative years in Southern Rhodesia—from a greater distance in both time and space than does the young Martha Quest—she struggles to find a "true" perspective within her romanticized memories; she determines that nostalgia must be resisted, for it distorts and falsifies memory. Early in the black notebook, Anna confesses her feeling that her first and only novel, *Frontiers of War,* utterly falsified rather than rendering honestly her deepest emotional experiences. She virtually repudiates it as an "immoral novel" because "that terrible lying nostalgia lights every sentence" (*GN* 63), capturing not the authentic version of events at Mashopi but "something frightening, the unhealthy, feverish illicit excitement of wartime, a lying nostalgia, a longing for license, for freedom, for the jungle, for formlessness" (63).[4] At her most cynical, she even characterizes this complex of self-deceiving feelings as a "nostalgia for death" (287).

One challenge a reader faces in attempting to understand the meaning of what Anna Wulf terms "lying nostalgia" is the impossibility of comprehending such observations independently of the Anna who names them. In the multiple notebooks and time frames of Lessing's narrative—encompassing Anna's memories from the 1940s, when she lived in Southern Rhodesia, to her experiences in London during the 1950s, when she tries to record more recent and current events in her life—she attempts to capture both the "raw" experiences and their myriad fictional transmutations. All of her memories are observed through a fragmented lens: the emotional and artistic crisis she undergoes and attempts to document from different perspectives and personas in her several notebooks.

Thus, "lying nostalgia" becomes a judgment about the difficulty—in fact, the impossibility—of recovering, through either memory or fiction, the "authentic" version of past experiences. Among the many strands that draw the multilayered narrative of *The Golden Notebook* into a kind of coherence, the unstable relations between past and present, between experience and language, between fact and fiction, and between subjectivity and authenticity pervade Anna's struggle with her various "selves" and thus occupy a significant place in the novel's multiple meanings.[5]

It is revealing to juxtapose Anna Wulf's struggle with "lying nostalgia" in her accounts of her experiences at Mashopi with Lessing's recent actual visits to the land of her formative years. In 1982, her first visit "home" since 1956, she returned to several emotionally significant places of her young adulthood, including Macheke—the Mashopi of *The Golden Notebook*—hoping to "sort out memory from what [she] had made of it" (*AL* 66). When she actually encounters specific places, she finds that she cannot disentangle her memories from her fictionalizations of them.

> What happened in Macheke I described, changed for literary reasons, in *The Golden Notebook*. But how much changed? All writers know the state of trying to remember what actually happened, rather than what was invented, or half invented, a meld of truth and fiction. It is possible to remember, but only by sitting quietly, for hours or sometimes for days, and dragging facts out of one's memory. . . . Mashopi was painted over with glamour, as I complained in *The Golden Notebook*. (*AL* 72)

One of the major occurrences of dissonance between Lessing's nostalgic recollections of places and their current incarnation transpires during her brief visit to the Macheke Hotel, fictionalized in *The Golden Notebook* as the Mashopi Hotel managed by the Boothbys. Lessing's fictitious version of it is so insistent that she cannot even recall the proprietor's actual name:

> Floating on moonlight, and on a hundred intoxications, I stepped carefully down, down the stone steps that were edged with the sweet-smelling plants Mrs. Boothby (Mrs. *Who?*) was so fond of and crammed into every crevice, and then . . . but it was impossible to see anything through this litter of planks, rubbish, broken bricks, neglected shrubs. No, this was impossible, there was perhaps another hotel . . . no, nonsense, this was the hotel, and here was the bar and here . . . if I were to sort out what had been here, and what I had made of it, then it would take . . . how long. Weeks? No, it was silly, useless, what was the point, and I must in any case drive on. (*AL* 76, emphasis and ellipses are Lessing's)

In each of her autobiographical accounts of her visits to southern Africa, Lessing struggles over whether to return to emotionally significant locations that have shaped her imaginative vision of herself and her past. Seven years after her emigration to England, during her first return home in 1956 (and the last before she was prohibited from reentry for more than two decades), she visited towns and areas that were important to her during her childhood and youth in Southern Rhodesia.[6] However, she could not bring herself to return to the location of her childhood home in the bush. The house itself, constructed of mud, cow dung, and trees, was no longer there, having been destroyed by fire some years before; Lessing also felt that she could only preserve her inner imaginative record of "home" if she did not have to confront the visual reality of its erasure. As she expresses it,

> One of the reasons I wanted to go home was to drive through the bush to the kopje and see where the house had been. But I could not bring myself to do it.
> Supposing, having driven seven miles through the bush to the place where the road opens into the big mealie land, supposing then that I had lifted my eyes expecting to see the kopje sloping up, a slope of empty, green bush—supposing then that the house was still there after all? (*GH* 55)

Instead, Lessing recovers the house in her imagination, rescuing it from erasure through an interior salvaging operation:

> For a long time I used to dream of the collapse and decay of that house, and of the fire sweeping over it; and then I set myself to dream the other way. It was urgently necessary to recover every detail of that house. For only my own room was clear in my mind. I had to remember everything, every strand of thatch and curve of wall or heave in the floor, and every tree and bush and patch of grass around it, and how the fields and slopes of the country looked at different times of the day, in different strengths and tones of light. . . . Over months, I recovered the memory of it all. And so what was lost and buried in my mind, I recovered from my mind; so I suppose there is no need to go back and see what exists clearly, in every detail, for so long as I live. (*GH* 55–56)[7]

Nonetheless, the nostalgic vision of "home"—and of "going home"— persisted. When Lessing returned to Africa in 1982, for the first time since her 1956 visit, she once again attempted to locate the Southern Rhodesia of her childhood; in *African Laughter,* as in *Going Home,* she simultaneously measures the progress of the contemporary Zimbabwe that has replaced it. During Lessing's reunion with her brother after twenty-five years, she is astonished that Harry has no memory of experiences they shared during childhood that are still extraordinarily vivid to her:

> "You don't remember things like lying in the rocks on Koodoo Hill and watching the wild pig—they were only a few feet away? Or hiding in the

long grass at the edge of the Twenty Acres to watch the duiker come down at sunset? Or climbing trees to hide so we could watch what went on in the bush?"

"No, I don't, I'm afraid." (AL 62)

Still, Lessing resists returning to the most emotionally powerful site of her past. Harry's mention of their childhood home arouses her deepest nostalgia for a place that no longer exists. She writes,

> As he mentioned the farm, a silent No gripped me. In 1956, I could have gone to see the farm, the place where our house had been on the hill, but I was driving the car and could not force myself to turn the wheel off the main road north, on to the track that leads to the farm. Every writer has a myth-country. This does not have to be childhood. I attributed the ukase, the silent No, to a fear of tampering with my myth, the bush I was brought up in, the old house built of earth and grass, the lands around the hill, the animals, the birds. Myth does not mean something untrue, but a concentration of truth. (AL 35)

During her six weeks in Zimbabwe in 1982, Lessing once again avoided visiting the site of her family home. Finally, on her return in 1988, she resolved to override her longstanding resistance and her brother's warning, "Don't go back, it will break your heart" (AL 314). His remark refers to the populations of wild animals that have vanished from the bush, casualties of the transition to more commercially viable farmland.[8] Nonetheless, Lessing finally determined that she "had to go back to the old farm" (301), in order to confront her own "myth-country."

> This business of writers' myth-countries is far from simple. I know writers who very early build tall fences around theirs and afterwards make sure they never go near them. And not only writers: all the people I know from former dominions, colonies, or any part of the earth they grew upon before making that essential flight in and away from the periphery to the centre: when the time comes for them to make the first trip it means stripping off new skin and offering exposed and smarting flesh—to the past. For that matter every child who has left home to become an adult knows the diminishing of the first trip home. (AL 301)

Approaching with trepidation that emotionally saturated place where yearning and resistance have long mingled, she muses, "Suppose one was able to keep in one's mind those childhood miseries, the homesickness like a bruise on one's heart, the betrayal—if they were allowed [to] lie in the mind always exposed, a cursed country one has climbed out of and left behind for ever, but visible, not hidden . . . would then that landscape of pain have less power than I am sure it has?" (305, Lessing's ellipsis).

One of Lessing's unanticipated discoveries is that the very improvements that have occurred in Zimbabwe since her departure in 1950 deprive her of the full impact of her return to the veld: paved roads speed her to a landscape she had hoped to reenter as slowly as the original rutted dirt lanes of her childhood had required. From the nearby town to the location of the old family house in the bush—the place that would "[confirm] so many dreams and nightmares" (312)—the journey has shrunk from an hour (or two, by foot) to a few minutes.

However, finally encountering with relief the actual place, "not one imagined or invented" (313), Lessing confronts her deepest nostalgia for the physical landscape of her childhood:

> I stood there, needless to say limp with threatening tears, unable to believe in all that magnificence, the space, the marvel of it. I had been brought up in this place. I lived here from the age of five until I left it forever thirteen years later. I lived here. No wonder this myth country tugged and pulled . . . what a privilege, what a blessing. (315, Lessing's ellipsis and emphasis)

What distinguishes this most recent autobiographical statement of Lessing's return to the landscape of her youth from the tormented struggles of her fictionalized persona Anna Wulf is the softening of the idea of nostalgia as a "lie." There is less a sense of loss than of recovery, even of wonderment, and acceptance of both what has been forgotten and what has been remembered, albeit inevitably colored by complex emotional shadings.

Although Lessing senses the strong presence of her parents' "ghosts" (AL 317) at the site of the family farm, she recognizes that her sense of loss is not only personal but general; "every day there are more people everywhere in the world in mourning for trees, forest, bush, rivers, animals, lost landscapes . . . you could say this is an established part of the human mind, a layer of grief always deepening and darkening" (318, Lessing's ellipsis).

The impulse to return to, reconstruct, or recover such lost landscapes of the past in some sort of "pure" form—uncontaminated by the alterations of time or later experience and understanding—is a central preoccupation expressed elsewhere in Lessing's *oeuvre*. In *Briefing for a Descent into Hell*, the locations that Charles Watkins, a professor of classics, visits during several hallucinatory journeys also suggest the ambivalent grip of nostalgia. His inner journeys are juxtaposed with the medical establishment's efforts to penetrate his amnesiac condition. In fact, amnesia functions in the novel as the antithesis of nostalgia: if nostalgia is the yearning to recover the self one knew in earlier, happier circumstances, amnesia is its involuntary erasure. Thus, at various moments, Watkins struggles to *remember* something vitally important—who he "is" and what his "mission" is—but the details continually elude him.

A central aspect of nostalgia—and a central point of connection between Lessing and Woolf—is a longing for such an ideal, harmonious world that is preserved through emotionally saturated memories of the past. Mario Jacoby proposes that the vision of an idyllic time and/or place in the past links two central concepts within human psychological development: the individual experience of the "intact world" of preconscious bliss characterized by the state of fusion or oneness with the mother, and the idea of a Golden Age or Edenic past that expresses the same sense of harmonious wholeness as a collective experience. Yet such locations (in either the individual or collective sense) are a fantasy. "There never were any good old days, there never was an 'intact world.' . . . The harmonious world which is now regarded as lost . . . never really existed. . . . The world of wholeness exists mostly in retrospect, as a compensation for the threatened, fragmented world in which we live now" (Jacoby 4, 5). Moreover, "to 'know' what Paradise means presupposes knowledge of its opposite, of the burdens and sufferings of earthly existence. The very idea of Paradise contains simultaneous grief over its loss" (Jacoby 26).

Thus, in *Briefing for a Descent into Hell,* nostalgia signifies not only personal yearning for significant lost places or persons but also a kind of collective human yearning for paradise and the lost innocence of an earlier world or earlier stages of human experience. Several of the locations in Charles Watkins's interior travelogues suggest this compensatory, lost/desired Edenic place, "a country where hostility or dislike had not yet been born" (*BDH* 36). Its contours and characteristics invoke the "myth-country" of Lessing's nostalgically recalled African childhood; in the first representation of this "lost landscape," golden leopard-like beasts become Watkins's companions in an idyllic terrain of lush forests, rivers, and savannahs. Eventually, after Watkins explores his domain and discovers the outlines of a vanished city,[9] he realizes that evil has somehow entered the idyllic place and understands his archetypal fall from innocence into the knowledge of good and evil: "I had arrived purged and salt-scoured and guiltless, but . . . between then and now I had drawn evil into my surroundings, into me . . ." (60).

The pattern of descent or entry into an idyllic location that is ultimately poisoned by human aggression or evil is repeated several times during the narrative, concluding with Watkins's lyrical recollection of his (imaginary) interlude with Partisan soldiers in Yugoslavia during the Second World War. He describes "vast mountains, in which we moved like the first people on earth, discovering riches at every opening of the forest, flowers, fruit, flocks of pigeons, deer, streams of running splashing water full of fish . . ." (233). A close friend asserts that Watkins never served in Yugoslavia.

Through the absolute discrepancies between who Watkins "is" to his relatives and friends and to himself—in his lyrical unconscious voyages and in his prosaic recovered identity (the latter restored through medical intervention)—Lessing explores, among other issues, nostalgic personal "memories" of innocence that are congruent with the fantasy of a harmonious Edenic past. Moreover, it is the shifting and selective nature of memory itself that is explored in the narrative through representations of complementary (if not contradictory) dimensions of Watkins's reality. Inevitably, by the time he is "restored" to his preamnesiac self, he has "lost" virtually all memory of his experiences in the interior realm, suggesting that each domain somehow cancels out the other. As he ruefully acknowledges to another psychiatric patient, "They say I lost my memory because I feel guilty. . . . I think I feel guilty because I lost my memory" (259).[10]

The yearning to return to an idyllic place in the past persists on an intergalactic scale as Lessing turns from "inner space" to "outer space" fiction. In Shikasta, for example, the Canopean emissary Johor returns after a long absence to the colonized planet Shikasta—a place he recalls as the paradisal Rohanda. His prejourney briefing includes a strong warning about the hazards of the now-degraded planet's innermost zone, Zone Six: its most characteristic feature is "a strong emotion—'nostalgia' is their word for it—which means a longing for what has never been or at least not in the form and shape imagined" (S 5–6). Johor knows that Zone Six is "a place that weakens, undermines, fills one's mind with dreams . . . that one had hoped . . . had been left behind forever" (7). Nonetheless, he and several other emissaries from Canopus submit themselves to the negative aura of Zone Six in order to influence selected inhabitants; their mission is to avert even further degeneration on the planet. Through documentary records of the emissaries' sojourns on Shikasta, the reader encounters Lessing's paean to a paradisal past along with her thinly disguised critical history of our own "Century of Destruction." Thus, Anna Wulf's—and even Johor's—critical judgment notwithstanding, Shikasta encompasses Lessing's ambivalent attitude towards nostalgia as both the domain of debilitating, falsifying memories and the inextinguishable yearning for a harmonious prelapsarian world.[11]

A "myth-country" located in the past—and in the imagination—also figures centrally in both Virginia Woolf's autobiographical writings and her fiction. The epiphanic "moments of being" that invigorate her fictional characters often originate in a yearning to return to or recover an idyllic scene or site. For Clarissa Dalloway, one such defining place is Bourton, where she spent a summer when she was eighteen. Recalling her passionate attachment to Sally Seton during that summer, she can still invoke the precise qualities of her feelings, preserved as if without alteration or distortion. "The strange thing, on looking back, was the purity, the integrity, of her feeling for Sally. It was not like one's feeling for a man. It was completely disinterested, and besides, it had a quality which could only exist between women, between women just grown up" (*MD* 50).

The central encounter in the narrative between Clarissa and Peter Walsh, with the ensuing ripples of recollection that it releases for both of them, pivots on nostalgia: their overlapping but differently colored memories and yearnings for the emotional intimacy and intoxication of their youthful romance at Bourton. "'Do you remember the lake?' [Clarissa] said, in an abrupt voice, under the pressure of an emotion which caught her heart, made the muscles of her throat stiff, and contracted her lips in a spasm as she said 'lake'" (43).[12] For Peter the image brings an inner wince of pain as well, as he is forced not only to confront his loss of Clarissa to Richard Dalloway all those years ago, but also to acknowledge that he still loves her.

In late middle age, Clarissa Dalloway thus looks nostalgically to the past, regretting the erosion of the freshness, the intensity, of her youthful passions. Still, Woolf—who believed that certain vivid memories retained their exact impressions intact in the mind, unmodified by the passage of time—permits Clarissa to preserve some of that vital fire of emotional truth in her adult life. The exhilaration she had experienced with Sally at Bourton survives in memory as the "radiance . . . the revelation, the religious feeling" (53) of their youthful encounter, a "moment of being" that she savors several times during the single day that forms the novel's present time.

The most emotionally saturated "myth-country" in Woolf's writing is not Clarissa Dalloway's Bourton, however, but the environs of St. Ives, Cornwall, where Virginia herself vacationed with her family during summers of her early years. Not only her first but, in her own estimation, her most central memory is associated with that landscape:

If life has a base that it stands upon, if it is a bowl that one fills and fills and fills—then my bowl without a doubt stands upon this memory. It is of lying half asleep, half awake, in bed in the nursery at St Ives. It is of

hearing the waves breaking, one, two, one, two, and sending a splash of
water over the beach . . . of lying and hearing this splash and . . . feeling
. . . the purest ecstasy I can conceive. (*MB* 64–65)

Later she emphasizes her feeling that nothing else in her early childhood was as valuable as the gift her parents gave her of those summer
holidays in Cornwall—"the best beginning to a life conceivable" (*MB* 110).
The account of St. Ives continues for several pages (110–17) as Woolf
describes in meticulous detail Talland House, its luxuriant gardens, and its
"perfect view—right across the Bay to Godrevy Lighthouse" (111). The latter
image of course became immortalized not only for Woolf but for her readers
as well in *To the Lighthouse.*

Woolf digresses briefly to examine the memory-making process itself,
as she mulls over "how many other than human forces affect us" (114). She
considers whether memory is an accurate record or "whether I am telling the
truth when I see myself perpetually taking the breath of these voices in my
sails, and tacking this way and that, in daily life as I yield to them . . ." (115).
Although she suspects this train of reflection "to be of great importance,"
Woolf puts it aside as "a vein to work out later" (115) and returns to her
vignette of St. Ives. Thus, she does not pursue the discrepancies between
"truth" and recollection, as Lessing's Anna Wulf does so insistently.

Woolf's idyllic memories of St. Ives are more significant when viewed
against her decidedly unnostalgic and unidealized descriptions of her childhood home at 22 Hyde Park Gate, London. Memories of that environment
are not softened by the scrim of nostalgia, for it was there that Woolf suffered
not only the deaths of several members of her immediate family—her
mother, stepsister, younger brother, and father all died within an eleven-year
period beginning when she was thirteen—but also the sexual advances of
her two half brothers.[13] Through memory and imagination she preserved the
image of her mother in particular, as well as other vanished members of her
family, as shields against a site so "tangled and matted with emotion" that
she felt "suffocated by the recollection" (*MB* 161).

## II. MOTHER

To the extent that nostalgia signifies not only "homesickness" or the yearning
for an emotionally significant place but also the longing for an absent,
emotionally important person, memory traces of *home* are inevitably linked
with those of *mother.* Both Virginia Woolf's and Doris Lessing's fiction and

autobiographical writings demonstrate this central emotional connection. Undoubtedly the fullest expression of nostalgia in Woolf's writing occurs in passages, both autobiographical and fictional, in which she attempts to recover the memory of her mother, Julia Stephen, who died when Virginia was thirteen. In "A Sketch of the Past," written when she was in her late fifties, Woolf admits that she remained haunted by the image of her mother until she was in her forties—until, in fact, she wrote *To the Lighthouse*. Before that time, "the presence of my mother obsessed me. I could hear her voice, see her, imagine what she would do or say as I went about my day's doings. She was one of the invisible presences who after all play so important a part in every life" (*MB* 80). Later she adds, "of course she was central. I suspect the word 'central' gets closest to the general feeling I had of living so completely in her atmosphere that one never got far enough away from her to see her as a person" (83).

Moreover, Woolf associated the death of her mother with the loss of the idyllic St. Ives. One summer, the Stephen family returned to Talland House to discover that the marvelous view of the lighthouse and bay had been spoiled by the erection of a hotel; soon, a real estate agent's sign appeared on their own lawn. "And then mother died. . . . Our lease was sold . . . and St. Ives vanished forever" (117). Thomas C. Caramagno, tracing the aesthetic expressions of Woolf's mood disorder in her fiction and autobiographical writings, proposes that manic-depressive illness itself might generate such nostalgia.

> Normal individuals react to the death of a parent, for instance, with sadness, mourning, and loneliness, but for the biochemically depressed this event takes on a huge biographical significance. Suffering an intense sense of abandonment and certain doom, convinced that they alone are inadequate and impotent, and feeling as helpless and as vulnerable as infants, these patients often look back nostalgically to what now seems to them an idyllic childhood union with an idealized parent, as they bemoan their loss or blame themselves for this fateful turn of events. (115)

In *To the Lighthouse*, Woolf imaginatively transforms "homesickness" by rendering into a consummate work of fiction her experience of the loss of her (idealized) mother as well as the idyllic setting of childhood with which that figure is profoundly associated. Like Julia Stephen, Mrs. Ramsay is an emotionally commanding presence who remains equally indelible in her absence, years after her death is matter-of-factly announced in the novel's middle section. Moreover, through a fictionalized persona, the artist Lily Briscoe,

.ores the pain still associated with the loss of that idealized mother. ɔbiographical commentary, Woolf observes, "if one could give sense of my mother's personality one would have to be an artist" [MB 85].) However, the motherless Lily of the first part of the novel worships Mrs. Ramsay in a manner that would characterize few actual mother-daughter relationships; idealizing the older woman, she literally desires to merge with her.[14]

> What device [was there] for becoming, like waters poured into one jar, inextricably the same, one with the object one adored? Could the body achieve, or the mind, subtly mingling in the intricate passages of the brain? of the heart? Could loving, as people called it, make her and Mrs. Ramsay one? for it was not knowledge but unity that she desired . . . intimacy itself, which is knowledge. . . . (TL 51)[15]

In the novel's middle section, the bracketed, understated announcement of Mrs. Ramsay's sudden death clearly mirrors Julia Stephen's unexpected death in 1895 at the age of forty-nine.[16] (Other bracketed statements of the deaths of Prue and Andrew Ramsay echo the loss of Virginia Woolf's half sister Stella and her brother Thoby to arbitrary, premature deaths.) While "Time Passes," the Ramsay house in the Hebrides—modeled after Woolf's mythologized St. Ives—remains empty and dark. The sense of literal and emotional absence represented through the deterioration of the unoccupied house recalls Woolf's observation about the years immediately following Julia Stephen's death: "with mother's death the merry, various family life which she had held in being shut for ever. In its place a dark cloud settled over us; we seemed to sit all together cooped up, sad, solemn, unreal, under a haze of heavy emotion" (MB 93).

In the novel's final section, Lily returns to the house in the Hebrides ten years later with the remaining Ramsays and confronts the undiminished power of Mrs. Ramsay's personality, despite her absence. Lily's nostalgic yearning is embedded in the effort of completing a (new) painting that, rather than capturing a realistic representation of Mrs. Ramsay, abstractly crystallizes her own feelings of attachment, longing, and loss. If nostalgia may be distinguished from simple memory by the presence of painful longing and a desire for the (impossible) restoration or recovery of that which has been lost, Lily experiences those feelings as she tries to recover Mrs. Ramsay's presence. Ultimately, in the novel's concluding passage, she reaches a cathartic moment that moves beyond the expression of longing to one of reconciliation with loss. Adding the final line that resolves the aesthetic and emotional dilemmas pursued through her painting, she acknowledges the moment of release: "I have had my vision" (209).

Thus, in the first part of *To the Lighthouse* Woolf creates a multifaceted vision of her mother, fabricated out of her own unrequited longing and loss, placing Lily to worship, childlike, at the maternal woman's knee—the way Woolf did (or imagined she did) as a child. However, in her autobiographical account, Woolf acknowledges more critically, "Can I remember ever being alone with her for more than a few minutes? Someone was always interrupting. When I think of her spontaneously she is always in a room full of people . . ." (*MB* 83). In the final section, the nostalgic yearnings, precipitated by the emotional finality of death, are balanced with a critical perspective toward Mrs. Ramsay that Lily would have been incapable of acknowledging ten years earlier. Phrased another way, the Mrs. Ramsay of the first part of the novel is a figure rendered from Virginia Woolf's nostalgic memories and fantasies, preserved from childhood, of her mother's *presence*. For the Mrs. Ramsay of the final part of the novel, Lily is the vehicle for Woolf's more critical exploration of the reverberations of her mother's *absence:* the emotional traces of nostalgia—and anger—triggered by irrevocable loss.[17]

Registering the cathartic effect of the process that she ultimately filtered through Lily Briscoe, Woolf analyzed the significance that writing about her mother (and father) in this novel had on her decades-long obsession:

> I suppose that I did for myself what psycho-analysts do for their patients.
> I expressed some very long felt and deeply felt emotion. And in expressing
> it I explained it and then laid it to rest. But what is the meaning of
> "explained" it? Why, because I described her and my feeling for her in
> that book, should my vision of her and my feeling for her become so
> much dimmer and weaker? (*MB* 81)

At the age of sixty-four, Doris Lessing—a few years older than Woolf when she wrote her autobiographical memoir—also attempted a "sketch of the past," no doubt prompted by her return to southern Africa after an involuntary decades-long absence. In it, she acknowledges the difficulty of articulating her earliest, painful memories as she attempts to achieve a balanced recollection of her parents, particularly her mother. Entirely unsentimental and unidealized, Lessing's recollection is almost antithetical to Woolf's: far from the self-sacrificing "angel of the house" embodied in Julia Stephen, Emily Maude Tayler is the quintessential rejecting mother. Lessing's memories are tainted by her knowledge from early in life that she was an unwanted child—that her mother, as she phrases it, "didn't like me" ("Impertinent Daughters" 61). Having wished for a first son, Maude Tayler repeatedly expressed her disappointment with her daughter, for whom she had chosen no name at birth (the attending physician suggested "Doris") and for whom she had "no milk. . . . I had to be bottle-fed from the start and I was half-starved for the first year and never stopped screaming . . ." ("Impertinent Daughters" 61).

Although a number of her novels suggest autobiographical sources in her own life, Lessing specifically labels *The Memoirs of a Survivor* her "attempt at autobiography."[18] Thus, her fictionalized representations of inter-generational female relationships deserve especially close scrutiny. Among other details that gain resonance in the context of Lessing's belief that her mother had rejected her from birth, the unnamed narrator describes "the sobbing of a child, a child alone, disliked, repudiated; and at the same time, beside it, I could hear the complaint of the mother . . . " (*MS* 145).

Lessing acknowledges in her autobiographical sketch that her memories of her mother are "all of antagonism, and fighting, and feeling shut out; of pain because the baby born two-and-a-half years after me was so much loved when I was not" ("Impertinent Daughters" 61). Not surprisingly, as she admits, "Writing about my mother is difficult. I keep coming up against barriers, and they are not much different now from what they were then. She paralysed me as a child by the anger and pity I felt. Now only pity is left, but it still makes it hard to write about her" ("Impertinent Daughters" 68).[19]

In the same sketch, a striking image of Lessing's parents reads as if it could have come from Woolf's *To the Lighthouse,* when Mr. and Mrs. Ramsay confront their mutually exclusive perceptions of the journey to the lighthouse—and of the world itself. As Lessing phrases it,

> I have an image of them, confronting Life in such different ways. He looks it straight in the face, with a dark, grim, ironical recognition. But she, always being disappointed in ways he could never be, has a defiant, angry little air: she has caught Life out in injustice *again.* "How can you!" she seems to be saying, exasperated, to Life. "It's not right to behave like that!" And she gives a brisk, brave little sniff. ("Impertinent Daughters" 57–58, Lessing's emphasis)

In fact, in certain ways Doris Lessing's significantly titled *Memoirs of a Survivor* is for Lessing what *To the Lighthouse* is for Woolf: an exploration of the nostalgic "lost mother" of childhood who is associated with the image of an idyllic vanished landscape of paradise or wholeness. However, the "lost mother" of Lessing's fiction is based less on her actual negative, rejecting mother than on a compensatory fantasy: the perfect parent of the imagination who offers unconditional love and acceptance.

As the narrator of *Memoirs* tries to make sense of the collapsing social world outside her window, she—another of Lessing's travelers in "inner space"—journeys symbolically through the wall of her flat to enter into another domain in space and time. There, she witnesses a young girl in various developmental stages. As the inner world the narrator apprehends beyond her wall becomes her "real life" (*MS* 18), the domain she visits "beyond the wall" ramifies into different layerings and emotional hues of experience and possibility. On the one hand it embodies the confining experiences of someone's actual past: variously, the young girl Emily and other females in the narrator's past, including her mother and her own earlier self at various stages of maturation. Significantly, Lessing's mother and her maternal grandmother were both named Emily.[20]

The location beyond the wall of the narrator's flat is understood as "a prison where nothing could happen but what one saw happening . . . with no escape but the slow wearing away of one [minute] after another" (42). Certain rooms trigger a powerful "tug of nostalgia for . . . the life that had been lived there" (41). A claustrophobic "child-space" (43), although apparently comprising Emily's experiences, is a location "as close to me as my own memories" (47). The narrator yearns at times to escape permanently into the inner realm, "simply to walk through the wall and never come back. But this would be irresponsible . . ." (24). Instead, rather than dismissing nostalgic memories as distortions that lie (as did Anna Wulf) or giving in to their painful but sentimental appeal, she determines to explore them and thus neutralize their debilitating power.

Hence, the domain beyond the wall also manifests sites of possibility, alternatives to the suffocating past enshrined in memory. "The space and knowledge of the possibility of alternative action" (42) offers the narrator the prospect of "restoration": revisions of experiences and locations both recalled and forgotten. She accepts responsibility for Emily as if she were her own daughter. Her choice may be understood, in light of Lessing's autobiographical admissions, as her attempt to achieve emotional reconciliation with her mother—herself a "poor girl brought up without affection" ("Impertinent Daughters" 55)—by reversing the generational obligations of the filial relationship. (In another ironic reversal, Lessing's mother also experienced "homesickness"—but for her, "home" was the England she had left behind for Persia and then Southern Rhodesia, before Doris's birth.)[21] In *Memoirs*, Lessing conflates her mother's nostalgia with her own: one of the narrator's fantasies or "fables" is pictured as a farm in Wales, far away from the collapsing city, characterized by "love, kindness, the deep shelter of a family" (34).

Late in *Memoirs,* the rooms the narrator has visited and at times helped to restore open out into layers of Edenic gardens that contrast sharply with the deteriorating, contaminated world she observes outside her flat. Ultimately, all walls dissolve and the nostalgic locations transmogrify into a place she can enter in present time. With Emily and others of their group, she is led "out of this collapsed little world into another order of world altogether" (217). The paradisal world they enter expresses the satisfaction of the desire to ameliorate "homesickness," to return to the state of ultimate harmony first known in the infant's attachment to its mother. As Jacoby phrases it, the longing for such a condition or place is ultimately "a longing for one's own well-being, which originally was dependent upon maternal care and protection, a longing to be cradled in a conflict-free unitary reality, which takes on symbolic form in the image of Paradise" (Jacoby 9). Thus are "home" and "mother" indissolubly bound through nostalgic memories.

In Lessing's *The Memoirs of a Survivor,* the figure who leads the narrator and the others into the ineffable is described in lyrical language reminiscent of Virginia Woolf's idealized fantasy of the lost mother of childhood. Coincidentally, the passage also contains an echo of the significant final phrase of *Mrs. Dalloway:*

> the one person I had been looking for all this time was there: *there she was.* No, I am not able to say clearly what she was like. She was beautiful. . . . I only saw her for a moment, in a time like the fading of a spark on dark air—a glimpse: she turned her face just once to me, and all I can say is . . . nothing at all. (*MS* 216, final ellipsis is Lessing's, emphasis is mine)

Suggesting an all-encompassing symbolic embrace that resolves the "longing for the mother as the 'containing world'" (Jacoby 7), "the world fold[s] itself up" (*MS* 216) around the nameless female figure who leads the narrator and the others into the blissful state that is the imagination's only antidote to homesickness.

## III. FIXING THE PAST

Following her return to Macheke/Mashopi to determine whether she could experience the place apart from her imaginative transformations of it in *The Golden Notebook,* Lessing wrote, "Memory in any case is a lying record: we choose to remember this and not that. . . . When we see remembered scenes from the outside, as an observer, a golden haze seduces us into sentimentality" (*AL* 72). As a description of the nostalgia-producing aspect of imagination, the language here is especially pertinent: the "lying record" of memory results from the inescapable filters of time and experience that separate the current self who recalls—"from the outside, as an observer"—from one's younger self whose experiences are recalled. Lessing's conviction that memory inevitably "lies" sharply contrasts with that of Woolf, who validates the undistorted accuracy of certain scenes from her childhood. While Woolf resists the possibility that, over time, memories are transformed by the evolving perspective of the observer-self, Lessing asserts the impossibility of recovering a "pure" version of any scene or experience in one's past.

Indeed, it is this difference in orientation, partly shaped by their different historical moments, that most distinguishes between the operations of nostalgia in Woolf's and Lessing's *oeuvres*. The modernist Woolf wrote during a time period in which collective loss (the devastations of one world war and a second one impending, the erosion of cultural stability, and the loss of the certitudes of traditional narrative form itself) corroborated the experiences of profound loss within her own personal circumstances. In both her fiction and her autobiographical writing, she attempts to "fix" the past—in both senses: to repair and to secure—at least in part by excavating nostalgic memories.

By contrast, Lessing is herself an exile who, reflecting (and reflecting on) her own experiences, continues to chronicle the dislocations of contemporary life—geographical as well as psychological and temporal. As Claire Sprague felicitously expresses it, "displacement, not arrival, is at the center of her imagination . . ." (*Rereading* 184). Thus, if the past is unequivocal for Woolf, it is entirely equivocal for Lessing. Through the lens of her postmodern orientation (a lens whose focus she herself helped to sharpen through her literary representations of her characters' fragmented psyches), Lessing questions the very fixity of the past that Woolf attempts to "fix," at the same time acknowledging the impossibility of achieving an unproblematic perspective in relation to either past times or places. Yet, despite the critique of "lying nostalgia" that Lessing articulates so persuasively through Anna Wulf in *The Golden Notebook,* a number of her other fictional and autobiographical writings betray the insistent grip of the lost landscape and the lost mother of her own formative years.

Nostalgia is the imagination's attempt to override, neutralize, or cancel loss. For Woolf and Lessing, that impulse fuels a desire not only to retrieve emotionally resonant memories but also to "mak[e] of the moment[s] something permanent" (Woolf, *TL* 161). Thus, I maintain that nostalgia is not simply, as Gayle Greene contends, "a forgetting, merely regressive, whereas memory may look back in order to move forward and transform disabling fictions to enabling fictions . . ." (298). Rather, the emotional resolutions that both Woolf and Lessing achieve through their aesthetic representations demonstrate the transformative significance of their fictional and autobiographical explorations of longing and loss, whether focused on idealized persons or places, or both. Though shaped by radically different historical, geographical, and personal circumstances, both authors explore and illuminate the writer's "myth-country"—"not . . . something untrue, but a concentration of truth" (Lessing, *AL* 35)—as they transform into art the lost mother of childhood and the lost landscape of home.

---

## NOTES

1. See Mario Jacoby, 5. David Lowenthal has located the meaning of the word *nostalgia* in medical history, "where it had been originally regarded as a disease with physical symptoms that were the result of homesickness: 'A physician found the lungs of nostalgia victims tightly adhered to the pleura of the thorax, the tissue of the lobe thickened and purulent. . . . To leave home for long was to risk death.'" (Lowenthal, *The Past is a Foreign Country* [Cambridge, 1985] 10. Cited in Shaw and Chase, 1).

2. Such vivid, almost photographically exact images are termed *eidetic* images.

3. In her wide-ranging analysis of the uses of memory in women's fiction, Gayle Greene discusses nostalgia in Lessing's *Children of Violence* and *The Golden Notebook* (see especially Green 302–3 and 308–10). She argues that, although nostalgia is not gender specific, it has "different meanings for men and women. Though from one perspective, women might seem to have more incentives than men to be nostalgic—deprived of outlets in the present, they live more in the past . . . —from another perspective, women have little to be nostalgic about, for the good old days when the grass was greener and young people knew their places was also the time when women knew their place, and it is not a place to which most women want to return" (296).

4. Betsy Draine, focusing on the relation between formal elements and meaning within Lessing's fiction, argues that Anna's nostalgia conveys a longing less for place than for a more abstract sense of order through form—"a yearning for the recovery of the sense of form, the stage illusion of moral certainty, innocence, unity, and peace. In effect, this yearning is a desire for unreality and nonexistence. Since the yearning can never

be fulfilled, it always leads to painful frustration and often to nihilism and despair" (Draine 71). Moreover, the notebooks each express a "pattern of opposition between nostalgia and awareness . . ." (72), including Anna-Ella's "long battle with nostalgia for the lost condition of naive commitment to an order of meaning" (81).

5.  I have explored these issues in greater detail elsewhere, concluding that "there is no single authoritative view of events" in *The Golden Notebook* (Rubenstein 102). Further, "all versions of Anna's experiences are fictions, though each is true in its own way. . . . The 'truth' is not in any one version of Anna's experiences but in what she—and we—understand by imaginatively fusing the various fragments and perspectives together" (Rubenstein 105–6). See also Greene, 308–10.

6.  Jennie Taylor, exploring *Going Home* as a text of colonial writing that blends autobiographical and political discourses, emphasizes the "interaction of difference, assimilation, and exile." Moreover, "*Going Home* implies arriving somewhere familiar, seeing it through a pentimento of memories, overlapping biographical and historical time, but as an alien who cannot be assimilated, either by the dominant white or subordinate black culture" (Taylor 60, 57). Although Taylor does not use the term *nostalgia,* her argument that Lessing "reinvents" crucial scenes from her past life in Africa "through the replacement of memory by desire" (63) coincides with what I term *nostalgia.*

7.  Nicole Ward Jouve, in her analysis of narrative and psychological aspects of *Children of Violence,* focuses on the "mud" of Lessing's original family home to symbolize Martha Quest's progressive loss of emotional connection to places and even to people. "[O]nce mud is left behind by the [*Children of Violence*] novels, once the mud house is lost, all sense of home is lost . . . [meaning] the ability of things, people, to *signify.* . . . [N]o house ever again has any weight of meaning [for Martha Quest]" (Jouve 81, emphasis in original). However, Lessing returns to the image of the mud house in *Shikasta.* (See Sprague, *Rereading 174*).

8.  In "Impertinent Daughters," Lessing describes the extraordinary richness and variety of wildlife that inhabited the bushland of her childhood:

> Every kind of animal lived there: sable, eland, kudu, bushbuck, duiker, anteaters, wild cats, wild pigs, snakes. There were flocks of guineafowl, partridges, hawks, eagles, pigeons, doves—birds, birds, birds. Dawns were explosions of song; the nights noisy with owls and nightjars and birds whose names we never knew; all day birds shrilled and cooed and hammered and chattered. But paradise had already been given notice to quit. The leopards and baboons had gone to the hills, the lions had wandered off, the elephants had retreated to the Zambesi Valley, the land was emptying. (65)

Later, she reiterates the "miracle of good luck" of her African childhood:

>We were surrounded by every kind of wild animal and bird,
>free to wander as we wanted over thousands of acres, solitude
>the most precious of our gifts . . . but our mother lay awake at
>night, ill with grief because her children were deprived, be-
>cause they were not good middle class children in some
>London suburb. ("My Mother's Life" 235, ellipsis in original)

9. The image of an Edenic city occurs throughout Lessing's work. It is a
leitmotif of *Children of Violence,* from the adolescent Martha Quest's
visionary fantasy of an ideal city (*MQ* 21) to the concluding volume of
the *Children of Violence* series, pointedly titled *The Four-Gated City.* As I
have noted elsewhere, "The image of the city also reproduces the
configuration of the sacred city, laid out with four cardinal orientations
whose center symbolizes the sacred center of the universe" (Rubenstein
127; see also 37–38, 56, 164).

   Ellen Cronan Rose traces to its sources in medieval texts the image
of the *città felice* in Lessing's work. Claire Sprague, in a chapter perti-
nently titled "From Mud Houses to Sacred Cities," also considers the
persistence of the image and its conflation of past and future fantasies;
she cites Frank E. Manuel and Fritzie P. Manuel's observation, in their
study of utopian thought, that "the nostalgic mode has been an auxiliary
of utopia" (Sprague, *Rereading* 155). Sprague traces the image of the
"archetypally lost city" from *Children of Violence* through Lessing's series
of intergalatic novels, *Canopus in Argos* (168–80).

10. See my fuller discussion of this narrative as a whole, in Rubenstein, *The
Novelistic Vision of Doris Lessing,* 175–99.

11. As Claire Sprague phrases it, "Lessing, who once seemed the quintessential believer in historical time, now seems a firm proselytizer for
archaic time" (*Rereading* 170).

12. Elizabeth Abel reads the recollected scene between Clarissa and Sally
Seton, interrupted by Peter Walsh's appearance, as a "psychological
allegory": "the moment of exclusive female connection is shattered by
masculine intervention . . . [suggesting] a revised Oedipal configuration:
the jealous male attempting to rupture the exclusive female bond,
insisting on the transference of attachment to the man, demanding
heterosexuality" (32–33). Abel also observes a kind of nostalgia in the
narrative, though one quite different in emphasis than the one I explore
here. As she phrases it, "Critics frequently note the elegiac tone which
allies *Mrs. Dalloway* with the modernist lament for a lost plenitude, but
nostalgia in this text is for a specifically female presence absent from
contemporary life" (42).

13. Woolf describes the "seductions by half-brothers" (*MB* 182) in "A Sketch
of the Past," especially 69, and in "22 Hyde Park Gate," especially 155.
Louise DeSalvo, exploring the significant implications of Virginia
Woolf's sexual abuse during childhood, concludes that "the pattern of
abuse lasted for many, many years, from roughly 1888, when [Woolf]
was six or seven, through 1904; that she was abused by more than one

family member; that it was a central formative experience for her; and that a pattern of abuse existed within the Stephen family" (*Impact* 101). Other Woolf scholars have challenged some of DeSalvo's assertions.

14.  In an early autobiographical commentary, written in her twenties, Woolf describes the relationship between her mother and her older half sister, Stella, in terms that both idealize the bond and suggest her own unfulfilled desires for merger with the mother they shared: "It was beautiful, it was almost excessive; for it had something of the morbid nature of an affection between two people too closely allied for the proper amount of reflection to take place between them; what her mother felt passed almost instantly through Stella's mind; there was no need for the brain to ponder and criticize what the soul knew" (*MB* 43).

15.  Ellen Bayuk Rosenman observes, "The double meaning of Lily's desire— as both a potentially fruitful aesthetic relationship and a dangerous emotional dependency—is hinted at by Lily's alternation of the terms 'knowledge' and 'intimacy,' as if she wanted to understand how her confusion of impulses might make sense" (101).

16.  Suzanne Raitt suggests that the bracketed statement of Mrs. Ramsay's death "signal[s] the violence with which we are forced to associate the decay of the house with that of Mrs. Ramsay, and to admit that wherever we look, she is in the end what we see. The brackets indicate at once a break in the narrative, and its essential truth" (56).

17.  A number of scholars have focused on the problematic relationship between Lily and Mrs. Ramsay in *To the Lighthouse,* including the possible parallels that may be drawn between the fictional characters and Virginia Woolf's relationship with her own mother, Julia Stephen. Using psychoanalytic approaches, Ellen Bayuk Rosenman and Elizabeth Abel both identify the intense, regressive, and ambivalent elements of the interrupted mother-daughter relationship as Woolf represented it through Lily's attachment to Mrs. Ramsay before and after her death. Rosenman, grounding her reading in object-relations psychology, observes that "Woolf's memory of Julia, written forty-seven years after her death, is specifically infantile, reconstructing the time when the mother is the child's whole environment. In Woolf's mind, Julia remains this idealized figure as if no other understanding of her had intervened since childhood" (Rosenman 7–8). Rosenman also suggests, "The original loss, for Woolf, is the loss of the mother, the 'centre' of St. Ives and childhood who is no longer present and who can only be approached through the compensatory gestures of art" (16).

Abel, revising elements of classic Freudian psychoanalysis from a feminist perspective, emphasizes the ambivalence of the attachment, noting that Lily is "buffeted by opposing impulses toward merger and autonomy in a pattern unbroken (and perhaps even intensified) by Mrs. Ramsay's death. . . . Lily functions simultaneously as the middle-aged artist whose completed painting 'of' Mrs. Ramsay concludes the novel that assuages Woolf's adult obsession with her mother and as an infant longing both to fuse and to separate" (Abel 68–69).

From a somewhat different position, Mark Spilka explores the consequences of what he terms Woolf's "impacted grief" (Spilka 120). He argues that in *To the Lighthouse*—Woolf's "elegy for her dead mother" (15)—she "returns to the childhood sources of her own blocked grief and successfully conveys the release of impacted feelings in a young spinster woman like herself; but, to avoid sentimentality and confusion, she circumvents the death which created that impaction, oversimplifies the life histories of her major characters, and so leaves untouched the most secret causes for her initial inability to grieve" (9).

Suzanne Raitt suggests that the idealized portrait of Mrs. Ramsay extends beyond Woolf's personal biography into an ambivalent attitude toward traditional and unconventional female roles: through her emphasis on Mrs. Ramsay's "feminine beauty," Woolf "appears to feel nostalgic for, as well as critical of, the ideal of Victorian womanhood" (Raitt 57).

Thomas C. Caramagno argues that "Woolf's preoccupation with her mother . . . stood for more than a neurotic longing to escape into the past. Julia became an emblem for Woolf's search for self" (Caramagno 153). Moreover, *To the Lighthouse* dramatizes Woolf's achievement of psychological as well as aesthetic equilibrium; Lily's resolution of her feelings about Mrs. Ramsay through her painting demonstrates that "the longing for mothering, for an idyllic past and manic omnipotence to overcome depressed helplessness, is replaced by adult self-sufficiency" (245). By the end of the narrative, "the body of the mother has been demystified; it is no longer seen as the only source of nurture and stability. . . . Woolf no longer desired to sacrifice her autonomy for the sake of becoming a child again" (269).

18. Lessing, quoted in front jacket copy of the novel.

19. Virginia Tiger, the first scholar to critique Lessing's autobiographical reminiscences of her mother, comments that the memoir "constitutes a critic's compost heap in whose mulch one sees seeded the many roots that have since taken fictional form" (7). Tiger briefly notes the correspondences between the autobiographical Maude Tayler and the figures of May Quest of Lessing's *Children of Violence* and Maudie of *The Diaries of Jane Somers*. Claire Sprague elaborates on Lessing's ongoing fictional representations and revisions of her knotted relationship with her mother (*Rereading* 108–28).

20. Lessing's mother later chose to go by her middle name, Maude ("Impertinent Daughters" 53).

21. Lessing remarked, in response to an interviewer's question about her mother's life in Southern Rhodesia, "Well, of course she wanted to go Home . . ." (Bertelsen 104).

# 3

—◆—

## WOOLF'S *BETWEEN THE ACTS*
## AND LESSING'S *THE GOLDEN NOTEBOOK:*
## FROM MODERN TO POSTMODERN SUBJECTIVITY

### Magali Cornier Michael

Virginia Woolf's *Between the Acts* (1941) and Doris Lessing's *The Golden Notebook* (1962) are transitional texts, in the sense that they contain both modernist elements and elements that push toward the postmodern. Exploring the links between Woolf's last novel, written as the world plunged into a second world war, and Lessing's postwar experimental novel yields insight into how women modernists developed certain subversive strategies that prefigure and anticipate the more radical challenges to Western metaphysics found in post–World War II fiction written by women. While Woolf's novel was published twenty-one years before Lessing's novel and is more firmly entrenched in modernism than Lessing's novel, both texts demonstrate a distinct movement from a modernist to a postmodernist notion of the subject. In addition, this push toward postmodern subjectivity is tied to feminist impulses in both cases.[1] After all, postmodern subjectivity's undermining of the binary logic on which the humanist subject is grounded potentially opens the way for the creation of new nonbinary notions of the subject, including notions of a specifically female subject.[2]

Although modernism begins to question the traditional humanist subject, the modernist subject's alienation and internal fragmentation is a direct result of the multiplicity of available perspectives rather than of some schism in *Being* itself (which would be postmodern). Modernists still tend to view the subject as always working toward a recentering and thus uphold the illusion of the subject as a coherent and unique entity grounded in an external reality that underlies all perspectives. For example, although the characters in Virginia Woolf's *The Waves* are reduced to named voices that tend to blur as they recount their alienation and fragmentation, the novel ultimately focuses on Bernard, who works toward a unity of consciousness. Woolf's novel suggests that there is no center of identity and that the self is fluid; and yet it also asserts that the selves it depicts are complementary and combine to form a complete and whole self, epitomized by Bernard's plural and yet unified consciousness.

In contrast, postmodernism posits a centerless, dispersed subject who is literally a composite of various socially and culturally constructed roles or positions—*not* perspectives—that cannot be reconciled. Rather than denying the subject outright, postmodernism calls into question the traditional humanist notion of the centered, rational, self-determining subject by situating the subject *within* culture and as a construction of culture.[3] Jacques Derrida, who has often been accused of doing away with the subject, in fact stresses that the "subject is indispensable" but "is a function, not a being" and that his aim is not to "destroy the subject" but to "situate it" by attempting to discover "where" the notion of the subject "comes from and how it functions" (271). In a similar vein, feminist critics such as Chris Weedon and Patricia Waugh have recently argued that the subject is "socially constructed in discursive practices" (Weedon 125) and "clearly *is* historically determined and situated" (Waugh 210). Moreover, the subject is not a static object but rather is always "in process" as it continuously moves toward a "becoming-other" than itself.[4] If the subject is a dynamic sociocultural function, then notions of the subject are open to transformation. Postmodern notions of the subject allow for the evolution of the subject and of specifically female subjectivities and thus have revolutionary potential for feminists—a potential not offered by traditional conceptions of the subject as containing an essential, centered, unchanging core. Indeed, I would argue not only that recent feminist fiction has been moving towards postmodern notions of the subject, precisely because they inherently allow for transformation, but also that germs of this movement can be located in the fiction of modernist women writers.

Insofar as postmodernism is both a reaction against and a continuation of modernism, the impulses disruptive of Western metaphysics used for feminist purposes in the fiction of post–World War II writers have their roots not only in contemporary existence, theory, and thought patterns but also in women writers' version of modernism in the first half of the twentieth century. As Andreas Huyssen has suggested, postmodernism's reaction against modernism is in effect a reaction against an institutionalized version of high modernism (185–90). Since the canon of literary high modernism conspicuously leaves out the work of women writers, precisely because it does not exactly fit the categories used to delimit high modernism, it is arguable that recent feminist writers *build from* rather than *react against* subversive elements within the novels of women modernists. Although the fiction of women modernists tends to be firmly grounded within modernism, these writers' particular focus on *women's* lives and thought patterns results in certain disruptions of traditional narrative and of Western conceptual modes—particularly subjectivity—that differ from those of their male contemporaries and that may be seen as germs of a movement toward the more radical disruptions created by more recent feminist writers.

To begin justifying this claim, an analysis of Virginia Woolf's writing is warranted, since she is arguably the most prominent literary predecessor of contemporary Anglo-American feminist writers. Woolf's access to the Hogarth Press, which she and her husband, Leonard Woolf, operated, meant that her books were published as soon as they were written and in a respected press. Furthermore, her central position within what became known as the Bloomsbury circle has given her a stature and recognizability that many of her contemporaries lack. All of this is not meant to take away from the undeniably high quality of her writing, but rather to help explain more fully why it has been more difficult for critics to ignore her work and why she is often the only woman writer to be included—if any are included at all— among the major modernist writers of fiction.

While *Between the Acts* remains grounded in modernist aesthetics, it also contains impulses and strategies that overtly push beyond modernism and that may explain why the novel has received less critical attention than some of Woolf's other texts. Since this posthumously published novel is harder to fit within the established framework of high modernism, it is often left out of critical discussions or course syllabi as unfinished, as an oddity, or as inferior.[5] However, *Between the Acts* is well worth examining, in that it highlights Woolf's sometimes contradictory conception of the subject and demonstrates more explicitly than some of her other texts the tension between the modernism and the movement beyond modernism that emerges from her writing in general and that is explicitly tied to her feminist impulses. Moreover, Woolf's novel functions as one side of a bridge to recent fiction that more overtly utilizes postmodern strategies and notions for feminist aims.

Doris Lessing's *The Golden Notebook* is one of the texts that make up the other side of this bridge. Like Woolf's novel, it remains grounded in modernism to a certain extent, and yet it also demonstrates a movement beyond modernism that surpasses *Between the Acts*. Lessing's novel stands as a monument in the history of post–World War II Anglo-American experimental fiction written by women, as it uses, challenges, and leaves behind the conventions and conceptual underpinnings of both realism and modernism. In particular, *The Golden Notebook*'s presentation of the subject steps decisively beyond realism and modernism as it opens up the way for and seeks to create new forms of female subjectivity.

— ◆ —

As early as 1924 in her essay "Mr. Bennett and Mrs. Brown," Woolf focuses specifically on the problem of the subject and its novelistic representation. Her view of the writer's task as an attempt to represent an elusive subject underscores her adherence to traditional notions of the subject as possessing an essential core and of art as mimetic, even if she questions the means by which representation can be achieved. Rejecting the notion that subjects or characters can be represented adequately in terms of their particular social and material contexts, Woolf insists that the goal of the modernists is to capture the essence of the subject. Yet her warning to readers not to "allow the writers to palm off upon you a version of all this, an image of Mrs. Brown, which has no likeness to that surprising apparition whatsoever" (28), implicitly acknowledges the difficulties of mimetic representation and of pinpointing an essential core within human beings. Although Woolf's discussion centers around a neutral or genderless subject, it is noteworthy that her representative subject is a woman and that she criticizes the means by which the Edwardian male novelists would have represented Mrs. Brown.[6] Her call for new ways of representing the subject thus seems to contain a more specific but as yet not verbalized call for new ways of representing a female subject, a challenge that she takes up in her own writing. Indeed, the notion of the female subject is central to most of Woolf's essays and fiction.

Female subjectivity is treated using strategies that pose more overt challenges to Western metaphysics in *Between the Acts* than in most of Woolf's fiction. *Between the Acts,* Woolf's last published novel, is torn between a modernist conception of the fragmented subject, possessing an essential self distinct from the social or surface self and from the outside world, and a (postmodern) notion of the fragmented subject as unstable, centerless, and dispersed.[7] Miss La Trobe is the epitome of the modernist alienated artist, presented as an isolated, lonely, and eccentric figure with a strong central core that allows her to create. Her modernist aesthetics surface in her belief that she can represent the essence of characters or subjects and that she can create a sense of unity. She is intent on finding new methods of representation but does not question the possibility of representation itself. Miss La Trobe's experimental play is a pageant of history that aims to bring together the members of the audience and make them "see" (98) historical events in their political and social contexts and thus assumes that a real or true history can be represented.

The modernism inherent in the depiction of Miss La Trobe as alienated artist, and of her play as an effort to find a new way of representing reality, is juxtaposed with a vision of the subject that pushes beyond modernism in the depiction of the audience and its reactions to the ending of the performance. In the last scene of the play, "The Present Time. Ourselves" (178), all the actors come out onstage with mirrors and other reflecting surfaces, which they point at the audience. This scene, which forces the audience to look at itself as "the looking-glasses darted, flashed, exposed" (183), steps decisively beyond modernism. The mirroring effect breaks down the barrier between audience and stage, audience and actors, and thus challenges the traditional distinctions between reality and fiction, life and art. The distorted and fragmented reflections of themselves that the members of the audience are forced to view visually emphasize the subject as fragmented, centerless, and dispersed and also blur the distinction between individuals:

> Now old Bart . . . he was caught. Now Manresa. Here a nose . . . There a skirt . . . Then trousers only . . . Now perhaps a face . . . Ourselves? But that's cruel. To snap us as we are, before we've had time to assume . . . And only, too, in parts . . . That's what's so distorting and upsetting and utterly unfair. (184)

The audience itself becomes a character in the play and in the novel, as individuals are revealed to lack unity, wholeness, separateness. The play's last scene creates the image of a fragmented subject with no distinct limits or center. The individuals in the audience are unable to evade their own distorted reflections; they are trapped in front of the spectacle of their own decentered and dispersed subjecthood.[8] Although on the one hand the play attempts to bring the audience together, on the other hand its depiction of the present through the use of mirrors denies the audience any sense of unity or wholeness: "the audience saw themselves, not whole" (185). Miss La Trobe's play thus both embraces and surpasses high modernism.

Isa is another modernist, alienated-artist figure—although she keeps her poetry secret from those around her—but her depiction at times steps beyond modernism. It is not clear, for instance, that she has an essential or core self, since she is so divided between her various roles as wife, mother, poet, romantic, lover. William Dodge takes notice of the multiple selves she takes up and discards: "he saw her face change, as if she had got out of one dress and put on another" when her little boy appears, and minutes later "again she changed her dress" (105) to address the nurse.

Isa feels trapped within marriage, within the old love-hate oppositional plot, and yearns for a new relationship between the sexes: "Surely it was time someone invented a new plot" (215). This acknowledgment of the need for structural changes is a feminist move with radical implications, which suggests that Isa is keenly aware of sexual politics and its role in subject formation. However, she lacks the strength to step out of the old plot even though she glimpses possibilities for change. She is unable to escape "the burden . . . laid on me in the cradle" (155) of being a woman in a male-dominated world. For example, she is powerless in the face of the double standard that allows married men but not their wives to philander: "She could hear in the dusk in their bedroom the usual explanation. It made no difference; his infidelity—but hers did" (111).

The movement toward a notion of the subject as a set of constructed roles rather than an essential core is further demonstrated in the novel's presentation of Isa's acute awareness of the sexual politics that affect her life in asides, in thoughts, in between the actions of the novel. This focus on the realm of the *in-between,* which is highlighted in the novel's title, calls attention to the ways in which Western culture masks and silences the workings of sexual politics in the construction of subjectivity in order to create the illusion of an essential central self. To highlight the realm of the *in-between* is a potentially radical move in that it disrupts a Western metaphysics that is grounded in binary thought, which attempts to negate all that lies in between hierarchically arranged polar opposites.

The novel's focus on silence—on what lies in between actions, words, and thoughts—thus functions as a politically charged device, emphasizing the cultural silencing of that which threatens the status quo. The material physical world enters the novel only as disconnected intrusions occurring in between events or thoughts. Although World War II is raging at the time the novel is set, 1939, war and the effects of fascism are only felt through isolated instances such as when "twelve aeroplanes in perfect formation" (193) fly over the audience in between the halting attempts of Reverend Streatfield to explain the meaning of the play once it has come to a close. Sexual violence also enters the novel in spurts; images of the gang-rape Isa has read about in the *Times* intrude into the gaps of her thoughts throughout the day. The juxtaposition of this picture of rape, which was "so real" (20), and the pastoral and traditional setting of the novel highlight the sexual politics implicit in the act of rape and its being silenced in the male-centered English family and culture:

> Every summer, for seven summers now, Isa had heard the same words;
> about the hammer and the nails; the pageant and the weather. Every year
> they said, would it be wet or fine; and every year it was one or the other.
> The same chime followed the same chime, only this year beneath the
> chime she heard: "The girl screamed and hit him about the face with a
> hammer." (22)

The short flashes of the rape scene take on at least as much importance as
the events being dutifully recorded at length by the narrative, so that the
realm of the *in-between* becomes a locus of attention. The novel's interest in
silences or gaps thus exhibits a feminist impulse by placing emphasis on the
sexual violence that remains unspoken and yet is powerfully present in
traditional settings and narratives. In some sense, war/fascism and rape/sex-
ism are in some ways being connected by being presented as the unspeak-
able, silenced elements within the traditional English family setting.[9]
Moreover, the novel demonstrates the ways in which the sexual violence that
is being silenced in effect constructs Isa's subjectivity: she remains unable to
act outside of the roles prescribed to her even though she acknowledges how
these roles limit and subdue her.

The novel's treatment of the issue of gender also demonstrates a
movement away from notions of an essential self. The novel highlights and
inherently criticizes the way in which gender is constructed and gender traits
assigned within a male-centered culture through sympathetic depictions of
characters derided for not fitting within accepted gender boundaries. Mr.
Oliver calls his grandson "a cry-baby" (13) and "a coward" (19) for being
frightened by the beak of paper meant to amuse him, thus embracing the
conventional notion that boys must be courageous and never cry. Miss La
Trobe is viewed as an oddity and an outcast because she breaks the set
standards for women. She is neither delicate nor demure; instead, she is
"swarthy, sturdy and thick set," she is sometimes seen "with a cigarette in
her mouth," she uses "rather strong language" (58), and she has lived with
an "actress who had shared her bed" (211).

But it is the character of William Dodge who calls the most attention
to the workings of social convention in the construction of gender. Again the
novel uses silence as emphasis. Giles angrily denounces Dodge's failures as
a man but leaves out the crucial condemnation:

> A toady; a lickspittle not a downright plain man of his senses; but a teaser
> and twitcher; a fingerer of sensations; picking and choosing; dillying and
> dallying; not a man to have straightforward love for a woman—his head

was close to Isa's head—but simply a ——— At this word, which he
could not speak in public, he pursed his lips. (60)

Homosexuality is taboo, since it threatens the neatly established association
of specific gender traits and roles with each of the sexes. Even Dodge views
himself as "a half-man," as a "mind-divided little snake in the grass" (73),
thus highlighting the extent to which individuals internalize the prescrip-
tions of conventions and to which subjectivity depends on cultural norms.

Although *Between the Acts* contains certain disruptive elements that
push beyond modernism, the novel nevertheless remains anchored in
modernism. With the exceptions of the scene in which the audience is
forced to watch its own reflection, the presentation of Isa as a conglomera-
tion of various roles or selves, and the depiction of gender as a product of
cultural norms, the novel asserts a modernist notion of the subject as
possessing an essential core beneath the surface fragmentation. The depiction of characters as possessing some kind of individual essence that makes
them autonomous and privileged separates the subject as essence from any
type of social, cultural, historical, or political context. Furthermore, the rare
intrusions of the politics of material existence help to create a subject that
is divorced from the world, thus upholding the traditional dichotomy
between the inner self and the outer world. Woolf's attempt to capture the
female subject by depicting the sensory world and individual experience of
daily life results in the almost total exclusion of the exterior material world,
and thus to a certain extent limits the possibility of political engagement.
On the other hand, the very intrusions of the politics of material existence
in between scenes, words, and thoughts call attention to all that is sup-
pressed in order to enforce the status quo. *Between the Acts* thus contains a
variety of features that anchor it firmly to the established canonized high
modernism, particularly in its emphasis on the whole integrated subject;
and yet it contains a number of elements that begin to disrupt traditional
Western metaphysics to the extent that the novel does not comfortably fit
within the institutionalized version of modernism, which itself remains
grounded in binary logic. The result is often a tension between modernist
notions and the germs of a movement toward a more radical challenge to
Western conceptual modes, a tension that may explain in part why *Between
the Acts* is often excluded from discussions of the modernist canon.

— ◆ —

Like Woolf's novel, Doris Lessing's *The Golden Notebook* (1962) is a transitional
text exhibiting a distinct movement from a modernist to a postmodernist notion
of the subject. In addition, this push towards postmodern subjectivity functions

as a feminist strategy. Lessing's novel is located within the context of the massive questioning of Western ideology that has dominated intellectual life since World War II. Like other literature of the period, *The Golden Notebook* responds to a new world of violence, terror, and chaos: the atomic bombing of Hiroshima and Nagasaki, Stalin's purges, South African apartheid, the instability of newly independent Third World nations. Within this disturbing context, *The Golden Notebook* attempts to situate and define a new female subject. Such a project of redefinition necessarily questions and problematizes the existing Western system of thought and values, particularly the system of binary oppositions that underlies Western metaphysics and shapes human consciousness as well as social structures and norms. Central to the novel are the dismantling of traditional notions of the subject and a movement toward the delineation of a new female subject that is not grounded in binarism.[10]

The Golden Notebook is a compilation of various texts. A short, five-chapter frame novella entitled "Free Women" is written in conventional narrative form. But the novella's chapters are interspersed by fragments of four notebooks kept by the central character of "Free Women," Anna Wulf. She uses each of the notebooks, distinguished by color, to record a different aspect of her life: the black notebook focuses on Anna the writer and on the memory of her early experiences in a communist cell in Africa; the red notebook deals with politics as it records her intensely conflicted relationship with the British Communist Party; the yellow notebook is a fictionalization of Anna's own life, particularly her recently ended love affair with Michael, written in the form of a novel entitled *The Shadow of the Third*; and the blue notebook is closer to a diary and tends to focus on states of mind. Eventually Anna ends each of the four notebooks and begins a new golden notebook, which records her descent into madness with her new American lover, Saul Green. The novel as a whole is also circular; it has no set beginning or ending. Near the end of the novel, Saul gives Anna the lines that begin the novella, "Free Women," and the novel as a whole, *The Golden Notebook*. Lessing's novel is thus constructed out of Anna's various pieces of writing: fragments of a novella and of five different notebooks, and the editorial notes that introduce and order these fragments.

Rather than merely presenting the character Anna, the novel contains various versions of a character called Anna as well as a writer and an editor also named Anna. This multiplicity of Annas on various levels calls into question not only conventional notions of character but also the humanist concept of the whole, unified, integrated self. There exists no essential Anna in *The Golden Notebook;* instead the novel offers many versions of Anna on several narrative levels, so that the name "Anna" can at best refer to a composite of various roles, functions, and representations. Anna is the editor of her various pieces of writing that she organizes to form the novel, *The Golden Notebook;* Anna is the author of various private notebooks; Anna is the author of a traditionally written novella entitled "Free Women"; Anna is the subject-character of the notebooks; Anna is a character in "Free Women"; and Ella is a fictional representation of Anna in the yellow notebook.

None of these Annas, however, *is* Anna. Instead, these versions of Anna suggest or approximate what the human being or character named Anna might be like.[11] Lessing's novel depicts a centerless subject who is literally a composite of various socially constructed roles or positions that cannot be reconciled: social self, political self, sexual self, gendered self, parenting self, artistic self. The only thing that unifies Anna is her name. In this sense Lessing is moving toward a postmodern notion of the subject as a socially and culturally constructed position.

Lessing has picked up on the postwar nihilism that has created a rift in *Being* and necessitated a reconceptualization of the subject as decentered and dispersed. While the challenge to the illusion of the subject as whole has most often been associated with postmodernism, it is potentially compatible with feminism in that it allows for the construction of an alternative conception of the subject. The movement toward postmodern subjectivity enables *The Golden Notebook* to approach a delineation of a new female subject that is not grounded in any transcendental or essentialist notions of *Being* but that instead posits the subject as a constructed set of positions and functions within a specific configuration of material and cultural conditions.[12] By underscoring the constructed quality of gendered roles, the novel attempts to explain both the fragmentation inherent in human beings and the breakdown of relations between the two sexes in a decaying society in which chaos reigns and roles can no longer remain fixed.

Since woman has traditionally been positioned on the object side of the classical dichotomy between subject and object, the first step toward creating a new female subject is to destabilize that opposition. *The Golden Notebook* takes up this challenge by positioning Anna as both subject or teller and object or character of her story. There is a constant process of difference and deferral as Anna shifts to occupy both and neither poles of this opposition. As editor, author, and character of *The Golden Notebook,* Anna's position within the dichotomy between subject and object is no longer stable.

The same is true of the related opposition between self and other. The Annas who are the objects of the notebooks and the characters of the various fictional pieces are the *Other* of the author-self Anna, and all of these Annas are ultimately the *Other* of the editor-self Anna. Anna's ability to both represent and recognize her *Other* in its various guises suggests that the novel conceives of the *Other* in modernist rather than postmodernist terms—the postmodern *Other* being precisely that which cannot be recognized or represented and yet which constitutes the self. Anna's recognition of her *Other* in the characters of her pieces of writing has much in common with Clarissa Dalloway's recognition of Septimus as her *Other* in Virginia Woolf's modernist novel *Mrs. Dalloway*. Yet Lessing does tug a little at the modernist conception of the *Other* in her presentation of Anna's *Other* in the form of versions of Anna, so that the *Other* is less vividly separate and more explicitly part of the subject herself than in the case of Woolf's Clarissa Dalloway.

The concept of the *Other* in *The Golden Notebook* is closer to the Lacanian *Other,* which seems to lie between the modernist and postmodernist *Other*. Jacques Lacan begins to disperse the subject by suggesting that it is composed of a dynamic interaction between a speaking subject, an alienated subject of identification or ego, identificatory objects, and an *Other* that for Lacan is knowable only inasmuch as it speaks through the unconscious—its language.[13] The Lacanian *Other* thus both constitutes and inhabits the human subject and is not directly perceivable. Anna's *Other,* discerned indefinitely in the fragments of her writing, similarly composes and is contained by the human being designated by the name *Anna*. The Lacanian *Other* is ultimately not postmodern, however, since it insists on a set structure to explain and tie together the dispersed elements that make up the human subject. *The Golden Notebook* likewise challenges but retains the opposition between self and other. In fact, it approaches a conception of the dispersed, decentered, postmodern subject only when it investigates madness, toward the end of the book. Since the novel conceives of both the self and other as constitutive of and contained by the subject, it does succeed in breaking down the hierarchical arrangement by which women have traditionally been placed in the position of *Other*. Anna is not *The Other;* she is a subject in her own right and encompasses the positions of both self and other.

Although she lives in a fragmented world in which roles and selves have become increasingly fragmented, Anna, the character and writer of notebooks, tries to hold on to a humanist concept of the whole integrated self by compartmentalizing her life. Anna rejects "[a]lienation. Being split" and tries to hold on to a "humanism" that "stands for the whole person, the whole individual" (360). She works to keep her roles as writer, communist, friend, mother, and lover distinctly separate: in a diary entry of the blue notebook, Anna admits that "[t]he two personalities—Janet's mother, Michael's mistress, are happier separated. It is a strain having to be both at once" (336). In her writing, Anna uses four separate notebooks to deal with various aspects of her life, feeling that otherwise "it would be such a—scramble. Such a mess" (266). Anna has convinced herself that the division of her life into four notebooks will stave off the chaos of contemporary existence and enable her to retain a concept of wholeness. She thus creates an artificial form of split personality to guard herself against *real* madness; but, in the end, she cannot sustain the inherent contradictions of this enforced division in the name of an illusion of wholeness. Not until Anna deliberately ends her four separate notebooks and begins to write in a single notebook does she finally accept the formlessness of life and of the individual.

Once she has accepted the world's chaos by willingly descending into madness and by writing in only one notebook, the golden notebook, Anna not only recognizes that "a world of disorder lies behind" (633) the surface of things and people, but she also accepts that she occupies a multiplicity of irreconcilable positions or selves. Although Anna feels "threatened with total disintegration" as she sinks into chaos through dreams, her experience of seeing herself "sleeping, watching other personalities bend over to invade her" (614) as she becomes "an Algerian soldier" (600) and a Chinese "peasant woman" (601) frees her from her divided self. Her acceptance of fragmentation and chaos as multiplicity and formlessness rather than as division pushes *The Golden Notebook* beyond modernism. By presenting fragmentation as a function of *Being* itself rather than as the result of a plethora of subjective interpretations, the novel has stepped decisively from modernism to postmodernism: after all, Anna's dream emphasizes that she fills a variety of subject positions. Postmodern identity can in fact be viewed as a set of dynamic roles, since postmodernism insists that human beings constantly take up and give up various sociocultural subject positions and thus have no singular, unified, stable subjecthood.

*The Golden Notebook*'s questioning of the conventional opposition between sanity and insanity in the latter sections of the novel serves as a means by which Lessing more decisively tests, explores, and dissolves the humanist notion of the subject. The male-centered nature of this dichotomy is particularly evident in the traditional association of sanity with reason, order, and men and of insanity with emotions, chaos, and women. Challenging what is essentially a deeply male-centered Western opposition therefore becomes a potentially feminist as well as postmodern move. Anna in fact plays into the conventional set of hierarchical oppositions when she attempts to hold on to her reason as a means of staving off chaos and madness:

> she set her brain on the alert, a small critical, dry machine. She could
> even feel that intelligence there, at work, defensive and efficient—a

machine. And she thought: this intelligence, it's the only barrier between me and—but this time she did finish it, she knew how to end the sentence. Between me and cracking up. Yes. (395)

As the novel progresses, however, the dichotomies between sanity and insanity and between reason and madness slowly disintegrate to the point of meaninglessness.

*The Golden Notebook* demonstrates that chaos can no longer remain outside the individual in a world in which "destruction" is acknowledged "as a force" (589) and in which "war" and "the immanence of war" are "the truth for our time" (591). The novel depicts Anna's wilful descent into madness as a means of acknowledging and accepting chaos and formlessness. Barbara Rigney suggests that in *The Golden Notebook* "[t]o go mad in a positive sense is to give up all certainty" and "to lose the distinction between the real and the not-real, between the self and the not-self" (75); madness itself thus undermines the traditional oppositions between self and other, self and world. Yet Rigney's assertion—that in the novel's world "[o]nly through the recognition of one's own madness as a reflection of the world's madness can a higher sanity be achieved" (74)—is problematic since it inherently assumes an opposition between self and world and between sanity and madness and posits the conventional term—sanity—as hierarchically superior and desirable. Lessing's novel questions the rigidity of these dichotomies and reveals that madness and sanity are not opposites but are merely culturally constructed labels for the two extremes of an unstable continuum: Anna recognizes that "the word sane meant nothing, as the word mad meant nothing" and that she "could see no reason why I should be mad or sane" (594).

The novel does not reverse the dichotomy and embrace madness, however, as is made clear by Anna's emergence from her exploration of insanity to go on and write "Free Women" and *The Golden Notebook*. Anna does not achieve "a higher sanity," as Rigney puts it, but rather reaches a point at which she accepts the continuous process of difference and deferral that destabilizes the rigid boundary between sanity and insanity. Anna understands that she can neither disown her own madness nor allow it to render her socially paralyzed:

> it's not a question of fighting it [madness], or disowning it, or of right or wrong, but simply knowing it is there, always. It's a question of bowing to it, so to speak, with a kind of courtesy, as to an ancient enemy: All right, I know you are there but we have to preserve the forms, don't we? (634)

Although the experience of her own madness allows Anna to transgress traditionally imposed limits or boundaries, she cannot let herself sink into madness and still function within a social system that depends on set forms. The novel thus calls into question the opposition between sanity and insanity, without putting emphasis on either term. Madness is depicted as both a symptom of and a cure for the fragmentation, formlessness, and violence of the contemporary world.[14] Lessing neither glorifies nor dismisses madness; she simply explores it.

The Golden Notebook presents madness in the form of split personalities and suggests that this state of consciousness parallels the fragmentation and chaos inherent in contemporary existence. Anna is disconcerted by Saul's inconsistent behavior, until she understands that he is struggling with madness and is in effect various persons:

> What was strange was, that the man who had said No, defending his freedom, and the man who said, pleading, It doesn't mean anything, were two men. I couldn't connect them. I was silent, in the grip of apprehension again, and then a third man said, brotherly and affectionate: "Go to sleep now." (562)

By presenting human beings as conglomerations of dispersed personalities, the novel reveals that the notion of a centered self is at best only an illusion. Saul's constant shifts from one self to another suggest that the human subject is in process and can never be fixed. Anna's own encounter with madness further emphasizes human beings' simultaneous occupation of various subject positions; she is "conscious of two other Annas, separate from the obedient child—Anna the snubbed woman in love, cold and miserable in some corner of myself, and a curious detached sardonic Anna, looking on and saying: 'Well, well!'" (562). Lessing seems to suggest that pathological split personalities are in effect only extreme versions of the schizoid contemporary subject.[15] Anna describes madness as "the place in themselves [people] where words, patterns, order, dissolve" and as something that "is there, always" (634). When Anna reemerges from her wilful descent into madness, she retains a split self. Saul refers to two of Anna's selves when he gives her the first line of "Free Women" and of The Golden Notebook: "I'm going to give you the first sentence then. There are the two women you are, Anna. Write down: The two women were alone in the London flat" (639). The novel's exploration of madness therefore enables it to push beyond the high modernist illusion of the unified centered subject.

The Golden Notebook is not a postmodern novel per se, since it holds on to the traditional agenda of telling an individual's story; but its mode of questioning and its attempt to find new notions of the subject show clear signs of a movement toward the postmodern, especially in its exploration of madness. The madness segments expose the gaps within subjectivity that have most recently been covered over by a bourgeois version of individualism and by high modernism's alienated subject and individual ego-self. No longer locked within the rigid opposition between subject and object, postmodern subjectivity encompasses both terms and neither term of the dichotomy. *The Golden Notebook* works toward a vision of a new subject independent of traditional binary oppositions and of imposed gender traits. The novel's Anna is not this new subject; however, by presenting multiple versions of Anna, the novel rejects illusions of the subject as unified or centered and pushes toward a postmodern notion of the subject: as decentered and dispersed, and always "in a process of 'becoming'" (Johnston 21). Assigning Anna to the position of madwoman, a position that traditionally has been marginalized because it threatens the status quo, enables Lessing not only to challenge the humanist subject but also to begin to fictionally create a new, specifically female, subject.

— ♦ —

Through its detachment from any one given position, postmodern subjectivity unveils notions of hierarchy and opposition as artificial constructions used by the dominant order to retain its position of power. In Woolf's *Between the Acts* and Lessing's *The Golden Notebook,* the movement toward postmodern subjectivity is tied to the novels' feminist impulses; both novels destabilize the binary system of thought that organizes the world, and perceptions of the world, according to a hierarchical opposition between the sexes. These two novels thus begin to make use of postmodern notions and strategies precisely because they allow for transformation, for creating new types of subjectivities that are not binary, hierarchical, and static. In this sense, these two novels anticipate the more radical subversions of traditional notions of subjectivity found in more recent feminist experimental fiction.[16]

Moreover, this analysis of *Between the Acts* and *The Golden Notebook* helps to document and explain the progressive movement toward more overt postmodern impulses in much recent feminist fiction. The tension within Woolf's novel between modernist and postmodernist notions of subjectivity not only suggest that *Between the Acts* is a transitional text, but also opens up the possibility that modernist texts written by women were already moving towards the postmodern, especially with relation to subjectivity, because of their interest in finding ways to depict the consciousness of *women*.[17] I am thus suggesting that women writers' version of modernism needs to be rethought, since it diverges from canonical high modernism, and that the movement toward the postmodern evidenced in recent feminist fiction has a history that can be traced back to the experimentation of women modernists.

---

## NOTES

1. I think that it is more accurate to talk of *feminist impulses* within fiction rather than of *feminist fiction,* since texts vary greatly as to the degree of their feminism. However, for the sake of efficiency, I will use the term *feminist fiction* in this discussion.

2. The traditional humanist subject is grounded in the system of hierarchical binary oppositions that underlies Western thought. Within this binary logic, the subject or self is defined in relation to a less powerful object or other. Since the oppositions, subject/object and self/other, coexist with other oppositions—such as man/woman, white/black, heterosexual/homosexual, civilization/barbarism—the privileged subject or self is associated with man, white, heterosexual, civilization; while the hierarchically inferior object or other is associated with woman, black, homosexual, barbarism. By undermining binary logic, postmodernism this makes possible nonbinary reconceptualizations of the subject. As Andreas Huyssen suggests, postmodernism challenges "the *ideology of the subject* (as male, white, and middle-class) by developing alternative and different notions of subjectivity," by "working toward new theories and practices of speaking, writing and acting subject," and by questioning "how codes, texts, images, and other cultural artifacts constitute subjectivity" (213).

3. In more general terms, Linda Hutcheon similarly argues that "postmodern discourses . . . do not deny the individual, but they do 'situate' her/him" (46).

4. See John Johnston's "Ideology, Representation, Schizophrenia: Toward a Theory of the Postmodern Subject" for a more in-depth discussion of postmodern subjectivity. Similarly, Chris Weedon suggests that subjectivity is always "in process, constantly being reconstituted in discourse every time we think or speak" (33), and E. Ann Kaplan discusses the "process toward subjectivity" (34).

5. This is not to suggest that there are no strong critical discussions of *Between the Acts.* What I'm suggesting, however, is that the novel has received considerably less critical attention than many of Woolf's other texts. Moreover, most of the critical discussions of *Between the Acts* are recent, which suggests that readers and critics are reevaluating this novel.

6. Woolf specifically refers to Bennett, Wells, and Galsworthy when she discusses Edwardian novelists.

7.   This latter notion of the subject as centerless, unstable, and dispersed
     has generally been associated with postmodernism. A few other critics
     have discussed *Between the Acts* in terms of postmodernism but have not
     focused specifically on the issue of subjectivity. See, for example, the
     work of Marilyn Brownstein, Pamela Caughie, and Alan Wilde.

8.   The fragmentation and distortion that result from the mirrors in Woolf's
     novel thus differs from the modernist fragmentation and distortion
     evident in something like Picasso's canvases. When a Picasso painting
     distorts the human body by presenting various perspectives of body
     parts simultaneously, the human figure nevertheless remains: no dis-
     persion of the subject occurs, and the subject retains a center. However,
     the multiple mirrors in Woolf's novel create a plethora of disconnected
     body parts, pointing to a subject that has no distinct limits or center. In
     addition, a Picasso painting retains the status of aesthetic object separate
     from its viewers. In contrast, the mirror scene in Woolf's novel breaks
     down the distinctions between audience and actors, life and art, reality
     and fiction.

9.   Patricia Joplin has argued more extensively that the novel links
     "patriarchy at home and its extreme form abroad, fascism" (210).
     Karen Kaivola similarly suggests that the novel links "gender divi-
     sions" and "brutality, militarism, oppressive economic systems, and
     imperialism" (50).

10.  Molly Hite similarly argues in *The Other Side of the Story* that "the critique
     of ideology" in *The Golden Notebook* goes "beyond narrowly Marxist
     principles to the more general set of presuppositions governing Western
     culture in the modern period, ultimately addressing the assumption that
     any world view can be adequate, that reality is the sort of thing that can
     be held together as a unified whole" (63). But she also asserts that novels
     by writers like Lessing are "recognizably distinct from the post-
     modernists" (2). In contrast, I am arguing that the effect of *The Golden
     Notebook*'s critique of Western metaphysics and use of various disruptive
     strategies is a movement toward the postmodern that coincides with and
     even propels the novel's more subversive feminist aims.

11.  Claire Sprague also notes that there are "many fictive Annas" (*Doubles* 45)
     in the novel and suggests that "Anna is a cosmos" (*Doubles* 56). I am also
     very much in agreement with Toril Moi's assertion that Lessing "radically
     undermine[s] the notion of the unitary self, the central concept of Western
     male humanism" in her rejection of "the fundamental need for the individ-
     ual to adopt a unified, integrated self-identity" (7).
          Molly Hite goes even further, claiming that "Lessing in effect intro-
     duces one of the defining features of postmodernism, the decentered
     subject" (Hite, "[En]Gendering Metafiction" 484). Although I agree with
     Hite, I think it is more accurate to suggest that Lessing is moving *toward*
     a postmodern notion of the decentered subject. I also think that the
     novel gives rise to more than just "two distinct Annas who can be neither
     reduced nor subordinated to one another" (Hite, *The Other Side of the*

*Story* 80): rather, the novel gives rise to a multiplicity of Annas on various narrative levels.

12. I thus agree with Molly Hite's assertion that "the problem with conceiving character in terms of preexisting forms is that such forms do not allow 'the future'—that is, anything genuinely new and unassimilated by the dominant culture—to be represented" (*The Other Side of the Story* 65).

13. For a good discussion of Lacan's conception of the human subject, see Ellie Ragland-Sullivan's *Jacques Lacan and the Philosophy of Psychoanalysis.*

14. Inta Ezergailis argues that Lessing's novel views madness "as both the extreme representation of the split ['cultural schizophrenia'] and an indication of a cure" (26). Elaine Showalter also suggests that the novel views "schizophrenia as an intelligible and potentially healing response to conflicting social demands" (238).

15. The work of Gilles Deleuze and Felix Guattari advances a notion of the subject as schizoid. For a discussion of the work of these two writers and of the postmodern subject as schizoid, see John Johnston's "Ideology, Representation, Schizophrenia: Toward a Theory of the Postmodern Subject."

16. More recent feminist fiction that radically subverts traditional notions of subjectivity includes a wide range of texts, from those that are highly experimental on a formal level all the way to those that appear very conventional in form: for example, Kathy Acker's novels, Brigid Brophy's *In Transit,* Angela Carter's *Nights at the Circus,* Fay Weldon's *The Life and Loves of a She-Devil,* Toni Morrison's *Beloved,* and Marilynne Robinson's *Housekeeping.*

17. My reading of the fiction written by women modernists other than Woolf, such as Gertrude Stein, Dorothy Richardson, H.D., and Djuna Barnes, backs up this assertion, although analysis of these writers' texts is beyond the scope of this chapter.

PART TWO

— ◆ —

# REDEFINING ROLES AND RELATIONSHIPS

# 4

— ◆ —

## THE "OUTSIDER-WITHIN": VIRGINIA WOOLF AND DORIS LESSING AS URBAN NOVELISTS IN *MRS DALLOWAY* AND *THE FOUR-GATED CITY*

### Christine W. Sizemore

Virginia Woolf is not only "the first canonized twentieth-century woman writer" (Marcus, "Pathographies" 807), but also the first urban woman writer, the one who describes in detail the twentieth-century city.[1] Although Claire Sprague argues that Doris Lessing is not influenced by Virginia Woolf in terms of style or form (*Rereading* 2), it is possible that Lessing learned from Woolf how to write about the city because both Lessing and Woolf use the standpoint of alienation to observe the city. It is precisely that alienation from the dominant culture, Hannah Wirth-Nesher argues, that allows a writer to perceive the modern city which is so

> heterogeneous and so vast that it . . . [can] not be perceived at one time. This [realization] is far more likely to occur when the author . . . has been by dint of the role society and history have assigned . . . [an] outsider, a minority member, or one who feels strongly the fragmented, secretive, and unfamiliar aspects of the city. (92)

Both Woolf and Lessing share an experience of being an outsider that allows each to observe the city from a different standpoint than someone who experiences the city only from within the majority culture. Both Woolf and Lessing can thus precisely delineate the fragmentation in space, in interpersonal relationships, and in time that is an integral part of living in a modern city. Woolf portrays this fragmentation in post–World War I London in *Mrs. Dalloway;* Lessing in post–World War II London in *The Four-Gated City.*

The particular outsider standpoint that both Woolf and Lessing share is like that defined by the African-American sociologist Patricia Hill Collins as the "outsider-within." Collins uses this term to describe the standpoint of African-American women, particularly those "ghettoiz[ed] . . . in domestic work." Collins explains that these women see "white power demystified" but they also know that they can never belong to their white "families." This "outsider-within" stance functions, Collins argues, "to create a new angle of vision" (11). Rachel Blau DuPlessis links both Woolf and Lessing to African-American writers in that they all share "double marginalization," Woolf as female and lesbian and Lessing as female and colonial (33).[2] Sara Suleri rightly cautions that "the marriage of two margins should not necessarily lead to the construction of that contradiction in terms, a 'feminist center'" (758), but Collins's "outsider-within" concept is general enough to describe new "angles of vision" without claiming that all standpoints come from exactly the same place. Certainly Alice Walker has been very clear in her revising of passages from *A Room of One's Own* for *In Search of Our Mothers' Gardens* that the history of enslaved African-American women is very different from that of "Shakespeare's sister," and that the obstacles preventing African-American women from writing were much greater than those Woolf describes. Nonetheless, Walker's very quotation from Woolf[3] acknowledges Woolf's initial depiction of the barriers all women writers must face. Furthermore, the existence of a strong African-American tradition of urban novelists— from James Baldwin to Ralph Ellison to Toni Morrison's *Jazz*—illustrates Wirth-Nesher's point that the outsider is the most sensitive perceiver of the urban environment. The best urban novelists seem to be those who are sufficiently within the majority culture to understand the elements of the city, but sufficiently outside it to be able to feel the fragmentation of the modern city and to judge its impact.

Although both Woolf and Lessing share the general standpoint of "outsider-within," their standpoints differ in terms of class, not only from the African-American domestic workers Collins describes, but also from each other. Virginia Woolf is an insider in terms of class and Doris Lessing is not. Although Jane Marcus asserts that "a salient sub-text in every Virginia Woolf novel is the voice of working class women, the heroic charwoman" ("Taking the Bull by the Udders" 149), many other critics, and even Lessing herself, disagree. Alex Zwerdling argues that although Woolf

> taught courses to working-class men and women, married a socialist, and held meetings of the Women's Co-operative Guild at her own house, the "lower orders" in her fiction are conspicuous by their absence. When they do appear, they are often given a generic identity, their individual characteristics expunged. (96)

In a 1962 interview Lessing makes the same point, saying Woolf is too ladylike:

> I've always felt this thing about Virginia Woolf—I find her too much of a lady. There's always a point in her books when I think—my God, she lives in such a different world from anything I've ever lived in, I don't understand it. I think it's charming in a way but I feel that her experience must have been too limited, because there's always a point in her novels when I think, "Fine, but look what you've left out." (Joyner 204-5)

Class differences, however, are not the only causes for feeling outside the dominant culture. Although Woolf is by class one of the "intellectual aristocracy" (Zwerdling 91), she strongly felt herself an outsider because of gender. Woolf used the term "outsider" to define herself from her earliest diaries in 1903 when she describes Vanessa and herself as outsiders alienated from the larger family circle, to her 1938 work *Three Guineas,* in which she proposes an Outsider's Society, to an October 26, 1940, diary entry in which she says she likes "outsiders better. Insiders write a colourless English" (Zwerdling 115). Woolf links her feelings of being an outsider to her perception of the city in *A Room of One's Own:*

> if one is a woman one is often surprised by a sudden splitting off of consciousness, say in walking down Whitehall, when from being the natural inheritor of that civilisation, she becomes, on the contrary, outside of it, alien and critical. (97)[4]

It is this "outsider-within" standpoint in which she combines insider status in terms of class and outsider status in terms of gender that Woolf brings to her portrayal of Clarissa and London in *Mrs. Dalloway.* Clarissa's insider status in terms of class makes her especially sensitive to the small changes in city life in the immediate post–World War I era that both illustrate the links with the past and foreshadow changes in public life and class structure.

Clarissa's sense of being an outsider in terms of gender and the power structure allows her the freedom to observe all the details of city life and to look around the city for a new community, one based not merely on class status but on a shared love for city life. The tone of the novel combines nostalgia for some of the people and places of the past whom Clarissa loved and celebration of the new promises of urban life.

Doris Lessing, born in a generation in which women were not shooed off the grass at universities or denied entrance to a library, did not feel as alienated as Woolf in terms of gender and did not experience the limitations of an upper-middle-class Victorian upbringing; nonetheless, Lessing vividly feels her outsider status as a colonial. Judith Kegan Gardiner explains that what this outsider status of "being a colonial-in-exile does is to put into play an oscillation whereby no place is home, home is ambiguous and ambivalent, here and elsewhere, and so there remains always a missing point of origin" (Gardiner, *Rhys* 13).[5] It is this sense of "outsiderness" that both haunts and gives freedom to Lessing's Martha Quest in *The Four-Gated City*. Martha Quest, as a white woman of English descent, is always in exile in Africa, but she can never be at home in London either. Lessing uses the same angle of vision that Woolf does, that of the "outsider-within," to portray contemporary London, but Martha Quest is even less an "insider" than Clarissa Dalloway. Her stronger sense of alienation from English culture erases any tone of nostalgia for the past. In fact she views England's past role as empire-builder with contempt. Martha joins Clarissa in a celebration of the city, but there is not for her so much a search for community as an exultation in the freedom that the contemporary city can give to a woman. At the same time, Martha as a survivor of World War II is even more aware of the dangers of complete destruction. The human mortality that Clarissa senses within herself as she approaches old age is seen on a global level by the younger, more contemporary Martha. In spite of these differences, however, it is the sharing of the mixed standpoint of outsideness and insideness that allows each protagonist to observe the city with such precision and to comprehend the fragmented nature of the modern city.

City planner Kevin Lynch explains that the modern city can not be conceptualized as a single entity; it can only be seen in fragments: "the city is a construction in space, but one of vast scale, a thing perceived only in the course of long spans of time. . . . It is seen in all lights and all weathers. . . . our perception of the city is not sustained but rather partial, fragmentary, mixed with other concerns" (*Image* 1–2). Many city inhabitants are so overwhelmed by the "vastness" of the modern city that they do not "see" it. Others restrict their observations to a particular place or neighborhood, like those writers whom Blanche Gelfant classifies as "ecological" novelists, authors who describe only a small "spatial unit" of the city (Gelfant 11).[6] The "outsiders-within" are the truest observers of the modern city because they look at the city with an already "split consciousness," as Woolf says, aware both of being inheritors of the civilization the city represents and yet of being profoundly alienated from it. This dual standpoint makes the perceiver of the city particularly sensitive to the incongruities of the modern city—specifically to the fragmentary nature of urban experience, both in the perception of urban spaces and of the people of the city—and to the city's changes through time. It is this "split consciousness" that creates the great urban novelists.

In *Mrs. Dalloway,* Woolf describes the combination of insider status in terms of class and outsider status in terms of gender in the character of Clarissa Dalloway. This "being Mrs. Richard Dalloway" (11) gives Clarissa a certain insider status in terms of class. The prime minister comes to her party, and some of her childhood friends are in powerful positions—for instance, Hugh Whitbread, who carries "a despatch box stamped with the Royal Arms" (5). Nonetheless, Clarissa feels alienated. She feels she has been exiled in her own house, banished upstairs by Richard to an attic room and narrow bed. Supposedly, Richard has convinced Clarissa to move upstairs after her illness so she can sleep without his interrupting her, but she feels solitary and rejected, "lying there reading . . . she could not dispel a virginity preserved through childbirth which clung to her like a sheet" (31). Clarissa feels strongly rejected by Lady Bruton, who invites Richard to lunch because he, as a public figure, can help her in her projects, but she does not include Clarissa. That rejection makes Clarissa realize even as she prepares for her party that a hostess has no power. Peter reflects society's attitude toward a hostess when he remembers that he tried to hurt Clarissa by calling her the "perfect hostess" (62).

Even the women in the novel who might *seem* important are shown as powerless. Although Clarissa envies Lady Bexborough—"slow, stately; rather large; interested in politics like a man" (10)—Lady Bexborough has no power to prevent her son's death in the war. Her opening of a bazaar seems hollow and ironic as she holds in her hand the telegram announcing her favorite son's death. Clarissa feels rejected by Lady Bruton, who has "the reputation of being more interested in politics than people; of talking like a man" (105); but Lady Bruton cannot write her own letter to the *Times,* and her project of encouraging respectable young people to emigrate to Canada is trivial and insignificant. Lady Bruton is finally satirized and dismissed as she drowses on her couch after lunch, snoring and dreaming of "commanding battalions marching to Canada" (112) while the men go back to their real work. Women may be interested in politics, as even Clarissa is in her parties for important people, but they are all still outsiders, and those who have an illusion of power—like Lady Bruton—are shown to be fools.

Unlike the other two women, however, Clarissa embraces her outsider status, and it gives her the freedom to perceive the city. Walking up Bond Street, Clarissa has "the oddest sense of being herself invisible; unseen; unknown" (11). It is from this viewpoint that Clarissa can observe the fragments that make up the city, each one significant in itself:

> Bond Street fascinated her; Bond Street early in the morning in its season; its flags flying; its shops; no splash; no glitter; one roll of tweed in the shop where her father had bought his suits for fifty years; a few pearls; salmon on an iceblock.
>
> "That is all," she said looking at the fishmonger's. "That is all," she repeated, pausing at the window of a glove shop where before the War, you could buy almost perfect gloves. (11)

Given the context of Clarissa's exhilaration at walking down Bond Street, her phrase, "That is all," does not refer to the paucity of goods available after the war, but rather to one detail's ability to stand for all that London can provide. It only takes one roll of cloth to signify that a tailor can produce a magnificent suit. It only takes a pair of gloves to link the stores of the present to the stores of the past. Whatever the privations of the war, the city still signifies an abundance of experience. Clarissa absorbs each detail of city space and appreciates all that each detail represents. She feels no need to arrange these details or to put them into a single context, as Richard Dalloway or Hugh Whitbread or even Peter Walsh would do.

Clarissa not only sees the fragmentary nature of city space, but from her perspective of the "outsider-within" she can identify with the outsiders of the city, even "the veriest frumps, the most dejected of miseries sitting on doorsteps . . . can't be dealt with, she felt positive, by Acts of Parliament for that very reason: they love life" (4).[7] Clarissa sees a variety of people as she walks toward the flower shop in Bond Street. Some she knows fairly well, such as Hugh Whitbread; others only slightly, such as Miss Pym, the florist; and others not at all. But she acknowledges and identifies with all of them in her love of the city. She accepts them as fellow urban citizens even though she knows only a fragment of their stories, or does not know them at all. Her standpoint allows her to feel a kinship with all city dwellers. Clarissa accepts the people of the city just as she accepts the passing motor car or the skywriting of the airplane or even the echoes of Big Ben. They are all fragments of city life. Clarissa does not know who is in the car or what the airplane is writing; she can tolerate indeterminacy and enjoy the urban fragments for themselves.

Big Ben, with its "leaden circles" (*MD* 4), represents time in the city. Clarissa's outsider-within status allows her to see two aspects of time: linear time and cyclical time. Big Ben represents linear time as it marks the passage of time during the day. In her essay on "Women's Time," Julia Kristeva identifies this kind of time as masculine, "the time of project and history" (Kristeva 36). Sometimes Clarissa also thinks of Big Ben as masculine, as, for example, when she introduces her daughter to Peter Walsh and the "sound of Big Ben striking the half-hour stuck out between them with extraordinary vigour, as if a young man, strong, indifferent, inconsiderate, were swinging dumb-bells this way and that" (*MD* 48).[8] Clarissa, however, later deconstructs this dominating sense of time, "his majesty laying down the law" (*MD* 128), by relating the clock to nature: "the leaden circles dissolving in the air" (*MD* 4, 94, 186) are like watery circles that result from something dropping on the surface of a pond. Julia Kristeva identifies this kind of time as that embraced by the second phase of feminism, time that "rejoins . . . the archaic (mythical) memory and . . . the cyclical or monumental temporality of marginal movements" (Kristeva 37–38).[9]

In *What Time is This Place* Kevin Lynch presents an insight about time slightly different from that of Kristeva. Although he does not associate his two different definitions of time with gender, he links cyclical urban time to nature, as Woolf does, and he gives a new perspective to historical time. The first aspect of time Lynch mentions is similar to Kristeva's cyclical time: "rhythmic repetition— . . . sleeping and waking, hunger, the cycles of the sun and moon, the seasons, waves, tides, clocks" (65). Here Lynch also links the repetition of clocks to repetitions in nature, as Clarissa does with her "leaden circles." Lynch calls his second aspect of time "progressive and irreversible change—growth and decay, not recurrence but alteration" (65). This progressive time is not the same as Kristeva's linear or historical time, because although progression has some linear characteristics, Lynch's definition makes it clear that progressive time can also be accompanied by a profound sense of mortality and loss, of decay as well as growth. Clarissa's recent illness makes her particularly aware of time as decay and change, and she links this changing aspect of time to the repetition of clock time: "For having lived in Westminster—how many years now? over twenty,—one feels even in the midst of traffic . . . a particular hush, or solemnity; an indescribable pause; a suspense (but that might be her heart, affected, they said, by influenza) before Big Ben strikes" (*MD* 4). Clarissa can accept her own aging and potential death and can also accept change in the city.

Clarissa's perception of urban time includes the positive achievements of progressive time, such as the airplane overhead; but it also involves the sadness and decay that time can bring in public life, as represented by the many references to the war throughout her sections of the novel, as well as those of Septimus. Clarissa balances the sadness that change can bring by invoking the cyclical time of memory, not only in the echoes of Big Ben but also in her observation of the shops in Bond Street which she used to visit with her family: "one roll of tweed in the shop where her father had bought his suits for fifty years. . . . a glove shop where, before the War, you could buy almost perfect gloves. And her old Uncle William used to say a lady is known by her shoes and her gloves" (11). The fragmentary sights of the city signify the potential abundance of the city, but they also represent both change and memory, progressive time and cyclical time. They trigger memories of the insider status of Clarissa's childhood when she was protected by her father and her Uncle William and her visible status of "lady," but they also remind her of her present position as outsider. Clarissa has long since discovered that any status that "being a lady" might have implied was illusory. Clarissa uses the details of the shops to link the time before the war, a time for her of childhood and protection, to the time after the war, a time which, in spite of the celebration of life represented in the city, still contained the tremendous losses suffered by all classes because of the war. Clarissa has no nostalgia for or any illusions about class status; but she does miss the familiar people of her childhood who have since died, and she is aware of her own impending death and the many deaths caused by the war. This awareness mutes the tone of the novel, but it does not destroy Clarissa's celebration of the city. The city has survived the war; the roll of tweed, the gloves are still visible in the city shops. "That is all" that she needs to trigger her observation of and appreciation of the city.

Like Clarissa Dalloway, Martha Quest in Doris Lessing's *The Four-Gated City* is an "outsider-within" the city of London, but Lessing's novel is set in post–World War II London. Martha is younger and more robust than Clarissa and does not consider herself a "lady." Furthermore, because of these qualities, Martha walks in more varied districts of the city than Clarissa and gets to know working-class people as well as those from the upper and middle classes. She shares with Clarissa, however, the standpoint from which she observes the city, that of the "outsider-within." As a white person, Martha is an insider in London in a way that she had not been growing up in Africa. Even as a woman, she feels free to walk around all parts of the city and not stand out. Nonetheless, her perception of the city is also that of an outsider, a colonial. For instance, when Martha first sees Trafalgar Square with her upper-class English friend Henry, "she looked at the haphazard insignificance of it, and the babyish statue" and laughs to think that "this . . . is the hub of the empire" (22). Martha realizes that, unlike Henry, she does not see these landmarks as symbols of nationalistic pride but rather as symbols of a destructive colonial domination. Geographer Yi-Fu Tuan argues that "[a]rchitectural space . . . articulate[s] the social order" (116), but one must add, only for insiders within that social order. Martha knows what the landmarks are supposed to mean, but she observes them from a different angle. From the standpoint of an "outsider-within," Martha Quest, like Clarissa Dalloway, sees the fragmentary nature of urban experience and the dual aspects of time operating in the city.

Like Clarissa, Martha feels a tremendous freedom in being "unknown" and thus able to walk around the city anonymously: "For a few weeks she had been anonymous, unnoticed—free. . . . Coming to a big city . . . means first of all, before anything else . . . freedom" (4). Martha is able to walk around a varied number of districts of the city because she too feels invisible and safe in her anonymity. Even among the prostitutes of Bayswater Road, Martha feels safe from being accosted by men because she clearly is an outsider and not one of the women waiting to pick up someone: "She was protected precisely by the line of girls for sale, who knew she wasn't one of their trade union" (33).

Because she is free to walk throughout the city, Martha can gather impressions of many different districts and spaces of the city.[10] Like Clarissa, she notes the many fragments that comprise city life. Martha starts one of her walks on the same Oxford Street that Clarissa does. She too notices the shops and the effect the war (World War II) has had on the availability of goods, but Martha looks with the eyes of a colonial. She realizes: "this is one of the streets whose name I've been brought up on" (32), but the reality of Oxford Street deconstructs for Martha the colonial myth of England's greatness. The clothes in the windows look shoddy and tasteless. Even "a yard of war-impoverished cloth can be woven with more sense or art" (32), she thinks to herself. Martha does not so much cherish the fragments of urban life, as Clarissa does. Rather Martha uses these fragments to come to understand what the real London is, as opposed to the mythic "hub of the empire" she has heard so much about. As a strong young woman and an exile who has not been brought up to avoid certain "dangerous" parts of the city, Martha continues her walk much further than Clarissa does. Martha notes the change in districts and in the classes of people who frequent them as Oxford Street and the shops turn into Bayswater Road, with its huge empty houses that had once been the homes of the wealthy, although now only prostitutes line the street. Martha even ventures into the squalor of Notting Hill and thinks about the differences between the city districts that she has just walked through:

> The "West End" was a market only. . . . The enormous piles [the houses] along the Bayswater Road had been and would be again a climate of money. But the streets from here to the canal were depressing . . . houses that . . . were cracked and leaning and dirty and wet, . . . boarded-up spaces full of rubble or water-filled craters. (34)

These fragments of city spaces allow Martha to perceive the great variety of post–World War II London, with both its wealth and its squalor, its surviving market places and its bomb-damaged empty spaces. Clarissa sensed the loss that World War I represented in her thoughts about the different men who died in the war; Martha, in her greater wanderings about the city, sees the physical results of World War II in the spaces of the city.

Martha gets to know individual Londoners from a variety of class backgrounds. She values her freedom and outsider status too much to live with any one group of people long and realizes that she knows only fragments of people's stories. Nonetheless, she knows lower-class Londoners much better than Clarissa, who identifies abstractly with the people of the city but does not live with them. Martha maintains her standpoint of the "outsider-within"; she never allows herself to become actually part of a group, but she stays with some individuals long enough to experience what their lives are like. When she first comes to London, Martha lives briefly with Iris, who runs a cafe, and she meets Stella, who lives down by the docks and is "the matriarchal boss of her knot of streets, among the body-proud, work-proud men who earned their wages by physical strength" (15). In her short stay with these women, Martha comes to know working-class life in a way that even her friend Phoebe, a Labour Party worker, does not. Phoebe knows statistics about the working classes, but she does not know individuals. When Phoebe asks Martha how she finds London, Martha thinks:

> And now, because it was Phoebe who sat there opposite, the past weeks changed their aspect and presented "London" to Martha as a series, containing dockland Stella, the cafe and Iris; Jack; Henry; and the people in streets and pubs. Fragments. (79)

Martha enjoys the variety of people whom she has met, but she admits that she only knows them as fragments. Her refusal to become an insider in any one group allows her to see fragments of lives in many groups. By accepting knowledge in fragments, Martha can maintain her freedom and see the breadth of lives that comprise a city.

Martha accompanies her own observation of the city with her knowledge of these people's lives, however fragmentary, and their perceptions of various aspects of urban life. When Martha walks through Iris's neighborhood, she walks "in a double vision, as if she were two people: herself and Iris, one eye stating, denying, warding off the total hideousness of the whole area, the other with Iris, knowing it with love" (10). As a colonial outsider, Martha critiques the spaces of the city, seeing the ugliness that colonial myths had tried to mask. Having lived "within" the neighborhood, however, even for a brief time, Martha can also see the neighborhood with Iris's eyes and Iris's love for her small bit of the city. Yi-Fu Tuan suggests that "[p]lace is security, space is freedom" (3). The insiders can see "place," the small parts of a city, such as a neighborhood, that have great meaning to someone who lives within it. The outsiders can see "space," the largeness and multiplicity of a city. Martha can perceive both in the city. As an outsider, a colonial, Martha notices the spaces of the city.[11] Borrowing Iris's viewpoint, Martha can see the "place" within the urban spaces.

Martha is also aware of the presence of time in the city. If, for Clarissa, time in the city is represented primarily by Big Ben's chimes that bring her back to the rhythms of life, for Martha—although she too occasionally hears Big Ben—the dominant aspect of time in the city is Lynch's "progressive" time. Martha carries with her as a talisman a fragment of a piece of wallpaper,[12] which she scraped off a wall at a bomb site. Like Clarissa, Martha recognizes both the decay and the growth of progressive time. Martha is aware of the destruction the war and the bombing of London have brought, but she also thinks of positive changes that the layers of wallpaper represent. She counts thirteen layers of wallpaper and thinks of the many different times people covered over their wallpaper and redecorated their homes. Each layer of wallpaper represented a change, a new investment for each family and a hope for their future: "Thirteen times had a wife or children said, Yes, that's very nice, I like that Dad; or had said, No, we chose wrong" (74). Like Clarissa, Martha can see the movement of time within the city in the small details of urban life.

Throughout the novel, Martha carries with her the sense of changing time in the physical city as well as in the lives of the inhabitants. Ten years after her arrival when Martha sees the rebuilding of London, she still remembers the earlier scenes of the bombed city:

> The city had lost its grey shoddiness; that dirty, ruinous, war-soaked city
> . . . it was gone. . . . She walked through this city and kept that other one

in her mind, so that a long street of fashionably bright buildings had behind it, or in it, an avenue of nightmare squalor, a darkness and a lightness together, the light so precarious a skin on a weight of dark, for these sagging old carcasses had been dabbed, merely, with paint: there was a surface of freshness. . . . London heaved up and down, houses changed shape, collapsed, whole streets were vanishing into rubble, and arrow shapes in cement reached up into the clouds. . . . it seemed as if the idea of a city . . . as something slow-changing, almost permanent, belonged to the past. (287–88)

Martha recognizes that the idea of the city as something permanent and unchanging is as unreal as the myths of colonialism. Behind the new city with its bright buildings and arrow-shaped skyscrapers, Martha still sees the war-ravaged city. Martha's vision gives new meaning to Tuan's understanding of "place as time made visible" (179) because Martha sees this part of the city both as it now exists and as it existed ten years ago. Like Clarissa's, Martha's perception of time in the city contains the aspects of both growth and decay, but Martha's vision is ultimately darker than Clarissa's. The destruction of London after World War II is more visible than that after World War I, and Martha retains the visual memory of bombed London behind the postwar urban renewal. Martha recognizes the new buildings as only a "precarious" skin over the former darkness. Clarissa feels a sense of loss in terms of the many lives lost in World War I, but for her the continuity of the shops and the streets in London represents a potential survival of civilization; Martha's sense of change is more foreboding. Martha sees a more damaged London after World War II, and she is aware not just of the technology of the airplane but of the atom bomb that the airplane can carry, and thus the potential loss of all civilization, of all cities.

By the end of *The Four-Gated City*—which itself is composed of appendices, fragments—this loss has occurred; Martha is dead and most of the cities of the world have been destroyed. Mark Coldridge, Martha's friend and one of the few survivors, reflects the only possible hope the novel suggests by thinking of cities in terms of cycles of history: "All those old cities, the olive trees, the vines, the fields, all gone, fusing the civilisations under them into seas of glass, . . . Nineveh and Tyre, and Sodom and Gomorrah, and Rome, Carthage, Balkh, and Cordova" (611). Those cities are gone, and so, in this time period set somewhere in the future, is London. Mark still dreams of "that perfect city, a small exquisite city with gardens and fountain's. . . . This although cities have become like people, refuse to be shovelled into the nearest incinerator" (610).

As Martha could have told him, Mark's dream is unrealistic; the small exquisite city where there are no outsiders or insiders, where the city can be perceived as a whole, not in fragments, is unlikely even as civilization begins from scratch with the few people left in the world at the end of the novel. But perhaps another kind of city is possible, maybe not exquisite, but vibrant and human. Ellen Cronan Rose notes that the utopian or ideal city has been a false image throughout *The Children of Violence* series; even "in *Martha Quest,* Lessing evokes the image of the ideal city when she is drawing attention to Martha's evasions of reality" (Rose, *Citta Felice* 372). By the time the series ends in *The Four-Gated City,* Martha has learned to perceive a real city. What is hopeful, in spite of the devastation with which the novel ends, is Mark's insight that cities are like people; they refuse to be completely destroyed. If they represent a particular place where one period in time is made visible, they also participate in the cycles of human history and rise again as human beings gather together to make space into place.

Both Woolf and Lessing succeed as urban novelists because they preserve two views of the city. Their protagonists can see the urban symbols and places that reflect the view from "within" the culture of the city, but they often see those places from a different perspective than characters like Hugh Whitbread or Henry Matheson who have never stepped outside of their culture. As outsiders, both Clarissa Dalloway and Martha Quest can see aspects of the city, fragments of city life, that insiders do not see, and they can tolerate and even appreciate fragmentation. Lynch argues that "the city is a construction in space, but . . . can be perceived only in the course of long spans of time" (1). Woolf and Lessing capture both these aspects of London as their protagonists see the literal constructions of shops or buildings that make up the city, but are also aware of change and the different movements of time in the city—from the small repetitive striking of a clock to the progressive growth of new buildings and the loss of old ones to the large cycles of time in which cities themselves rise and fall. Both Woolf and Lessing have created "outsiders-within" who use alienation creatively to read the modern city.

---

## NOTES

1. See Susan Squier's book *Virginia Woolf and London: The Sexual Politics of the City.*
2. Jane Marcus also links Woolf to Jewish writers, saying that her "position as 'daughter of an educated man,' a self-styled 'outsider' in British

society, may be likened to the position of the Jewish intellectual in
Weimar Germany" ("Thinking Back" 2).

3.  Walker quotes part of *A Room of One's Own* and adds her own bracketed
    interpretations to highlight the differences:

    any woman born with a great gift in the sixteenth century
    [insert "eighteenth century," insert "black woman," insert
    "born or made a slave"] would certainly have gone crazy, shot
    herself. . . . a highly gifted girl who had tried to use her gift for
    poetry would have been so thwarted and hindered by contrary
    instincts [add "chains, guns, the lash, the ownership of one's
    body by someone else, submission to an alien religion"]. (*In
    Search of Our Mothers' Gardens* 235)

4.  Squier footnotes this passage in her discussion of issues of gender, class
    and outsider status in Woolf's essays "Street Haunting" and "Street
    Music" (Squier 44–51).

5.  Sprague also comments on Lessing's exile status and experiences of
    alienation: "English, white, female, Lessing grew up at least thrice
    alienated in colonial Africa. . . . Her [Marxist] politics made her a fourth
    kind of exile" (*Rereading* 1–2).

6.  Gelfant discusses James Farrell as typical of this kind of novelist in *The
    American City Novel*. See Sizemore (3–4) for a brief discussion of several
    British women "ecological" novelists.

7.  Squier also comments on this passage, noting that "the urban environ-
    ment, by its very disparate, varied nature, nurtures egalitarian social
    relations" (96).

8.  Marcus reflects this aspect of time when she calls Big Ben "a great masculine
    bully, dominating the lives of the citizens" ("Thinking Back" 6).

9.  Johanna Garvey notes that throughout the novel the water imagery func-
    tions to subvert "masculine visions . . . of urban space [and] . . . institutions"
    (60). For a discussion of the application of other of Kristeva's ideas to *Mrs.
    Dalloway,* see Jean Wyatt, "Avoiding Self-Definition: In Defense of
    Women's Right to Merge (Julia Kristeva and *Mrs. Dalloway*)." *Women's
    Studies* 13 (1986): 115–26.

10. The chapter on Lessing in *A Female Vision of the City* discusses not only
    the urban districts that Martha walks through but also the city's bound-
    aries and edges that Martha is especially sensitive to. (See Sizemore
    29–47.)

11. Yi-Fu Tuan recounts theologian Paul Tillich's experience of Berlin as
    being like the sea. Both gave Tillich "the feeling of openness, infinity,
    unrestricted space" (Tuan 4).

12. Sprague also calls this fragment of wallpaper "talismanic," but she relates
    it to Martha's acceptance of layers of her own identity (*Rereading* 89).

# 5

— ◆ —

## MOTHER-DAUGHTER PASSION AND RAPTURE: THE DEMETER MYTH IN THE FICTION OF VIRGINIA WOOLF AND DORIS LESSING

### Lisa Tyler

In her now classic work on motherhood entitled *Of Woman Born,* Adrienne Rich laments Western culture's loss of the "mother-daughter passion and rapture" once celebrated in the ancient Greek myth of Demeter and Persephone (237). In order to appreciate Rich's lament, it is necessary to recall the events first described in the Homeric *Hymn to Demeter,* the oldest known version of the myth, which opens with the young Persephone at play with her friends in a flower-filled meadow. When she reaches to pluck an especially beautiful narcissus, the earth opens, and she is abducted and raped by Hades, god of the underworld. Demeter, grieved by her loss, refuses to allow seeds to sprout or plants to grow, and famine threatens humankind. A concerned Zeus—who earlier had given Hades his permission to take Persephone—asks that Persephone be restored to her mother. Hades agrees, but feeds her several pomegranate seeds, thus ensuring that she must return to the underworld to spend part of each year with him. She is then reunited with her mother, and fruitfulness is restored to the earth (Athanassakis 1–16; Foley 1–27).

The myth explains the changing of the seasons—winter returns when Persephone must leave her mother each year—but it also suggests the rich possibilities of the mother-daughter relationship.[1] For example, feminist psychoanalytic critic Marilyn Arthur argues that the Demeter myth centers on "the achievement of a successful identification with the mother," which works in the myth as a "form of female solidarity . . . whose basis is the special and particular comfort, affection, and general gratification which women are able to offer one another" (31). She suggests that this mother-daughter bond, which is central to the myth, is "a female solidarity which is discovered in the context of a patriarchal world" (30).

Virginia Woolf and Doris Lessing both explore this female solidarity in their revisions of the myth. Both writers were assuredly familiar with the myth, despite their relatively unorthodox educations. Lessing's knowledge of classical mythology is most evident in her novel *Briefing for a Descent into Hell,* in which the protagonist is a classics professor (Singleton 69). Woolf learned to read Greek so that she, like her male counterparts, could read the classics untranslated; one critic has even suggested that Woolf probably knew more Greek than James Joyce did (Herman 266). She greatly respected classical scholar Jane Harrison, and critics have begun to trace Woolf's use of Harrison's work in her writings.[2]

Woolf and Lessing use the myth in their fiction to subvert the traditional heterosexual romance plot, essentially by replacing it with the cyclical story of the preoedipal bond, separation, and reunion.[3] The conventional expectation for a woman character is that she be involved (often passively) in a heterosexual romance with a man whom she ultimately marries, thus concluding the plot—or, alternately, that she becomes involved in an illicit romance and dies. Examples of the former include *Evelina, Jane Eyre, Bleak House,* and the novels of Jane Austen; examples of the latter include *Wuthering Heights, Tess of the D'Urbervilles,* and *The Mill on the Floss.* Works in which the central character is male sometimes add to the heterosexual romance a search for the father; *Great Expectations* is perhaps the best example of such a plot. In the works of Woolf and Lessing, however, women characters often specifically *reject* the romance plot. Mrs. Dalloway, for example, recoils from the excessive intimacy it demands, and the unnamed narrator of Lessing's "Flavours of Exile" retreats from what she perceives as the violence of heterosexuality. And instead of searching for the lost father, these women search for a mother or mother figure from whom they have been separated, often by men.

In fiction by Woolf and Lessing, the mother-daughter relationship is extraordinarily powerful for women and *remains* powerful for both mothers and daughters long after the daughter reaches adulthood. Perhaps most important, Woolf and Lessing suggest that heterosexual relationships fail many women and that women, unlike men, do not find in heterosexual relationships the emotional closeness and support they need; therefore women often turn (or return) to each other for emotional support (Chodorow 200). As Terence Hewet complains to his fiancée in Virginia Woolf's *The Voyage Out,* "I don't satisfy you in the way you satisfy me. . . . You don't want me as I want you—you're always wanting something else" (302).

Rachel's intense longing for her mother—and more generally, for intimate, loving relationships with other women—echoes the longing expressed in the myth. The mother and daughter in the Homeric *Hymn* experience an intense desire for each other's presence and physical closeness, a desire that today we might term *homoerotic.* In fact, classicist Helene P. Foley notes that in the Homeric *Hymn to Demeter,* the Greek word used for Persephone's longing for her mother connotes sexual desire (131). A young girl's love for her mother is, of course, not specifically lesbian, but, like the young boy's oedipal love, it encompasses the desire for physical and sexual intimacy as well as the more socially acceptable need for attention, affection, and care.

While not literally "lesbian," the homoerotic desire described here seems to fit within the "lesbian continuum" Adrienne Rich has proposed, which embraces not just "genital sexual experience with another woman," but "many more forms of primary intensity between and among women, including the sharing of a rich inner life, the bonding against male tyranny, [and] the giving and receiving of practical support" (Rich, "Compulsory Heterosexuality" 51). Certainly Woolf, who seems to have been a lesbian, has written much more extensively of the mother-daughter romance than has the apparently heterosexual Lessing. Perhaps it is easier for lesbians to see the romance inherent in the mother-daughter relationship. This homoerotic desire makes what might be termed a lesbian reading—a reading alert to the possibilities of homoerotic romance between women—not only possible but necessary for a fuller understanding of the fiction involved.

Those of us who are heterosexual (and perhaps, given the heterosexism of our culture, homosexual readers as well) often have great difficulty even *seeing* homoerotic romance as a plot. In *Mrs. Dalloway,* for example, Clarissa is preoccupied with her daughter throughout most of her day; she worries rather more about her than she does about Richard, and indeed, Elizabeth is one of the focal characters of the story—yet Elizabeth's admittedly brief segment, unlike the longer passages centering on Clarissa, Peter, and Septimus, receives remarkably little critical attention. Similarly, Doris Lessing's short story "The De Wets Come to Kloof Grange" has traditionally been discussed in terms of colonialism and culture clash; the mother-daughter romance on which Lessing's story focuses simply becomes invisible. More generally, writers who foreground homoerotic romance between mother and daughter (or between women in general) are liable to see their work dismissed as plotless, trivial, or sentimental. It is, I think, exceedingly difficult for women writers to portray positive mother-daughter relationships without incurring such charges. Louisa May Alcott's *Little Women* is the most obvious example, but a case could also be made for such disparate works as Enid Bagnold's play *The Chalk Garden,* Edith Wharton's novella *The Old Maid,* Amy Tan's novel *The Joy Luck Club,* and popular films like *Beaches, Terms of Endearment, Steel Magnolias,* and *Fried Green Tomatoes.*

Despite our difficulty in perceiving and valuing homoerotic romance between women, we can *learn* to become better readers. In an essay entitled "'Women alone stir my imagination': Reading Virginia Woolf as a Lesbian," Pamela J. Olano contends that "readers without lesbian experience, but open to lesbian possibilities, can develop the skills needed to read from a lesbian location and thus to open the space into which the lesbian narrative can come" (161). Olano further observes that lesbian narratives are "often expressed in an intertextual code" (162). The myth of Demeter and Persephone, I want to argue, is one such code, and in this essay I want to trace its presence in three novels by Woolf and three short stories by Lessing (with particular attention to "The De Wets Come to Kloof Grange"). I chose these works because each opens with an unresolved mother-daughter romance and each manifests several, if not all, of the motifs of the myth: the lyrically beautiful celebration of the mother-daughter relationship, the abrupt and often violent break with the mother and consequent grief of both women, the daughter's frightening confrontation with a violent heterosexuality which she experiences as a rape, and the desire for (if not necessarily the achievement of) a mother-daughter reconciliation. In several of the works I will discuss, either gardens or floral images play an important symbolic role, metaphorically representing the lost unity, the joy of reunion, or both.

Identifying those motifs helps us to trace in all of these works the often implicit or palimpsestic plots of homoerotic romance and the daughter's search for the mother that might otherwise be hidden from readers accustomed to plots centering on heterosexual romance and the son's search for the father. These writers' use of myth to inform their works also gives a depth and resonance to plots that readers operating on heterosexist assumptions might otherwise all too easily dismiss—as for example, with the initially slight-seeming short story, "Among the Roses," in Lessing's latest collection, *The Real Thing.*

Neither of these writers is sentimental about the possibilities of homoerotic romance in a male-dominated society; both writers recognize that women cannot always offer each other the support they need. Mrs. Ramsay in *To the Lighthouse,* for example, does not support Lily's desire to become an artist, presumably because she considers marriage a safer alternative, and Helen Ambrose insensitively dismisses Rachel's reaction to the kiss that Richard Dalloway forces on her. Mothers and daughters (both biological and surrogate) often prefer men to each other, for sexual, social, pragmatic, economic, or personal reasons. Again, Mrs. Ramsay is the supreme example, valuing her husband more than Lily and her sons more than her daughters. The mother-daughter romance falters, at times, because women are taught not to value each other. As Susan Gubar explains, "the grievous separation of mother and maiden implies that in a patriarchal society women are divided from each other and from themselves" (305).

Woolf clearly acknowledged this separation in her work, often by making her female protagonists motherless. Woolf's own experiences resonate throughout her work; she had a particularly troubled family, and her introduction into heterosexuality was even harsher than Persephone's. Virginia Woolf lost her mother when she was thirteen and her older half sister when she was fifteen. She was molested by one of her half brothers when she was six and by the other after their mother died.[4] As a teenage girl, she must have felt much like Persephone, trapped in an underworld where she was repeatedly raped; unlike Persephone, she had no mother to save her. Only gradually did she find other women who could mother her and, if not undo her abuse, at least help her to overcome it—including her sister, Vanessa; a number of important women friends; and her lesbian lover, Vita Sackville-West.[5]

Not surprisingly, then, given her own experiences, Woolf seems in her first novel to be particularly preoccupied with one of the myth's three elements, the daughter's separation from the mother and her induction into the underworld of violent heterosexuality. That novel, *The Voyage Out,* is arguably her most overtly autobiographical.[6]

*The Voyage Out* opens with a mother, Helen, grieving at her separation from her children (9–11); another mother, Clarissa Dalloway, later expresses the same sorrow (56). Ironically, both of these women have voluntarily left their children at the behest of their respective husbands. Thus Woolf simultaneously attributes the separation of mother and children to the father and criticizes the mother's compliance with the father's wishes—perhaps because of her own anger that her mother had literally (in Woolf's mind, at least) worked herself to death in service to the men in the family.

The novel's protagonist, Rachel, is a Persephone-like figure, young, unformed, passive, innocent, and completely ignorant of sex (*VO* 96). Helen mentally compares her to a six-year-old and sees her as a victim (25, 37). Evelyn Murgatroyd tells Rachel she looks as though she had "lived all [her] life in a garden" (248), an image reminiscent of the meadow of flowers from which Persephone is abducted.

Masculinity and heterosexuality are associated with violence throughout the novel (DeSalvo, *First* 61), just as they are in the Homeric *Hymn*. Rachel exclaims that "men are brutes" (*VO* 82), and Hewet says that the ordinary man is a bully (212). Helen suspects Rachel's father "of nameless atrocities with regard to his daughter" (24). Certainly he hits her (28). Richard becomes a metaphoric rapist when he abruptly kisses Rachel (76); the event is rapidly followed by the image of "withered rose-leaves" (79).[7] That rape is echoed: Evelyn Murgatroyd is seized and kissed by Sinclair, and she condemns men as cowardly, undignified beasts (246-47). When Hewet and Rachel stumble across Arthur and Susan making love, Susan looks "not altogether conscious," and they cannot tell "whether she was happy, or had suffered something" (140). Not surprisingly, Rachel thinks of love as an assault (Apter 17).

Marriage is consistently portrayed in negative terms (*VO* 241–42). Rachel herself advocates separatism, complaining that the sexes bring out the worst in each other (156). Terence Hewet, who is to induct Rachel permanently into the underworld of heterosexuality, is compared to a god (224), thus linking him to Hades, the god who abducts Persephone. Like the other representatives of heterosexuality in this novel, Terence seems to consider violence inherent to sexual relations. Earlier, fearing he had mis-placed a book borrowed from Hirst, he had compared himself to a murderer of children (143)—an ominous suggestion given the comparison of Rachel to a six-year-old. He later shakes a fist at her and scuffles with her until he throws her to the floor, ripping her dress in the process (298).

Rachel herself is torn between Helen, her surrogate mother, and Terence, her fiance (311); she is, therefore, not unlike Persephone, who is torn between Demeter and Hades. Rachel is clearly frightened by what she perceives as the violence of heterosexuality (Naremore 49), but the possibil-ity of lesbian sexuality with Helen seems violent, too;[8] Helen more or less knocks her down to roll in the grass with her (283). Moreover, Helen's abandonment of her own children for no apparent reason does not bode well for her protection of Rachel (DeSalvo, *First* 37, 39); nor does her laughing dismissal of Richard Dalloway's kiss (*VO* 80). Rachel says of the dance, "This is my idea of hell"—but Helen enjoys dancing. Helen is unwaveringly loyal to heterosexuality, the pairing off that the dancing virtually parodies (152, 159). As Louise DeSalvo notes (*First* 57), Helen does not protect Rachel so much as threaten her.

Rachel dies because she has no mother to protect her from male brutality and abuse. Richard Dalloway can seize her and kiss her and blame her for tempting him, and neither Helen nor Clarissa will stop him. More seriously, the women around Rachel do not dissuade her from marriage, as she seems, unconsciously, to want them to do; instead they encourage her engagement. Rachel wants Helen to love her enough to save her from rape. That is what Hirst implies when he counsels Hewet against "[p]utting virgins among matrons" on their expedition (110); matrons might defend the virgins from the men. But Helen will not defend her from the depredations of men. Rachel is unable to find a Demeter, a satisfactory surrogate mother to protect her from male sexuality, and flowers, which traditionally symbolize the reunion of mother and daughter in the myth, simply remind Rachel of death (35). She therefore escapes the dangers of heterosexuality by dying (DeSalvo, *First* 94–95), even as she enacts her own loving return to Theresa, her dead mother.[9] And in Rachel's death, unlike Persephone's, rebirth seems impossible (Fleishman 21). Woolf's divergence from the myth here disappoints readers' expectations and emphasizes Rachel's vulnerability and despair.

If Rachel consummates her mother-daughter romance in death, Lily Briscoe of Woolf's novel *To the Lighthouse* is similarly tempted but ultimately resists such a consummation, preferring instead a purely imaginative reunion with Mrs. Ramsay. Lily, whose very name is a flower, is a Persephone figure, virginal and small (77, 156). She is compared to "corn under a wind" (130), and, Mrs. Ramsay thinks to herself, she "is so fond of flowers" (156). The younger woman seeks the kind of preoedipal unity with Mrs. Ramsay that an infant shares with its mother (79).

Mrs. Ramsay is clearly a goddess figure, "[w]ith stars in her eyes and veils in her hair, with cyclamen and wild violets. . . . [s]tepping through fields of flowers" (25).[10] She feels that she becomes one with trees, streams, and flowers (97), and she reminds others of Greek temples (291). Woolf describes her as "very clearly Greek, straight, blue-eyed" (47), and like Demeter, the august Mrs. Ramsay presides over a "sanctuary" and preserves "some secret which certainly Lily Briscoe believed people must have for the world to go on at all" (78). When the regal mother of eight goes to join her guests at dinner, "like some queen" she "looks down upon them, and descends among them, and acknowledges their tributes silently, and accepts their devotion and prostration before her" (124)—much as the Greek goddess might have responded to those who worshipped her. The dinner party itself, like the Eleusinian mysteries celebrated in Demeter's name, is a kind of fertility rite at which the newly engaged couple "must be danced round with mockery, decorated with garlands" (151). Mrs. Ramsay and her guests are "celebrating a festival" (151) complete with "olives and oil and juice" (150), and in a particularly nice pun, the hostess is described as having "led her victims to the altar" (153).

In this novel, as in *The Voyage Out,* masculinity is once again associated with violence. Jasper is shooting birds (*TL* 41). James contemplates murdering his father (10), and his father, in turn, torments him with a weed (49–50).[11] Mr. Ramsay is moreover perpetually reciting lines from Tennyson's "Charge of the Light Brigade," a poem commemorating a particularly bloody (and futile) battle (29, 31, 49). His very presence is apocalyptic: "Every time he approached—he was walking up and down the terrace—ruin approached, chaos approached" (221).

And once again, heterosexuality is unpleasant, at best; when Andrew and Nancy accidentally come upon Paul and Minta kissing, they recoil in disgust (115–16). Lily believes that the worst human relations "were between men and women" (139) because love inexplicably transforms lovely young men into bullies (154). She later tells herself, "she need not marry, thank Heaven: she need not undergo that degradation" (154). Prue Ramsay's marriage is fatal (198–99), and Lily thinks of Prue's death in terms that rather pointedly recall the myth: "She let her flowers fall from her basket, scattered and tumbled them on to the grass and, reluctantly and hesitatingly, . . . went too" (299).

In this revision of the myth, it is Demeter, and not Persephone, who undergoes the (metaphoric) rape, which occurs when Mr. Ramsay ruthlessly insists that his wife fulfill his outrageous need for sympathy and support (Rosenman 96): "into this delicious fecundity, this fountain and spray of life, the fatal sterility of the male plunged itself, like a beak of brass, barren and bare" (*TL* 58). And it is the Demeter figure of Mrs. Ramsay, rather than the Persephone figure of Lily, who dies. Without Mrs. Ramsay, Lily thinks, the world is no longer fruitful: "It was all dry: all withered: all spent" (224). In the daughter's search for the mother, she has no torch, only "matches struck unexpectedly in the dark" (240). She grieves extravagantly for her loss: "And then to want and not to have—to want and want—how that wrung the heart, and wrung it again and again!" (266). When Lily does imaginatively envision Mrs. Ramsay's return, she sees her wearing a wreath of white flowers, returning through purple fields of lilies or hyacinths (269–70)—much as if the maternal figure had metamorphosed, through Lily's resurrection of her, into a Persephone yet unmolested by men.

Mrs. Ramsay cannot help Lily escape heterosexuality; on the contrary, helplessly implicated within it herself (Rosenman 95), Mrs. Ramsay encourages Lily to marry (Heilbrun 137). Her power, like Demeter's, is severely circumscribed by the patriarchal society in which she lives; in that society, marriage is perceived as a woman's only protection from rape, and even that protection is hardly secure, as Mrs. Ramsay's metaphoric rape by her husband makes clear. In such a society, women like Lily who do not wish to marry must remain alone and at risk; only in *Mrs. Dalloway* was Woolf openly able to suggest another alternative.

Lily Briscoe is a "woman seeking intimacy with another woman, not her mother but toward whom she turns those passionate longings" (Rich, *Of Woman Born* 228). Unlike Rachel, she is able to survive only because she is neither impelled into heterosexuality nor imperiled by men's violent sexual advances; like Rachel, she values her relationships with women (and especially her relationship with the dead maternal figure) more than her relationships with men. But it is in *Mrs. Dalloway*, "Woolf's most overt celebration of lesbian sexuality" (Cramer 178), that Woolf is able to envision a daughter's successful reconciliation with a *living* mother.[12]

In this novel, it is Clarissa who is Demeter, goddess of vegetation. She is associated with flowers from the opening sentence, and flowers are specifically and repeatedly associated with motherhood throughout the novel.[13] Clarissa notes, for example, during her morning excursion, that "June had drawn out every leaf on the trees. The mothers of Pimlico gave suck to their young" (9). Clarissa's former suitor, Peter, in thinking of her, comments to himself, "She enjoyed practically everything. If you walked with her in Hyde Park now it was a bed of tulips, now a child in a perambulator . . ." (118). The parallel structure links flowers to maternity, just as later, at Clarissa's party, Sally Seton, the girlfriend of Clarissa's youth, is remarkable both for her five sons and for her conservatories (286). Perhaps most telling of all is the only moment in the novel in which Clarissa's own mother is mentioned: She is recalled "walking in a garden" (267).

Like Mrs. Ramsay, Clarissa, too, is compared to a goddess (*MD* 43). Peter, in telling Clarissa he is in love, speaks "not to her however, but to some one raised up in the dark so that you could not touch her but must lay your garland down on the grass in the dark" (66). And Clarissa's command to "Remember my party to-night!" (72) recalls Demeter's command in the *Homeric Hymn* that the people of Eleusis celebrate rites to propitiate her (Athanassakis lines 273–74).

If Clarissa is a Demeter figure, then Elizabeth, her daughter, is assuredly a Persephone. Like Helen Ambrose contemplating Rachel in *The Voyage Out,* Clarissa, in thinking of her daughter, above all stresses her youth and inexperience: "In many ways, her mother felt, she was extremely immature, like a child still, attached to dolls, to old slippers, a perfect baby; and that was charming" (*MD* 209). Elizabeth reminds people of the flowers, water, and springtime associated with the young maiden of the myth (186, 204, 205, 287, 294). Like Persephone, she tends to be passive (204).

Doris Kilman is the Hades figure in Woolf's revision of the myth; she tries to take Clarissa's daughter away from her. Her very name suggests violence, death, and perhaps masculinity, as well. Clarissa pronounces her a denizen of the underworld, "one of those spectres with which one battles in the night; one of those spectres who stand astride us and suck up half our life-blood, dominators and tyrants" (16–17). She later thinks of her in terms of Victorian melodrama: She is "Elizabeth's seducer, the woman who had crept in to steal and defile" (266).

Unlike Helen Ambrose and Mrs. Ramsay, whose first allegiance is always to their husbands, Clarissa, like her daughter, sees her relationships with women as emotionally primary. Although she apparently loves her husband and enjoys seeing her old flame Peter once again, she spends most of her day contemplating her connection to two women—mourning the loss of her intensely intimate relationship with Sally Seton, and longing to repair her troubled relationship with her daughter Elizabeth. Psychoanalytic critic Elizabeth Abel sees in this novel a palimpsestic plot that further underlines the novel's association with the Homeric *Hymn to Demeter*. She describes Clarissa's reminiscences as "Woolf's subversive account of the force required to break the daughter's attachment to her mother" (144 n.4). Sally is a maternal figure for Clarissa despite their closeness in age, much as Virginia's sister Vanessa seems to have been for Virginia. Abel suggests that Peter's intrusion into what Clarissa calls "the most exquisite moment of her whole life" (*MD* 32), the moment when Sally Seton kisses her, "suggests a revised Oedipal configuration: the jealous male attempting to rupture the exclusive female bond, insisting on the transference of attachment to the man, demanding heterosexuality" (Abel 32–33). Clarissa certainly describes his intrusion in violent terms that recall both Richard Dalloway's kiss in *The Voyage Out* and Mr. Ramsay's demands in *To the Lighthouse*: "It was like running one's face against a granite wall in the darkness! . . . She felt only how Sally was being mauled already, maltreated; she felt his hostility, his jealousy, his determination to break into their companionship" (53). Peter thus becomes a Hades figure, violently intervening in a mother-daughter romance. In an earlier manuscript, Woolf was even more explicit: Peter asks Clarissa outright, "Why didn't you marry me?" and Elizabeth walks into the room, almost as if in answer to Peter's question (Charles G. Hoffman 182).

Woolf links Peter more explicitly to Hades later, when she shows us Peter envisioning himself as "a romantic buccaneer" (*MD* 80); it is hardly coincidental that Demeter says that she was attacked by what some translations term "pirates" (Foley 8, line 24). As Makiko Minow-Pinkney notes (68), Peter even enacts a symbolic rape of Clarissa by "tilting his pen-knife towards her green dress" (*MD* 60). No wonder, then, that Clarissa and Sally share Demeter's (and Rachel Vinrace's, and Lily Briscoe's) apocalyptic view of heterosexuality: "they spoke of marriage always as a catastrophe" (50).

During her party, Clarissa vicariously dies when she learns of Septimus's death, and her return to her party constitutes a rebirth. And it is at the party that the daughter is returned to the mother. Woolf openly equates the daughter's decision to attend her mother's party with Persephone's return to Olympus; when she turns toward home, the clouds Elizabeth sees "had all the appearance of settled habitations assembled for the conference of gods above the world" (210). Only when Woolf imagines, in Clarissa, a mother who can put her ties to women above a heterosexual relationship, can she envision a successful (if not altogether rapturous) mother-daughter reunion.

Unlike Woolf, Doris Lessing is not known for her portrayals of loving mothers and daughters. It was, after all, her fiction which inspired Lynn Sukenick to coin the term "matrophobia," defined as a woman's fear of becoming her own mother (519). Lessing's two best-known works are *The Golden Notebook* and her *Children of Violence* series; in the former, the protagonist's mother is barely mentioned, and in the latter, the protagonist's mother remains a lifelong enemy with whom she is never satisfactorily reconciled. There is some evidence, however, that Lessing's focus has since changed; in her *Diaries of Jane Somers,* she presents a moving mother-daughter relationship, although, as is typical of women in such positive relationships in Lessing's work, the two are not biologically related. Her most recent collection, *The Real Thing,* seems obsessed with maternity, including among its protagonists the teen mother in the opening story, two middle-aged mothers of adult daughters, a mother on government aid, the title character of "The Mother of the Child in Question," and patients in the "Womb Ward." Even the title of the collection's title story arguably refers to shared parental love and the precedence it takes over romantic love.

While the mother-daughter relationships in Lessing's novels have been analyzed and discussed, those in her short stories have largely been neglected.[14] One of the most intriguing is that presented in "The De Wets Come to Kloof Grange," in which an Englishman hires a new assistant, an Afrikaner whose wife finds adjustment to the isolation of the veld difficult. The story's central (and focal) character, Mrs. Gale, is a Demeter figure. She is associated with the corn; her husband describes her as "an elderly Englishwoman, as thin and dry as a stalk of maize in September" and observes that she has "small flower-blue eyes" (106). But unlike Woolf's mothers, she rejects her archetypal role, brushing off the beauty of Africa's vegetation with the one-word complaint, "Mosquitoes!" (103) and "impatiently" tending her torch-like "lamp, which did not burn well" (104).

Her reactions foreshadow her failure to respond to the Persephone-like Mrs. De Wet, who is so young that Mrs. Gale initially mistakes her for Jack De Wet's child rather than his wife (112). The girl—as the narrator calls her—wears flowered dresses (114, 116) and is later compared to "a queen who has been insulted" (123).

While Mrs. De Wet is not, like Persephone, abducted and raped, her life changes nearly as abruptly, as she confesses to Mrs. Gale: "He met me in a cinema and we got married next day" (112). Mr. De Wet is a Hades figure who physically abuses his young wife (114, 126). He brings her down to an underworld home, a house of death: "It looked dead, a dead thing with staring eyes, with those blank windows gleaming pallidly back at the moon" (108). And like Persephone, this girl, too, grieves for her loss—a loss which Mrs. Gale herself has experienced and which the older woman belatedly realizes she could have done much to mitigate:

> ". . . I am so lonely. I wanted to get my mother up to stay with me, only Jack said there wasn't room, and he's quite right, only I got mad, because I thought he might at least have had my mother . . ."
>     Mrs. Gale felt guilt like a sword: she could have filled the place of this child's mother. (118)

That the older woman has shared this experience is clear. Mrs. De Wet speaks to Mrs. Gale, at least initially, "as one girl to another" (113), telling her of late-night walks. Mrs. Gale remembers similar experiences in an acrimonious conversation with Major Gale: "'Tell that fine young man that his wife often goes for long walks by herself when he's asleep. He probably hasn't noticed it.' Here she gave a deadly look at her husband. 'Just as I used to,' she could not prevent herself adding" (123). Mrs. Gale also recalls staying up late trying to undo her own separation from all she had loved: "writing letters, reading old ones, thinking of her friends and of herself as a young girl" (118). Her letters to and from her old friend Betty help her preserve this sense of herself as a Persephone who "came to exile in Southern Rhodesia" (104).[15]

If the young Mrs. Gale was not exactly raped, neither was she an entirely willing sexual partner: "What a relief when he no longer 'loved' her! (That was how she put it.) Ah, that 'love'—she thought of it with a small humorous distaste. Growing old had its advantages" (106). She later remembers getting up to read letters "in the early days after her husband had finished his brief and apologetic embraces" (118).

Upon her arrival, she changed the farm's name from Kloof Nek to Kloof Grange, to remind her of home (107), and even her furniture suggests her nostalgia: "Africa and the English eighteenth century mingled in this room and were at peace" (104). But Mrs. Gale has overcome much of her initial loneliness, as the peace of the schizophrenically furnished room perhaps implies. It is her husband, Major Gale, who makes the most explicit reference to the myth, telling her, "You always complain I bury you alive" (105). Ironically, it is in response to his comment that Mrs. Gale most clearly acknowledges her change of heart: "In fact, she had learned to love her isolation, and she felt aggrieved that he did not know it" (107).

Although she plans to do well by her new neighbor-woman, this Demeter is unwilling or unable to rescue Persephone. Mrs. Gale is cold and critical (115). She repeatedly experiences anger at Mrs. De Wet's situation (115, 122, 123, 125, 127), but her anger lacks the efficacy of Demeter's. Young Mrs. De Wet waits expectantly for her rescue, alternating between "bright chatter" and "polite silences full of attention to what she seemed to hope Mrs. Gale might say" (119). But the older woman has nothing new to tell her: "Mrs. Gale was saying silently under breath, with ironical pity, in which there was also cruelty: You'll get used to it, my dear; you'll get used to it" (121). She openly rejects the girl's mute appeals; the girl backs away from her husband and "reache[s] for the older woman's hand," but Mrs. Gale does not respond—"this was going too far" (113). The older woman recognizes her failure, "[b]ut she felt more comfortable with the distance between them, she couldn't deny it" (119).

She offers to show Mrs. De Wet her lavish garden, believing that it will have a salutary effect (119). It is there that the older woman finds consolation, but the girl does not share her response to the greenery; this Demeter has failed to rescue her daughter from the underworld, and the long-sought-for reunion of mother and daughter does not take place. As she leaves, Mrs. De Wet "lag[s] up the path behind her husband like a sulky small girl, pulling at Mrs. Gale's beloved roses and scattering crimson petals everywhere" (121).

When the girl inexplicably disappears, Mrs. Gale responds much as Demeter did; she, too, begins to destroy vegetation, in a way that underscores her similarity to Mrs. De Wet: ". . . [Mrs. Gale] was walking crazily up and down her garden through the bushes, tearing blossoms and foliage to pieces in trembling fingers" (125). She refuses to sleep or eat or even sit down (126).

In the final moments of the story, when she belatedly attempts to take the side of the abused wife against her violent and insensitive husband, Mrs. Gale's failure becomes brutally clear: "Mrs. De Wet heaved herself off the floor, rushed on Mrs. Gale, pulled her back so that she nearly lost balance, and then flung herself on her husband. 'Jack,' she said, clinging to him desperately, 'I am so sorry, I am so sorry, Jack'" (127). Abandoned by Demeter, this Persephone has chosen to love her abductor; in this, she is more like Mrs. Gale than either woman recognizes.

Nancy Chodorow notes that men are often unwilling or unable to provide the intensely close personal relationships that women need (203). Women therefore try to recreate the closeness they experienced with their mothers in one of two chief ways. First, they try to build relationships with other women, but given Western society's homophobia, they frequently find intimate relationships with women outside the family difficult to achieve. The second way in which women try to recreate these bonds, according to Chodorow, is by giving birth themselves and thus reexperiencing the closeness of the mother-child bond through their relationships with their own children (200–1).

In attempting to reassure the hysterical Mrs. De Wet, Mrs. Gale recalls her initial sense of isolation and thinks, "But that was before she had her first child. She thought: This girl should have a baby; and could not help glancing downwards at her stomach"; Mrs. De Wet "said resentfully: 'Jack says I should have a baby. That's all he says'" (118). Clearly, both Mrs. Gale and Mr. De Wet are simultaneously correct and culpable; a child would probably help the girl by giving her the closeness she craves—but so could either her husband or the only woman available to befriend her. Mrs. Gale later realizes that advising the girl to have a child amounts to acknowledging the impossibility of intimate heterosexual relationships (Budhos 39). Mrs. Gale responds to Mr. De Wet with anger; "'You don't realize,' said Mrs. Gale futilely, knowing perfectly there was nothing he could do about it. 'You don't understand how it is'" ("DW" 122). "There's more to women than having children," she later contends (123). But part of her anger is, or should be, at herself, for failing the girl as much as the girl's husband has. Like Helen Ambrose and Mrs. Ramsay, Mrs. Gale is too deeply committed to heterosexuality to acknowledge its failures—or to feel comfortable with the younger woman's homoerotic desire for her love. In their initial meeting, the girl tells Mrs. Gale how she and her husband had met: "It seemed as if she were in some way offering herself to the older woman, offering something precious of herself" (112). It is Mrs. Gale's failure to accept this offering, to respond to a woman in need, that drives Mrs. De Wet to behave as she does.

If Doris Lessing is skeptical about the possibility of close relationships among women, she is even less sanguine about the possibility of creating and maintaining a deep affective relationship with men, as she demonstrates vividly and lyrically in her short story "Flavours of Exile." "Flavours of Exile" simultaneously makes the most overt reference to the Demeter-Persephone myth and—superficially at least—seems of these three stories to be the one least concerned with mother-daughter relationships. In the story, a young girl, enamored of a boy at a neighboring farm, waits for a pomegranate on her mother's tree to ripen and then tries to show it to the boy who is the object of her love. Disgusted, he picks up a stick and brutally smashes the fruit.

The pomegranate, with which the girl identifies, is surely an allusion to the myth, and William's act of brutality is a symbolic rape (Allen 8). The story's narrator uses sensual imagery to link the classical myth of Demeter and Persephone with both the Biblical poetry of the Song of Songs and the modernist poetry of W. B. Yeats, as I have elsewhere argued (Tyler, "Classical"). The story contrasts the female narrator's sensuality with her young friend William's savagery, echoing the contrast in the myth between the idyllic unity of the mother-daughter relationship and the harshly uncaring coercion of Hades' rape. Like Rachel in Woolf's *The Voyage Out,* the unnamed protagonist of Lessing's story seems trapped; compelled into heterosexuality by society, she is nonetheless frightened and repulsed by the violence that, in this story at least, seems to be inherent in masculine sexuality.

Like Woolf, who began rather bleakly, but later, in *Mrs. Dalloway* especially, became tentatively confident about the possibilities for women's relationships with each other, Lessing has written most optimistically about the mother-daughter relationships in one of her most recent stories, "Among the Roses."[16] In this story, which appeared in *Ladies' Home Journal* before it was published in the collection entitled *The Real Thing,* a mother, Myra, reencounters her daughter Shirley in the rose gardens of Regents Park. It is clear that mother and daughter have missed each other during their three-year separation after a quarrel: "Soon Shirley came in, and Myra's heart hurt at the sight of that face," and Shirley looks "discontented," "sad," "alone and lonely" ("AR" 120, 121). Shirley has had a series of unsuccessful heterosexual relationships, including a marriage to a physically abusive man she still speaks of with "admiration" (122); ironically, she later shrieks to her mother, "You always put up with everything" (124) and seems to be angered by those qualities in her mother that she most dislikes in herself.

Shirley has evidently taken up gardening, at least temporarily, to become closer to her mother, and Myra responds by inviting her to visit, an offer that Shirley accepts, adding offhandedly that she has missed her mother (123). Despite nearly beginning to quarrel all over again, both women are obviously trying to patch up an admittedly difficult relationship that nonetheless remains important to both of them. That they manage, despite their prickliness with each other, *not* to quarrel—"At least, not yet" (124)—suggests the depth of their need for each other. Their reunion is tense, tentative, and probably temporary, but it *is* a reunion, and between a biological mother and daughter at that (a rarity in Lessing's fiction, and Woolf's as well).

Both authors seem, in the works discussed here, to see heterosexual intercourse as inherently violent. They suggest that women's connections with each other *came first;* as Patricia Cramer observes of Woolf's fiction, "This pattern representing the arousal of sexual and emotional intimacy between women checked by a male intrusion suggestive of rape shows that Woolf saw male sexual violation as a curb on her sexual feelings and not a cause, as some have suggested, of her lesbian identification" (186). Unlike Woolf, Lessing has in her writing sometimes seemed harshly critical of lesbianism (see for example the lines from *The Golden Notebook* quoted in Rich, "Compulsory Heterosexuality" 26). Her characters have sometimes made comments suggesting that lesbians are bitter, frustrated heterosexual women who have turned to other women after giving up on men, and the lesbians she portrays in *The Good Terrorist* are unpleasant and disturbing women. But the characters in both Woolf's novels and the short stories by Lessing that I have analyzed in this essay assuredly fit within Rich's lesbian continuum by sharing each other's inner lives, bonding (at least in limited ways) against male tyranny, and giving each other practical support. These women characters choose to return to these connections for the nurturing and support they need, and they do so, or try to do so, in spite of the extraordinary range of forces aligned against them, forces that Rich documents in her essay on "Compulsory Heterosexuality and the Lesbian Existence." That their reunions are muted and sometimes lack the "passion and rapture" Rich calls for is, I think, an effect of women's exhaustion at overcoming the barriers to relationships with each other that Rich herself identifies.

To unite with each other, women must implicitly deny the psychological self-sufficiency of the heterosexual couple. A woman like Helen Ambrose or Mrs. Ramsay must stop devoting so much of her time and attention and care to men and begin devoting more of that solicitousness to other women. But a woman must be financially and emotionally independent in order to take that risk. Many women must also overcome cultural homophobia— their own as well as others' fears of even the appearance of too intimate a relationship with other women. They may have to combat the kinds of class and ethnic differences that the bourgeois British Mrs. Gale and the working class Afrikaner Mrs. De Wet find insurmountable in "The De Wets Come to Kloof Grange."

Perhaps the most difficult psychological barrier to overcome is the generational difference. Mothers frequently find it difficult to allow their daughters opportunities that the mothers themselves were denied. Elizabeth

Dalloway, for example, has a host of educational and career opportunities that were not available to Clarissa—opportunities that Clarissa therefore has difficulty appreciating. In "Among the Roses," Shirley's sexual freedom simultaneously intrigues and frightens her mother, the quietly conventional Myra. A mother who has learned to repress her own sexuality may not be pleased to see her daughter's enthusiastic participation in the sexual revolution. Even the most loving mother may feel ambivalent about the wider range of choices available to her daughter. And these are only the *internal* barriers to women's intimacy. I have not mentioned the obstacles that domestic violence, sexual abuse, economic hardship, geographical distance, and other external factors can present to women's relationships with each other. Struggling with such differences, the women characters in the fiction of Woolf and Lessing might well be diffident and subdued in rapprochement, rather than ecstatic.

These stories replace the traditional Freudian oedipal plots of heterosexual romance and the search for the father with homoerotic romance and the search for the mother. Woolf and Lessing are realistic in acknowledging that homoerotic romances also fail. But both women are nonetheless creating new plots for women, telling new stories in which Chloe likes (or at least wants to like) Olivia, stories in which women's relationships with each other matter as much as, or even more than, their relationships with men. In devising new ways to talk about women's lives, Virginia Woolf and Doris Lessing genuinely celebrate the passion and rapture of the mother-daughter romance.

---

## NOTES

1. In my discussions of the symbolism and psychological implications of the myth, I am indebted to Mara Lynn Keller and C. Kerenyi. For an excellent introduction to the Homeric *Hymn to Demeter*, see Helene P. Foley's edition, which includes the text of the hymn in both English and Greek, a commentary on its text, and interpretive essays, including the article by Marilyn Arthur cited later in this essay. In her edition of the hymn, which was published when this essay was in revision, Foley, a classicist, discusses the myth's elements of mother-daughter romance (118–37) and its influence on later writers (151–69).
2. See for example Eileen Barrett, Patricia Cramer, Carolyn Heilbrun, Judy Little, Patricia Maika, Jane Marcus (in "Pargeting"), Madeline Moore, Annabel Robinson, and Sandra Shattuck.
3. Madeline Moore similarly sees the myth as central in Woolf's fiction, although she explicates its presence primarily only in *The Voyage Out*,

*To the Lighthouse,* and *Between the Acts,* and her understanding of *The Voyage Out* differs from mine. On the nature of Woolf's homoerotic rather than heterosexual plots, see Rachel Blau DuPlessis (61), Susan Stanford Friedman (169), and Carolyn Heilbrun (70–71).

4.  For Woolf's own account of these experiences, see her *Moments of Being.* Martine Stemerick gives a brief overview of Virginia Woolf's relationship with her mother and her half sister Stella; see also Moore (10–15). Ellen Bayuk Rosenman presents a more thorough discussion of the relationship and its influence on Woolf's fiction. For the best book-length discussion of the troubled dynamics of the Stephen family, see Louise A. DeSalvo's moving and highly readable *Virginia Woolf: The Impact of Childhood Sexual Abuse on Her Life and Work.*

5.  For an overview of Virginia Woolf's relationships with other women, see Jane Marcus's "Virginia Woolf and Her Violin: Mothering, Madness, and Music." On the influence of her lesbianism on her writing, see Blanche Wiesen Cook and Patricia Cramer.

6.  See George Ella Lyon for a brief discussion of the themes of the body and sexuality in *The Voyage Out* and in Woolf's own life (111–18). Christine Froula has suggested that Woolf attempted in this novel to transcend the traditional marriage plot but was unable to do so—an inability that Froula links to Woolf's breakdown immediately after finishing the novel (68). Jessica Tvordi has presented a somewhat strained lesbian reading of this novel, but she focuses on Rachel's relationships with Helen and Evelyn and barely touches on the mother-daughter relationship.

7.  Christine Froula also compares the kiss to a rape (73); for similar interpretations, see also Rachel Blau DuPlessis (52) and Helen Wussow (101, 103).

8.  It is perhaps doubtful whether, in her ignorance, Rachel is even *aware* of the possibility of lesbianism. When Clarissa Dalloway tells her she will enjoy walking someday, Rachel assumes she means walking with a man; "I wasn't thinking of a man particularly," Clarissa responds (*VO* 64). Even the less sheltered Susan blushes in mortification at the idea of lesbianism (*VO* 136).

9.  As Mitchell Leaska emphatically concludes, Rachel practices withdrawal as a means of self-defense (38). Nancy Topping Bazin sees Rachel's dream and hallucination as reflections of Rachel's desire to return to the womb (66). Rosenman also sees Rachel's death as a return to her mother (23, 29–30).

10. I am not the first to see the archetypal dimensions of *To the Lighthouse;* virtually every critic of the novel mentions Mrs. Ramsay's goddess-like quality. See Blotner for a detailed explication of the relationship between this novel and the Homeric *Hymn to Demeter.* Blotner, however, offers a more positive interpretation of Mrs. Ramsay than I do. See also Fleishman (especially 109–29) and Anne Golomb Hoffman. In "'The Deceptiveness of Beauty': Mother Love and Mother Hate in *To the*

*Lighthouse,*" Jane Lilienfeld discusses the ambivalence implicit in the portrayal of Mrs. Ramsay; Lilienfeld's article, the best on the novel's conflicted mother-daughter relationship, informs my understanding of the novel. Like Lilienfeld, Susan Luck Hooks and Marjorie McCormick both suggest an ambivalent role for Mrs. Ramsay, casting her as the Great and Terrible Mother. See also Marianne Hirsch (113) and Madeline Moore (74, 85–86).

11. For a discussion of the violence implicit in this scene and in the novel's family dynamics in general, see Jane Lilienfeld's excellent essay entitled "'Like a Lion Seeking Whom He Could Devour': Domestic Violence in *To the Lighthouse.*" Donna Risolo constructs a lesbian interpretation of *To the Lighthouse,* arguing that Mrs. Ramsay is both female-identified and lesbian; Risolo, too, briefly mentions the myth (245).

12. For a more comprehensive discussion of the Demeter myth and mother-daughter relationships in *Mrs. Dalloway,* see Tyler's "Our Mothers' Gardens" (128–65).

13. On Woolf's floral imagery and its association with female sexuality, see Cramer 183–86.

14. For discussions of the mother-daughter relationships in Lessing's novels, see for example Rebecca J. Lukens, Katherine Fishburn, Grace Stewart (specifically 84–89), and Claire Sprague (*Rereading,* especially Chapter 6). Because Lessing's novels have received so much more attention than her short stories, I have chosen to focus on the Demeter myth in her short fiction. It is, however, an important structuring device in her Jane Somers novels, *The Diary of a Good Neighbour* and *If the Old Could . . .* ; her *Marriages between Zones Three, Four, and Five* is an almost literal retelling of the myth in many respects.

    An earlier version of the analysis of "The De Wets Come to Kloof Grange" was presented at the Sixth Annual Women's Studies Conference, Western Kentucky University, September 24, 1992. Because I have elsewhere discussed the other two stories I deal with in this essay (see Tyler, "Classical," and note 16, below), I have chosen to discuss this story at somewhat greater length.

15. Even the name Mrs. *Gale* suggests a possible allusion to another young woman who is involuntarily displaced to a strange and colorful alien land but who yearns only to return home—Dorothy Gale of Frank L. Baum's *The Wonderful Wizard of Oz.* For a discussion of the mother-daughter dynamics of Baum's novel, see Evelyn Silten Bassoff.

16. The analysis of "Among the Roses" is a condensed version of an argument fully presented in an essay entitled "Our Mothers' Gardens: Doris Lessing's 'Among the Roses,'" forthcoming in *Studies in Short Fiction.*

PART THREE

— ◆ —

# CREATIVITY, CONSCIOUSNESS, AND THE PRIVILEGED MIND

# 6

— ◆ —

## THE FEMALE BODY VEILED:
## FROM CROCUS TO CLITORIS

### Ruth Saxton

In many ways so different in their examinations of female subjectivity, Virginia Woolf and Doris Lessing share a striking discomfort with their female characters' bodies. This aspect of their writing makes problematic the role of literary foremother that they have played for so many of us. In the first half of the century, Virginia Woolf defined two tasks of the woman writer. First, she must kill the angel in the house. Second, she must truthfully write the female body: "the book has somehow to be adapted to the body" (*ARO* 81). Woolf did the first too well. She conflated the Victorian angel with the maternal figure and killed both in her texts. She was less successful at the second, claiming in "Professions for Women" that the task of telling the truth about woman's body remained for future generations of women writers. She could not reconcile woman's body and mind except in fantasy. In the second half of the century, Doris Lessing seems to succeed where Woolf fails, writing about the female body in all its realistic, even clinical, detail, including menstruation, pregnancy, abortion, childbirth, varieties of lovemaking, illness, weight gain and loss, aging, and deterioration. In reality, in spite of all her attention to woman's body from adolescence into postmenopausal old age, Lessing, like Woolf, perpetuates a deep schism between mind and body, in which the female body is seen as a shell that severely limits woman's experience and both distorts and disguises her identity.

The female body is a locus of interest in both writers' texts, and their portrayals of the body are worth examining in terms of the ongoing discussion of female identity that circulates around and through novels by women. Woolf and Lessing, whether celebrating a female sentence or claiming the legitimacy of a fictional woman's perspective, raise questions about the nature of femaleness and its relation to the body. Both writers simultaneously portray female embodiment as a celebratory source of female artistic authenticity and as a dangerous delimiter and hindrance that must be overcome.

Although their fiction portrays a multiplicity of female characters, the privileged position in novels by Woolf and Lessing is that of the imaginative or thinking woman who is aligned with artistic production rather than maternal or erotic plenitude. Although these female protagonists are figured and configured from many angles in both writers' texts, they are all defined by their relation to the body. The body is the text of a woman character; she, we, other characters, all read her body and her relation to that body. In Woolf's texts, the female body is imagined rather than substantial, and the female character is relatively unconscious of her own degree of control over her body as text and the extent to which she is read by others. In Lessing's texts, the female body is biologically and socially charged, and the female character is highly conscious of her control over how her body is read as well as of the extent to which others read her, especially in middle age. However, both writers insist that, though a woman's body is her fate, and though she may be somewhat able to control the product of her body as text, her body is, like her clothes, a surface, a covering, a temporary and illusory source of power.

For both Woolf and Lessing, the female body is central to woman's experience of her identity, and yet each writer argues that "true" self and identity are somehow disembodied for woman, that body is only a container of consciousness, a trap, a disguise. Discomfort with being female remains constant in both writers. In both writers, the privileged position for the female is a position removed from maternal reproduction: in Woolf, the artist figure; in Lessing, the thinking woman who has outgrown her reproductive capacity. In Woolf, only a female character who resists reproductive sexuality can create a female text. In Lessing, only a female character beyond active sexuality is ready to develop and create her self and her art. Woman can either procreate or create, but never simultaneously. In Woolf, the one precludes the other; in Lessing, protagonists often are mothers first and only then can create.

In Woolf's fictional world, woman cannot simultaneously exist as an artist and mother, as mind and body. Women characters in Woolf's novels are either thinking/dreaming mind (the Artist) or maternal body (the

Mother). This dichotomy appears in her first novel, *The Voyage Out,* between Rachel Vinrace, as potential musician, and Helen Ambrose, the aunt who within the timeline of the plot is surrogate mother and mentor for Rachel into the ultimately dangerous heterosexual plot of courtship and marriage. *The Voyage Out* introduces the basic predicament of the Woolfian protagonist, the female artist whose body is caught up in the heterosexual love plot, who yearns for a bond with the maternal, and whose sexual body threatens not only her artistic autonomy but her very life.

Woolf first calls attention to Rachel's body as text to be read by showing us the varying readings of it by adults aboard ship, later in her first experience of heterosexual desire and her engagement to Terence, and finally in her death, which figures Rachel as a text subject to interpretation both within the novel and among critics of the novel. Rachel's body is the locus of the irreconcilability of her art and her sexual desire. Rachel is atypical of young women in Woolf's novels in that, after the death of her mother, Theresa, she is raised by maiden aunts and a seafaring father, isolated from any maternal education concerning her body, and allowed to develop primarily on her own. Through undirected pursuit of her music and reading, she lives primarily in her mind as a thinker/dreamer unaware of the possibilities and dangers of her body.

Unlike later Woolfian protagonists, Rachel, surprisingly naive for her twenty-four years, is not highly conscious of a price to be paid for yielding to desire. Unlike Clarissa Dalloway, she is not conscious of the material risks of following her passions rather than her head in making a judicious choice of husband. Unlike Lily Briscoe, she has neither a highly tuned sense of gender inequities nor a compelling urge for merger with a maternal figure. Though deeply upset by the conflicting feelings she has in the presence of Richard Dalloway and the profound sense of invasion and fear evoked by his unsought kiss, Rachel seems to desire Terence. He does not force himself on her. She struggles to balance competing tugs between her desire for intimacy and the boundaries necessary for solitude and art, but she seems genuinely to want a physical relationship with Terence, a relationship Woolf refuses to allow, killing her almost immediately after she becomes engaged to Terence, just as she is beginning to feel the power of her own sexuality. That death makes no sense to other characters in the novel, who read it not only as a tragedy, but also as if it were a litmus test of their own beliefs. Within the context of Woolf's later novels, however, Rachel's death is simply the first of a long line of deaths—each one reinforcing the assumption that to remain a thinking/dreaming mind, an Artist, woman must avoid fulfilling her sexual desires. If she enters the heterosexual plot, she dies. Physical desire is safe only in yearning after what she cannot realize, from which perspective it can enrich her art. The body is a risk and traps woman.

Rather than portray physical union, Woolf explores her characters' desires to know one another at the level of consciousness and portrays their desire in highly charged metaphors. We think readily of Lily Briscoe with her longing to really "know" Mrs. Ramsay. That attempt to know others is apparent throughout Woolf's fiction, from *The Voyage Out* to *Between the Acts*. Although the knowing of others in Woolf is a knowing of their being, mind, or feeling, surprisingly the actual text of that reading is often some detail of the body—facial features, hands, or even general shape and size. For example, Helen notices Rachel's face and lack of color and assumes from that detail that Rachel is weak and lacks beauty. Rachel notices Helen's tall figure, draped in purple shawls, and assumes she is romantic.

Since most people assume that their first impressions of others are somewhat accurate, we as readers may initially accept characters' readings of physical traits as accurate guides to personality or character. However, Woolf shows the danger in reading body in this way. Helen Ambrose considers Rachel weak. Rachel Vinrace considers Helen romantic. Helen assumes Rachel has no opinions of her own and is abused by her father. Rachel assumes Helen is elderly and exotic. It is important to recall, however, that within the novel these initial readings eventually are revealed to be inaccurate. Rachel gets along fine with her father, and Helen is only sixteen years older than Rachel. Those initial readings may seem harmless, yet the final individual readings of Rachel's death are just as superficial, revealing more about the characters who make them than they do about Rachel or the meaning of her life.

Woolf frequently creates a triangulated situation involving two parallel pairings of a female protagonist, one with a male and one with a female. These two types offer two competing contexts for reading that protagonist. In *The Voyage Out*, one pair contains Rachel and Helen; the other pair contains Rachel and Terence. These two types of intimate relationship are familiar ones to Woolf readers, the one between two women, often a variation on the mother/daughter relationship, a buried plot of sensually charged possibility in the text, more compelling than the one between a woman and a man—the more traditional marriage plot. A pull toward intimacy and merger dominates in the woman/woman pair, whereas a profound sense of difference and an attempt to establish boundaries dominate in the woman/man pair. The sexualized blurring of boundaries between female bodies here points to the theme of desire for female merger in later works.

In the pairing of Rachel and Helen, Woolf sets up what becomes a familiar trope on the relationship of two women, a relationship she continually tries to excavate throughout her work. In this trope, the beautiful embodied woman who is herself implicated in the marriage plot tries to educate the artist woman into the path the maternal/embodied woman has chosen. (Clearly both women have bodies. I am using this term as differentiator between artist/thinker and primarily traditional defined maternal/woman.) The dreamer/mind woman is drawn toward intimacy with the safe, maternal/embodied woman. This intimacy is never realized, though Woolf hints at its potential power through erotically charged metaphors. One member of the woman/woman pairing dies in Woolf's novels. The artist woman has greater potential as an artist if her body does not attract the attention of men. Her art then can develop in relative peace, apart from the onslaughts of courtship, marriage, childbirth, and family life, all of which deplete woman in patriarchal society. Yet this survival as artist is at incredible cost in that it requires the symbolic death of her body.

Helen perceives major differences between herself and Rachel, seeing Rachel as very young, dull, not pretty, having less depth and potential than herself. Nevertheless, Helen tries to educate Rachel concerning her body and sexuality, resulting in the young woman's initiation into the courtship and marriage plot. Helen as the safe maternal figure, a surrogate for Rachel's dead mother, is exempt from the familiarity as well as the conflicts which would occur if she were Rachel's actual mother. Woolf creates in her a sisterly function, a sororal rather than parental relationship. She is a go-between for Rachel and the young men at the hotel. Her own physical, bodily presence attracts the favorable attention of both men and women, and that bodily presence is important. She initiates the introduction of Rachel to Mr. Hewet and Mr. Hirst, the two apparently marriageable young men, openly discussing with them the dreadful naiveté of the female sex, and even requesting their help in educating Rachel. She initiates the evening walk to the hotel which results in their invitation to the dance. At the dance, she, not Rachel, thoroughly enjoys the earthy passion of dancing, though her husband refuses to attend, and she also accompanies Rachel on the outing arranged by Hirst. The presence in the text of Ridley, her scholarly husband, is muted and nonphysical. This retiring Greek scholar with no taste for dancing or adventure, unable to "read" his own wife, is indirectly linked by Woolf with Hirst, the young scholar whom both Rachel and Helen consider "ugly in body, repulsive in mind" (201). In a revealing comment, Helen even wonders whether there is some connection between scholarship and maltreatment of the body.

Helen is linked far more with Rachel than with her husband, Ridley. He exists in the background, a reminder that she is considered safe as a companion for Rachel. As a married woman she is free of impropriety in her adventures with younger men and women at dances and on the extended trip up the river. Though within the text Helen is more linked with Rachel than she is with her husband, she nevertheless sees Rachel only in terms of her potential role in the marriage plot, not as potential artist. In fact, she is somewhat amused by Rachel's music and does not have any sense of its importance to Rachel, except as a background for her own action, a situation that mirrors her sense of Ridley's scholarship as background to her own life. For example, when the accompanist at the dance retires for the night, Rachel fills in at the piano. Helen continues dancing until morning; we are given no indication that Rachel would have preferred dancing with a partner to her own impassioned performance alone at the piano. This hint of her potential to become an artist is totally disregarded by Helen, who sees her only as product in the marriage quest.

Woolf assumes the heterosexual love plot is vexed and sets up the issues early. Whereas in her representation of the woman/woman pair of Rachel and Helen Woolf points to the theme of desire for merger in later works, in her presentation of the woman/man pair, Woolf accentuates the woman's preoccupation with establishing and maintaining boundaries between herself and her lover. Though Rachel is drawn toward Terence, and repeatedly says she is in love, that she feels happiness, and that she wants to know Terence, as readers of Woolf, we know that she would lose her freedom in marriage. In this plot, the woman risks becoming trapped in a bodily exchange, with the potential loss of her mental and artistic freedom.

Throughout the scenes in which Terence and Rachel become acquainted, Woolf repeatedly calls attention to Rachel as body: "Her body was very attractive to him." Terence, when looking at Rachel, notices her dress, her shape, her head, her face, her lips, her large gray eyes, her hand, her fingers. She realizes Terence pleases her; he notices the "very small individual things about her which made her delightful to him." She touches his face and has a sense of his body as unreal (282). He connects his looking at her with musings on men's power over women, a power similar to the power they have over horses, and although he assumes that woman's willingness to obey men must be based on an erroneous (because inflated) view of men, he, nevertheless, assumes marriage usually includes such obedience (212). This passage for Woolf readers echoes the passage in *A Room of One's Own* in which woman reflects man at twice his normal size; Terence seems to assume that in marriage Rachel will inflate his image.

Woolf calls unusual attention to Rachel and Terence's awareness of each other's bodies in the passages in which they try to read each other. He responds to her body; body is crucial to their pairing. When Rachel looks at

Terence, she considers him good looking in the sense of general health and notes especially the size of his head and eyes as well as the sensitivity of his lips. She reads the breadth of his forehead as revealing "capacity for thought" (216). When he looks at her he begins to feel desire and to think of obedience; when she looks at him, she thinks about his thinking. Although Terence alludes to former experiences of falling in love, experiences felt in his body, his response to Rachel is surprisingly chaste. Likewise, she feels some stirrings of sexualized feminine power, but her observations of his body do not stray beneath the neck. This is a cerebral and mental attraction, yet the idea of bodies being so present expresses the sexual plot beneath this surface. Reciprocal male/female love makes Rachel feel her own womanliness, her independence, her calm and certainty, her completeness and happiness. "Very gently and quietly, almost as if it were the blood singing in her veins . . . Rachel [becomes] conscious of a new feeling . . . [says] to herself, with a little surprise at recognizing in her own person so famous a thing: 'This is happiness, I suppose'" (283).

Yet, under Terence's gaze after he first refers to her as a woman, Rachel becomes self-conscious and concerned about a loss of her freedom, a possibility of repressing her "wild music." She does have stirrings of power as she begins to feel what she and Terence explain as being "in love" with each other, and she experiences the apparent paradox of wanting to be understood and not wanting to lose an iota of her freedom. She wonders, "Why did he sit so near and keep his eye on her? No, she would not consent to be pinned down by any second person in the whole world," and she insists she likes walking alone and not mattering to anyone: "I like the freedom of it—I like . . ." (215). She and Terence alternate between a desire to merge with one another and an equally strong desire to escape from each other into their own realms of art and accomplishment—whether in the novel or music.

Those lusty athletic bodies like Susan's and Arthur's may produce healthy children, but Woolf provides no similar image of Rachel and Terence. Woolf has earlier mentioned kisses, some stirrings of desire, a longing for intimacy, but there has been very little sense of a physical Rachel until her fever. Illness and death provide Rachel's "escape" from marriage, ironically an escape from the body located in the body. Woolf's description of Rachel's body when ill is almost our only indication of Rachel's experience of her body. Whereas in health, Woolf gives the reader no account of Rachel's bodily sensations, in portraying Rachel's illness, Woolf describes Rachel's physical sensations in concrete detail: The headache is a "pulse in her head . . . each thump seemed to tread upon a nerve, piercing her forehead with a little stab of pain" (328). She registers sensations of extreme heat and cold.

Her body becomes increasingly important daily. "She was completely cut off, and unable to communicate with the rest of the world, isolated alone with her body" (330). She is conscious of pain "but chiefly of weakness" (346). She is "conscious of her body floating on the top of the bed and her mind driven to some remote corner of her body, or escaped and gone flitting around the room" (347).

After her death, Rachel's presence in the novel is as a crucial text to be read, particularly by those furthest removed from the inner-circle of family and friends, who all try to make sense of her death, forced by that death to think of their own beliefs, significance, and mortality. Just as characters in the novel project onto Rachel's death their own views about what kills her, readers project their views of what kills the female artist. For some characters, Rachel's death must have a reason or life itself has no reason. For such characters, it might have been prevented by refraining from the expedition, washing vegetables properly, not drinking the local water, each explanation focusing on a physical cause of death. For Woolfian readers, Rachel's death might have been prevented by her not falling in love with Terence, not becoming engaged, not participating in the British colonial plot, perhaps even keeping her mother alive or having another chance in another plot. Rachel falls in love, is conflicted over questions of intimacy and independence, is feverish and hallucinating, and dies before she can explore any of her new desires or fears. And, life goes on for those who loved her: Terence and Helen.

The two most memorable passages in the novel each contain the triangle: Rachel, Helen, and Terence. One scene is set in the meadow just following Rachel's decision to marry Terence, when she and he are trying to explain themselves to each other before being joined by the rest of their group. The other scene is set in the bedroom, which has become a sickroom and death chamber rather than the setting for marital bliss. Rachel is central to both scenes, her body the contested space. In the first scene, Terence and Helen apparently kiss above Rachel's head, and we are given a rather confusing and erotic visual description, slightly out of focus. In the second scene, Rachel's sensations and hallucinations dominate, surrounded by Terence's thoughts and Helen's actions. These two passages have a power that makes them stand out from the rest of the novel, as if they were separately framed set pieces inserted into the text. Each is filled with highly charged images, and each contributes to contradictory readings of Rachel's body as icon in the competing plots of woman as body versus woman as mind.

The first charged scene occurs in the midst of Terence and Rachel's attempts to explain themselves to one another—their faults, their histories, their feelings. Suddenly Woolf inserts the line: "A hand dropped abrupt as iron on Rachel's shoulder" (283). The line is abrupt and has connotations of assault. We are told that she fell beneath it and that "through the waving stems" of grass, Rachel saw a figure "large and shapeless against the sky." We may expect to be told that Terence has passionately thrown her down in the grass, but instead are surprised by the statement: "Helen was upon her" (283). Woolf's ambiguous wording invites multiple interpretations and possible projections of the reader's own biased assumptions about either the man/woman pairing or the woman/woman pairing. The textual description is then rather hard to follow. We are given bits of information: "rolled this way and that," and "she was speechless and almost without sense" (283–84). When she at last "lay still," we are told all the grasses have been shaken "by her panting." The passage—with its physical motion, rolling in the grass, loss of speech, panting—certainly suggests passion and eroticism. What are we then to make of the statement "Over her loomed two great heads, the head of a man and woman, of Terence and Helen"? Why are Terence and Helen kissing and laughing, speaking of love and marriage in the air above her? Are we to read in their actions a complicity in the initiation of Rachel into the marital love plot? What are we to make of her realizing "Helen's soft body, the strong and hospitable arms, and happiness swelling and breaking in one vast wave" (284), a clearly eroticized vision of Helen by Rachel? What are we to make of this woman/woman sexual energy? Is it Rachel's lesbian awakening? a maternal vision?

Whether Helen is actually or imaginatively present to Rachel, it is important that we are given no sense of Rachel's body in the passage. The scene has sexual connotations certainly, but they are quite different from the earlier descriptions of hair, eyes, mouth, face. Any erotic appeal in this passage is of Helen's body. The kissing, laughter, even speech is transferred from Rachel to Helen. The movement of the passage is from Rachel and Terence walking apart from the group to Helen and Terence immediately above Rachel's head, to Rachel "too" (along with Terence?) "realizing" Helen's soft body. The passage concludes with the trio being joined by all the rest of the group. Helen is the link between the newly engaged male/female pair and the rest of society. The mother/woman initiates the connection between the artist/woman and the socially sanctioned heterosexual plot, at the same time being the container for a female libidinal energy, lesbian desire.

The second triangulated scene or set of scenes takes place in Rachel's bedroom, where her mind distorts her surroundings and we are aware of her delirium. Rachel's images here are feverish as she sees scenes on, and even through, the walls. We are told that Helen and Terence take turns at her bedside, but it is only when Helen calls in a nurse that Rachel's perception of the woman at her bedside transposes into an elderly woman, and Rachel calls out "Terence!" She blurs the images of Helen, the nurse, and a little deformed old woman, and when Terence is at her bedside, she sees "the old woman with the knife" (335). When Terence kisses her four days later, although she has her eyes wide open, she sees "an old woman slicing a man's head off with a knife" (339). In the six days that follow, Rachel is "unable to keep Helen's face distinct from the sights themselves" (341) and struggles to grasp "a reason behind" the "plot," "adventure," "escape" involved in those sights she cannot dismiss. Woolf tells us that Rachel has a sense of "tormen-tors" who mistakenly think she is dead. Is Woolf linking Helen and Terence as tormentors whose attempts to induct her into the marriage plot, to bring her to life, are a mistaken reading of her? The nurse, when asked to comment on Rachel's condition, suggests it may be the moon which "affects the brain . . ." (344) or the month of May. The moon is a traditional feminine body symbol, and May is the traditional month for pagan witchcraft celebrations.

Woolf parallels the earlier triangulated scene in the grass in these sickroom scenes just before Rachel's death. Helen, who has always appeared strong and determined, becomes like a child and Terence takes her in his arms where she clings "crying softly and quietly upon his shoulder" (346), reminding us of the kiss above Rachel's head in the grass. Woolf here gives us Rachel's sensations in words similar to those in the grass, mentioning "a wave" which "seemed to bear her up and down" and is then "replaced by the side of a mountain." Rachel again sees Helen's form above her where it appears "gigantic size, and came down upon her like the ceiling falling" (347), reminiscent of the "iron hand" of the earlier passage. But Terence, not Helen, causes the "greatest effort" for Rachel, for seeing him "forced her to join mind and body in the desire to remember something" when what she wishes is "to be alone" (347). In the earlier scene in the grass we are given motion—rolling, grass shaken, words like "love," "marriage," "soft," "strong," "hospitable," "happiness," "swelling," "breaking." In the sickroom we see deformity, decapitation, Helen blurring into the nurse into the woman with the knife, Terence's kisses followed by Rachel's vision of an old woman slicing off a man's head. Her desire is for escape, to be curled up at the bottom of the sea—another female trope.

The surface plot, which leads the reader to expect the marriage of Rachel and Terence, is abruptly truncated. The ending feels more like a puzzle Woolf is making for us than a story of "real" characters. Just as characters within the novel read Rachel's death and search for meaning, so we read her death, left with speculations and questions. The readings of Rachel by characters within the novel all overlook the competing plot of woman as artist versus woman as body. Does Rachel die because she is motherless and has not been inducted into the heterosexual plot early enough? As woman who would be artist, does she die because she tries to be both sexual and artist? Woolf does not allow Rachel to become artist or to consummate her sexuality with either Terence or Helen. She implies that physical death avoids the inevitable spiritual death ahead of Rachel, the living death implied in becoming like any of the other married women in the novel. Whichever way we read Rachel's life and death, we must conclude that the body of the woman is contested space.

In *To the Lighthouse,* Woolf mirrors several of the elements of *The Voyage Out,* foregrounding the woman/woman pairing of younger woman artist and older woman surrogate mother, the dreaming mind with the maternal body. Here, as in *The Voyage Out,* the mother surrogate tries to initiate the younger artistic woman into the heterosexual plot she herself has chosen, but Lily, unlike Rachel, resists. Here Woolf investigates more fully than earlier the choices between being artist or mother/wife. Some things are similar to those in *The Voyage Out:* like Helen, Mrs. Ramsay is mother. Unlike Helen, she is mother to eight, not two, children and is surrounded by those children. Whereas in *The Voyage Out,* Helen tries to form Rachel in her likeness, in *To the Lighthouse,* not only does Mrs. Ramsay try to form Lily, but Lily also tries to form Mrs. Ramsay on canvas. Mrs. Ramsay, the epitome of the mother-woman in Woolf's fiction, dies part way through *To the Lighthouse,* leaving the surrogate daughter as survivor, a reversal of the pattern in *The Voyage Out.* Nevertheless, although Woolf allows Lily to survive and suggests that her artistic production of Mrs. Ramsay will endure beyond flesh and blood, that survival does not allow Lily to experience any pleasure in her body. The most intense desire in the text is that of Lily for Mrs. Ramsay, a feeling which is only equaled by the intense sense of grief and loss in the wake of Mrs. Ramsay's death.

Lily Briscoe is defined more explicitly as an artist than Rachel, though she too is untutored. She is not just potential artist; she lives by and for her art. Also, unlike *The Voyage Out,* in this text Woolf provides the interiority of the female artist. She also allows the artist to live, although she does not allow her to have any active sexual definition. Woolf sets up the trope: a woman cannot be in a heterosexual union and also create; she cannot have access to a woman/woman union except in imaginative fantasy. Female artistic production requires the death of the sensual body.

Woolf complicates woman's mind/body split in *To the Lighthouse* through Lily's interior balancing of the costs to woman regardless of her choice. Woolf writes, "Such was the complexity of things": that Lily, in the presence of Mrs. Ramsay, feels "violently two opposite things," that love between men and women is "beautiful" and "exciting" and yet "the stupidest, the most barbaric of human passions, and turns a nice young man . . . into a bully with a crowbar . . ." (154). Mrs. Ramsay's insistence that "William and Lily should marry" (42) and that "an unmarried woman has missed the best of life" (77) is countered by Lily's self-knowledge, her thoughts of her father, her home, and most of all of her painting. Her painting centers her thoughts in the midst of the dinner party when she is acutely aware of expectations she should be nice to young men, should bolster the male ego. Ten years later, Lily is even more self-assured, and in facing her blank canvas, realizes it provides a frail barrier but is "sufficiently substantial to ward off Mr. Ramsay and his exactingness" (223). Lily, unlike Mrs. Ramsay, discovers that Mr. Ramsay's need for sympathy can be satisfied with simple praise of his boots.

By not participating in the marriage plot, Lily escapes the constant depletion of the wife/mother role. At the dinner party, as in the rest of her life, Mrs. Ramsay knows that her individual, separate guests become a community only because of her exertion: "the whole of the effort of merging and flowing and creating rested on her . . . if she did not do it nobody would do it" (126). Not only her husband, and the male guests, but also the children and even Lily come to Mrs. Ramsay for some essence, some vitality, and "[s]o boasting of her capacity to surround and protect, there was scarcely a shell of herself left for her to know herself by" (60). Though Lily is convinced later in life that "one could not imagine Mrs. Ramsay standing painting, lying reading, a whole morning on the lawn" (291), Woolf hints that Mrs. Ramsay, if not totally giving to others, might have been an artist, whether in her storytelling or in her creation of illusion, draping the boar's head in her shawl, arranging the magical dinner party. Lily escapes the depletion of the mother/woman who in "[g]iving, giving, giving . . . had died" (223), but she also misses out on the love, the power, the general sense of importance to others, which remains after death and inspires Lily's art. Not only does Woolf have Mrs. Ramsay die, and Lily die to her own sexuality in choosing to be artist, she further emphasizes the explicit threat of the female body even to the nonartist woman by having Prue, the daughter who had adored her mother "as if there were only one person like that in the world" (271), die in childbirth. By *To the Lighthouse,* the body explicitly represented as heterosexualized is dangerous in various degrees to all women, even to the nonartist woman, and that danger is precisely what the artist wishes to avoid.

Mrs. Ramsay considers forming Lily in her likeness, but Lily is resistant, compelled not only by her art and her desire for self-preservation, but also by her desire for Mrs. Ramsay. Lily does not wish to attract men. She is acutely aware of their expectations, and of those shared by Mrs. Ramsay, that it is a woman's duty to minister to men, to bolster their egos, to offer just the right word or assurance of sympathy that would allow them to assert their superiority. She is bruised by Charles Tansley's insistence that "[w]omen can't paint, women can't write" (75). She reveals no inclination toward marriage, though she does feel a bit left out of the radiance shared by Minta and Paul Rayley the day they become engaged. Rather, she, like everyone else in the novel, adores the beautiful Mrs. Ramsay.

We know that Mrs. Ramsay is beautiful because of the many references to her beauty, and because others call her beautiful, but Woolf does not provide a portrait of her actual bodily appearance. Charles Tansley experiences her beauty as "stars in her eyes and veils in her hair, with cyclamen and wild violets" (25), and both he and the man digging in a drain are captivated by her beauty. Mr. Bankes, in a telephone conversation with Mrs. Ramsay, imagines her as "very clearly Greek, straight, blue-eyed" (47). Mrs. Ramsay seldom thinks of her own beauty, and yet when snubbed by Mr. Carmichael her immediate internal defense is to think of herself as a woman whom other men have found beautiful and then to feel somehow "shabby, worn out . . . cheeks . . . hollow . . . hair . . . white." Immediately after his disregard of her beauty, she considers herself "no longer a sight that filled the eyes with joy" (66) and turns more fully to the maternal act of reading aloud to her son. Her internal sense of her beauty follows this pattern of comparison between former and present beauty two other places in the text: once when looking in a mirror and dressing and once at the dinner party when Minta arrives in a rosy glow. In all three instances Mrs. Ramsay recalls herself as formerly having power over men because of her beauty and yet presently feeling a loss of such power because of her age (she is fifty) and the duties of family life (there is Mr. Ramsay with his need to be sheltered from bills and domestic responsibilities, and there are eight children plus assorted guests). However, none of the men except Mr. Carmichael is oblivious to her beauty or gives any hint of considering her less attractive because of her age. When others speak of her it is in terms of her influence, her aura, her vitality. Mrs. Ramsay is not only beautiful, she is naturally beautiful.

Instead of portraying Mrs. Ramsay's beauty itself, Woolf portrays her influence on others and gives us their perceptions of her beauty and forcefulness. Four passages that reveal her effect on others include the scene in which Mr. Ramsay comes to her for sympathy, her walk with Charles Tansley, James's experience of the bid for sympathy by his father, and Lily's musings about the possibility of intimacy with her.

Mr. Ramsay's demand for sympathy results in a scene in which she "seemed to pour . . . a rain of energy, a column of spray . . . animated and alive . . . burning and illuminating . . . fountain and spray of life." In each case, we are given a series of references to energy and its affect on the other, who is not primarily gazing on a set of particular physical attributes. The sexual energy of this passage is not located in anatomical parts, a smile or a set of eyes. Charles Tansley's description is romantic and tells us more about her affect on him than about her actual appearance. "Stars," "veils," "cyclamen," and "violets" create a mood, not a portrait. Similarly, Woolf describes James's experience of Mrs. Ramsay, like that of Tansley, in metaphor: "a rosy-flowered fruit tree laid with leaves and dancing boughs" (60). These images of a fruitful tree and a column of spray combine phallic and female images, creating a sense of Mrs. Ramsay as an epic woman, containing ultimate power, combining earth and sky.

Unlike the three differently aged males, Lily does not see Mrs. Ramsay in lyrical or romantic terms. Instead, she wonders about the "deceptiveness of beauty" (78) and searches for the "spirit in her, the essential thing" as well as the possibility of intimacy. Lily tries to get behind the shell of the body to a self separate from that body. In spite of her claim that a woman can't worship another woman, Lily adores Mrs. Ramsay and questions how to achieve unity with her, whether by the body, the mind, the brain, or the heart, wondering "Could loving . . . make her and Mrs. Ramsay one?" She repeatedly questions how one knows another person "sealed as they were" (79). Here again Woolf uses erotic images, waters mingling in one jar, tablets in the heart, a bee circling around a dome, with the eroticism located in intensely charged metaphors into which a reader can project female desire. Yet, Woolf does not tell us how Mrs. Ramsay or Lily Briscoe experience their bodies. Bodily sensation exists only in fantasy space, ellipses, metaphors, not in lived specific experience.

The body is surprisingly absent even in the passages we read as sexually charged. For example, Woolf creates a word picture of Lily seated "on the floor with her arms round Mrs. Ramsay's knees, close as she could get, smiling to think that Mrs. Ramsay would never know the reason of that pressure . . ." (79). We are allowed to ask questions, to guess, but we are not explicitly told the reason of that pressure, although we recognize Woolf's ellipses as places she invites us to imagine. Is Lily longing for preoedipal union? for sexual connection? for fusion to Mrs. Ramsay's life-force energy? What follows the passage is a series of questions about how to achieve unity with an adored object. Woolf mentions the body, the mind, the brain, the heart as possible means to make Lily and Mrs. Ramsay one. She mentions loving, "as people call it," and we are free to interpret that phrase as making love. The object of such loving, however, is not given as a satisfaction of desire, as pleasure, as particularly physical and embodied, but rather as a means of achieving unity of consciousness. The sense of the passage is a longing. Ten years later, admitting that Mrs. Ramsay's power over her was so great she has escaped marriage only "by the skin of her teeth" (262), Lily asks how she can "express in words these emotions of the body? express the emptiness there? . . . It was one's body feeling, not one's mind . . . to want and not to have . . . " (265–66). That yearning may be read as Woolf's coding of lesbian desire, but the reader can also read the passage as desire to be encircled in the all-encompassing love of the mother.

The longing for female merger expressed as a mother/daughter bond in *To the Lighthouse* is located in remembered female friendship and on-going occasional responses to women by Clarissa Dalloway. In *Mrs. Dalloway* we find the most startling evocation of erotic female/female longing in Woolf, in the match in the crocus passage:

> It was a sudden revelation, a tinge like a blush which one tried to check and then, as it spread, one yielded to its expansion, and rushed to the farthest verge and there quivered and felt the world come closer, swollen with some astonishing significance, some pressure of rapture, which split its thin skin and gushed and poured with an extraordinary alleviation over the cracks and sores! Then, for that moment, she had seen an illumination; a match burning in a crocus; an inner meaning almost expressed. (47)

The metaphor is one which encompasses and symbolizes Woolf's fantasy of the female body, notable in its beauty, power, and finally in its status as metaphor. This erotic passage occurs immediately following Clarissa's interior monologue about maintaining her virginity through marriage and childbirth, failing Richard "in that way," and sometimes feeling for a woman the feelings she assumes men have for women. The passage resonates with Clarissa's earlier memory of Sally Seton at Bourton. Clarissa recalls dressing for dinner, arranging her hair, all in an ecstasy because of Sally's presence in the house. No other memory is as beautiful or evocative, as filled with delight and vitality. Clarissa celebrates Sally's unconventionality, her flaunting of tradition, her breaking of rules, and most importantly that kiss, which set Clarissa afire and then was so harshly interrupted by Peter Walsh, as if she had run into a granite wall, echoing the "iron hand" of *The Voyage Out*.

Woolf creates beautiful embodied maternal women, yet the female artist herself is disembodied at some basic level. Helen Ambrose, Mrs. Ramsay, and Sally Seton are all beautiful and charismatic, attracting men and women to themselves without apparent effort. Each marries and lives out the heterosexual marriage plot without textual evidence of extraordinary suffering. But, hidden in each novel is a submerged plot of female/female desire originating in the artist woman for the maternal woman, a desire expressed not in language of the body but in strongly charged metaphors of nature and of energy, flowers and fire. In contrast to the iron hand, the beak of iron, the granite wall, she envisions the grassy meadow, the chambers of the mind, the match in the crocus. The impossible image of fire in a flower is metaphorically sexual; the female erotic is absolute art. Woolf suggests a fantasy of a new body/mind relationship, and her texts represent a longing for such idealized female space. The imagistic metaphor also calls attention to her own status as artist, as woman not hindered by reproduction, and therefore having access to that "incandescence" necessary for successful artistic production.

Lessing's portrayal of sexual activity as well as her acute attention to biological stages of female development, particularly in reference to the reproductive cycles of a woman's life, at first glance suggests that she, unlike Woolf, has managed to come to terms with the female body: to truthfully "write the body" without fear of shocking or offending the imagined reader. However, while Lessing does write about the female body in detail, like Woolf, she is conflicted in her portrayal of that body. Her protagonists, like those of Woolf, are aligned with thinking or dreaming mind, self-consciously inhabiting their bodies in sharp contrast to peripheral female characters who are relatively "at home" in their bodies. In Lessing, the "artist" women have sexual experiences, but unlike "body" women, they are self-conscious and reflective. Martha Quest, protagonist through five volumes of the *Children of Violence* series, for example, is a thinking/dreaming character who—though she marries, gives birth to a child, and has numerous sexual experiences—always feels deeply split between mind and body. Lessing's protagonists combine the beauty of a Woolfian "body" woman like Mrs. Ramsay with a highly developed mind and are thus acutely aware of their physical appearance and painfully conscious of the ways in which others read their bodies as texts.

While Woolf's depiction of the female body is often only suggested or veiled in metaphor and she invites future generations of women writers to go beyond her efforts, Lessing meticulously writes the female body: vaginal versus clitoral orgasms, menstruation, defecation, physical aspects of sexual passion, childbirth, illness, death. Yet in spite of seeming initially to be so "body" attentive, especially in contrast to Woolf's repression of the body or reliance on metaphor, Lessing is as conflicted about the female body as is Woolf. Bodies are other: in *The Four-Gated City,* Martha Quest "had worn brown bare arms" (5), and her mother and fellow sea voyagers look out from within the "disguise they wore, white hair, graveyard faces, unsightly bodies" of old age (265). Lessing reinscribes the divisive split between mind and body, portraying the female body as cage and female biology as a trap, and privileges in her fiction the consciousness that has transcended the body.

Woolf exposes the social restrictions of feminine heterosexual roles, suggesting woman can avoid those restrictions if, like Lily Briscoe, she chooses art rather than marriage, or if, having chosen marriage, in a more vexed scenario like Clarissa Dalloway, she is frigid within her marriage. We recall, for example, Clarissa's memory that she chose Richard Dalloway rather than Peter Walsh because with Richard she could be more separate. Lessing, however, locates female restrictions in the objectification of the female body, an objectification that must be experienced and then outgrown rather than rejected at will by the female character. At most, a character can diminish such objectification through conscious strategies of camouflage and disguise. For example, Kate Brown in *The Summer Before the Dark* undergoes a transformative summer in middle age after raising four children in a traditional marriage, and returns home from her summer's experience boasting a wide band of graying hair. In Lessing's fiction as in Woolf's, woman's body is locus of the problem of female identity. However, Lessing, unlike Woolf, does not offer alternate sexual choices—lesbianism or celibacy—as viable ways to avoid submersion of identity. Rather, the Lessing protagonist must go through the "normal" trajectory of (heterosexual) femininity—loss of virginity, childbirth, menopause—during which she is continually conscious of herself as "body" before she can shed that carapace and gain access to greater self-knowledge.

In Lessing's fiction, women experience their bodies as separate from themselves because of patriarchal societal objectification of women's bodies. Lessing locates a split between female self and body in adolescence, when young female characters discover a new power and trauma in their budding sexuality as their bodies metamorphose from those of little girls to those of young women. They flaunt their new "body power" before mothers, disguise and accentuate it in costume changes before mirrors and with friends, and experience the power of their changed bodies as both heady and frightening in the presence of young men. Just as Rachel's budding sexuality in Woolf's *The Voyage Out* is immediately perceived as a precursor to marriage and elicits from her paradoxical feelings of happiness and a need to maintain her freedom (215), so Kate Brown in *The Summer Before the Dark* recalls an early scene in which she was a young woman filled with the double desire of a Lessing protagonist at the entree to sexuality (13). She recalls "wearing a white embroidered dress designed to expose and conceal throat and shoulders" (13). Split between the call of heterosexual femininity and the life of the mind, the young Kate was conflicted with desires to be a beautiful, angelic "marvelous being" like her dead grandmother and to study Romance languages and literature in the university like her still living grandfather (14).

Beyond adolescence, the sexually active young woman in Lessing's novels experiences a sense of internal division when she is admired exclusively as a body. Martha Quest, in her first sexual encounter with Douglas Knowell, resents his "self-absorbed adoration" of her body and his comments on her legs, arms, and breasts; and "during this rite, she remained passive, offering herself to this adoration" and yet feeling "quite excluded" from it (*MQ* 220). She feels deeply split as he expresses near reverence for her "perfect body" as if she were merely an assortment of breasts, buttocks, curves, and hollows to satisfy his male cravings. For a woman to recognize that she is perceived as a sexual object is to be aware that she is always subject to male approval or disapproval of her outside rather than her inside, to be constantly conscious of her appearance to men, and therefore always to be adjusting her internal thermostat, registering whether or not she desires male attention, and dressing and acting accordingly. We see Martha's various experiments with cosmetics, hairstyles, diet, and fashion to please men as well as her camouflage in an oversized matronly coat when she wishes to hide her body from unwanted attention on the London streets at night.

The adolescent or young woman's changing body propels the Lessing protagonist into ready-made social expectations of courtship, marriage, and maternity regardless of her own inclinations. If, like Mary in *The Grass is Singing*, as an adult woman she still feels and dresses like a little girl, content with nonsexual male and female friendships, she is subject to gossip by her friends and urged to change, not only her dress but also her ways. An announcement of Mary Turner's death begins *The Grass is Singing*, and Lessing locates the origins of her death both externally with roots in a racist colonialist society and internally with psychological roots in her parents' disturbed and disturbing relationship. Nevertheless, it is only after Mary, at the urging of her friends, is catapulted into the courtship plot with its fragile illusory basis in romance novels and films, that Mary, like Rachel, begins her descent toward death, an unusual plot pattern in Lessing's novels. While portraying the cost to Mary of adaptation to society's standards that to be an adult she must marry and experience sex with a man, Lessing locates the cause of her death in racism and sexism rather than in the heterosexual expectations of society.

Unlike Mary Turner, most of Lessing's female protagonists have active sexual lives. In Jane Somers's words, they have "had all that good sex" (*DJS* 6).

They are neither celibate like Lily Briscoe nor frigid like Clarissa Dalloway. Lessing does not eschew sexuality, rather she seems to expect her protagonists to be sexually active. Characters like Mary Turner, Lynda Coldridge, and Alice Mellings of *The Good Terrorist,* who apparently have no sexual drive, are portrayed as somehow wounded by their earlier family lives, children of mismatched parents, women who are deeply alienated from their surrounding societies. Yet while sexual activity may be pleasurable and while it is portrayed as a necessary part of becoming a mature woman for Lessing's protagonists, the problems she highlights for her female characters are heightened between puberty and menopause because of the ways in which the reproductive female body is objectified in patriarchal culture. In spite of their sexual exploits, Lessing's protagonists are seldom truly at home in their bodies, however skilled they become at seduction and lovemaking. Determined not to be prudish, informed by sex manuals, able to achieve orgasms, successful in pregnancy and breast feeding, her protagonists are neither spontaneous nor passionate women. They seem always to be withholding some part of themselves as if it would be dangerous to let their bodies gain precedence over their ever watchful minds. Martha Quest, for example, feels like a "rider who was wondering whether his horse would make the course . . . [regarding] this body of hers, which was not only divided from her brain by the necessity of keeping open that cool and dispassionate eye, but separated into compartments of its own" (*PM* 63). Lessing's protagonists think about everything—their experiences, their appearance, their bodies, others' reactions and responses to them. Even in sex, one senses them watching, analyzing, feeling an internal division. Lessing describes Martha and Jack in bed in *The Four-Gated City* as "two bodies . . . face to face." Their intentional conscious control of phases and rhythms of sex leads to a state in which "sex, heart, the currents of the automatic body were one now together," yet above these, Martha is conscious of "her brain, cool and alert, watching and marking" (62).

From the point of view of protagonists who never are completely comfortable in their bodies, "body" women such as Martha's friend, Maisie, or Kate Brown's friend, Mary Finchley, are enviously perceived as not compartmentalized, as somehow whole. Mary, unlike Kate, wears whatever she pleases and has sex with whomever she desires, seemingly without damage to her husband or children, and Kate views her as of a different species. Kate describes Mary as "really quite different from me . . . 'a savage woman' . . . She hasn't any sense of guilt" for following the dictates of her body (*SBD* 225). Martha Quest, unlike her friend Maisie, for example, experiences sex and pregnancy as a trap, although she wishes they could enlarge rather than narrow her life. Yet this state of undifferentiation is seen by Lessing's protagonists, by Lessing herself, as somehow "lesser" and more simplistic than divided status. A startling example of the protagonist's equation of undivided "body" women with simplicity appears in *A Proper Marriage* in the young Martha's sense of envy for "simple women of the country who might be women in peace, according to their instincts, without being made to think and disintegrate themselves into fragments" (63). A troubling extension of this conception of body/simplicity/primitivism occurs in the early weeks of her marriage, when Martha feels as if she is "always accompanied by that other, black woman, like an invisible sister simpler and wiser than herself . . ." whom she envies "from the bottom of her heart" (63). Here Martha replicates the standard male ideas regarding men and women in relation to mind and body, thus aligning herself with white men and seeing African women as "other" through the double prism of gender and race.

The protagonists, in contrast to other characters who are often their friends, feel deeply alienated from and imprisoned by their bodies. Lessing seems to equate this division and alienation with intelligence and more desirable, valuable female subjectivity than "happily embodied" characters offer. The memorable scene in which Martha and her friend Alice, in the final stage of their pregnancies, momentarily escape their sense of body/mind division stands out because it is so unusual in this work. The scene of the two women frolicking naked in a muddy red pothole filled with rain water stands out in its joyous celebration of their bodies in nature, with frog, snail, and green snake, oozing life force and a joyous sense of rebellion. They shout in "exultation" and "triumph" and "[loosen] deliciously in the warm rocking of the water" (*PM* 134). The snail is "glistening and beautiful," the snake "lithe," but the feeling is quickly replaced by the more normal sense of objectification as the two women dash back to their car "panic-stricken," where they "must" quickly dress, before they are "exposed and visible" (135). As soon as they think about being discovered, their sense of division returns. This scene hints at the possibility of body joy if no men are present. It is notable precisely because it is an exception and is so quickly curtailed by the characters themselves and by Lessing as writer. The internalized presence of the male gaze destroys their sense of wholeness. In a different world, one reminiscent of Woolf's fantasy of nonpatriarchal possibility, such as Al•Ith's matriarchal Zone Five in *The Marriages Between Zones Three, Four, and Five,* pregnancy, for example, could enrich woman's life; whereas in the patriarchal Zone Four, as in the world of Martha Quest, pregnancy is constricting, and the female body is experienced as a trap, a sense returned to at the end of this scene.

Still, in spite of glimmers when the female body is celebrated, both writers, Woolf and Lessing, imply that unself-conscious fleshiness is a trap for women. In Woolf it seems that the heterosexualized body is a social trap which possibly may be avoided by the single, nonmale-defined lesbian or artist, but in Lessing all female bodies are inherently traps. Neither art nor lesbianism is suggested as an escape from the entrapment of the female body in Lessing. Rather, she suggests that for the thinking woman the time will come, usually unbidden, in middle age when she loses interest in her sexuality and senses in a new way the extent to which she is *not* her body but her mind.

Lessing repeatedly portrays middle-aged female characters who experience their release from the constant pressures of sexuality as a boon, even as they envy the young. She writes of middle age as an eventual escape from the tyranny of the sexually defined trap of woman's body. At this stage, her protagonists confront their bodies in mirrors, mourn years of collusion with patriarchal standards of female appearance, and, with a profound sense of the extent to which their bodies are merely temporary containers of some truer, essential self, begin to nurture that invisible self. Occasionally this acceptance of the benefits and freedom of aging is preceded by a frantic attempt to prolong youthful appearance and hold off old age, as in Martha's and Kate's attention to fashion makeovers in midlife. However, when her female protagonists recognize the benefits of old age as an escape from sexual objectification in heterosexual exchange, they begin to enjoy that poignant anonymity achieved paradoxically because of the extent to which their bodies disguise them. When Kate Brown returns to her familiar neighborhood dressed in a large hat and poorly fitting dress, appearing quite different from usual, and realizes that her best friend, Mary, does not recognize her, she is "relieved" and "elated" (*SBD* 148), "delighted" that "knowing people" is so "easily disproved" (151).

Like the Woolfian protagonist whose situation is triangulated, containing two parallel pairings, one with a male and one with a female, throughout her life the Lessing protagonist inhabits similarly triangulated relationships, also in parallel male/female, female/female pairings. However, Lessing complicates her triangles, reflecting shifts within the pairings rather than simply contrasting two constant configurations as in Woolf.

In *The Four-Gated City,* Lessing creates triangulations similar to those we earlier saw in Woolf. The female protagonist, Martha, is portrayed in two parallel pairings—one with Mark Coldridge and one with his wife, Lynda Coldridge. Resonating in the background of both pairings are Martha's earlier pairings with former husbands and lovers and the pairing of Mark's and Lynda's marriage. These earlier pairings have failed as such: Lynda has escaped marital and societal expectations in her apparent madness, and Martha has abandoned her husband and child because of her fear of repeating the dismal trajectory of the nuclear family plot.

Like Woolf, Lessing sees the woman/woman bond here as less vexed than that of the woman/man; however, unlike Woolf, Lessing requires her protagonist to experience both bonds sequentially. And, unlike Woolf, Lessing's woman/woman bond is not one which is informed by a fantasy of lesbian sexuality or of preoedipal *jouissance*. It is, rather, a post-erotic friendship which replaces the erotic with a spiritual or political energy understood as healing. Even with all of her previous sexualized body experience, including multiple affairs, couplings, marriages, middle-aged Martha has additional lessons to learn before she is ready to move beyond the experiences of her body. Lessing requires Martha to fulfill the roles of surrogate wife and mother within the Coldridge household, to painstakingly excavate her own past, including relations with her mother, and to once again fully experience the temptation of escape through lovemaking and bodily pleasure with Mark, before she is ready to learn from Lynda and begin to develop her own mental powers. In the male/female pairing, Martha is tempted to forget her own inner needs. Sex is presented as almost narcotic, blocking pain, blocking growth in middle age: "The room was outside pain. It vibrated with shared intimacy, trust, happiness, love. . . . this place of smooth warm bodies" (239). To develop her inner life, Martha must discipline her body, and that includes moving beyond sex: "If it is a question of survival . . . then one gets up an hour earlier. . . . You drink less brandy and eat less and even dismiss the lover" (299–300). Martha realizes that "when it's a question of survival, sex the uncontrollable can be controlled" (301). In the pairing with Lynda, Martha learns to "read" Lynda accurately, seeing meaning in her "madness" where others see chaos, and begins to tune in to an alternate mode of communication which depends *entirely* on the development of mental powers. Martha, like Lynda, develops her powers of intuition and telepathy, making possible intercontinental communication when technological modes of communication fail after a series of major breakdowns and crises in the civilized world.

Interestingly, unlike Woolf, Lessing does not limit childrearing and nurture to male/female relationships, and she does not portray nurture as necessarily depleting. Even in a female/female relationship, the nurture of children and the qualities usually associated with the maternal do not disappear. After the apocalyptic ending of *The Four-Gated City*, in an appendix to the conventional novel, Lessing reveals through a series of "found manuscripts" that Lynda and Martha's telepathic abilities—in concert with others' abilities to "tune in" to wavelengths overlooked by ordinary people— have contributed to the escape of a small group of people who begin life anew after the apocalypse on an island. There a generation of mutant children with heightened mental powers represents the hope of a future for humanity.

In *The Diaries of Jane Somers,* Lessing again creates a triangle with parallel pairings. The female/female pair includes Jane Somers and Maudie Fowler, with their dead husbands in the background, and the male/female pair includes Jane and Richard, with his absent wife in the background. In *The Diaries,* Lessing puts a spin on the triangle scheme: here, both pairings provide Jane with something essential. With Richard, Jane experiences a revised courtship/marriage plot, and with Maudie she experiences a revised mother/daughter plot. What is conspicuously different in this male/female pair is the lack of physical sexuality; Jane and Richard do not consummate their relationship. And, in the mother/daughter revision, the relationship is chosen rather than a biological given. In each, the bodily connection is revised. Lessing offers a vision of the male/female pairing that does not deplete or constrict the woman and of the mother/daughter bond that, like that of Woolf's Lily and Mrs. Ramsay pair, is chosen and leads to artistic production by the daughter. Jane writes Maudie's life.

Here, like Martha in *The Four-Gated City,* Jane has had ample sexual experience of her body earlier in her life. More acutely than any other Lessing character, including Kate Brown, Jane as a fashion editor at *Lilith* knows how to create an image of the body, and over the years has dedicated countless hours to realize her desired image. Yet, Jane's middle-aged romance depends entirely upon shared conversation rather than any union of bodies. Lessing depicts a glorious spring romance between Jane and Richard that depends entirely on secret meetings, walks, meals together, and an anonymity in which neither reveals past or present details outside the time they spend together. When they arrange to spend a night together, they are unable to consummate their relationship because of a resistance to being naked together at midlife, haunted by ghosts of their younger selves, their younger bodies, in his adult son and an old photograph of her as a beautiful young woman. Their sense of their appearance, of themselves as artifacts, is at least partially responsible for their inability to enjoy one another's bodies, and yet Lessing suggests that the physical desire grows from a nostalgia associated with earlier relationships at a time when Jane, at least, no longer identifies her sexuality with her physical-ity. Their physical desire for one another remains unconsummated, because, Lessing suggests, it reflects not their present desire for the other but nostalgia for younger selves. However, that self and its physicality is already past. When Richard leaves for America, Jane actually seems relieved, left with her profession and her role as surrogate mother. Lessing suggests here as in *The Four-Gated City, The Marriages Between Zones Three, Four, and Five,* and *The Summer Before the Dark,* that the sexually active body is simply a way station to female change, growth, and maturity. Her work and biologically displaced maternity are seen as more important, more true to Jane's identity, than any sexual relationship could be.

What lingers with far greater intensity than the male/female relationship in *The Diaries* is the profound relationship between Jane and Maudie, a friendship with intense feelings through which Jane learns how to feel, how to love, how to care. She also faces the female body not as beautiful artifact to be petted and groomed and used as a high-powered tool to create an image, but as a demanding machine with its requirements for food, hygiene, and bodily processes. Mounting difficulties of age and illness in Maudie bring Jane face to face with the limitations of the body and with her own mortality. She becomes less preoccupied with her object status and more active in life as subject: She feels alive in the everyday enjoyment of sunshine, rain, good food, her bath. In the presence of Maudie and among the very old, Jane exclaims "I love—all of it, all of it. And the more because I know how very precarious it is" (166). After Maudie's death, Jane asks basic but profound questions about the relationship of body to spirit and is left haunted by the sense that Maudie must have been more than her body. "I cannot make myself believe that this furious bundle of energy which is Maudie is going to disappear altogether" (234). In *The Diaries,* what matters ultimately is not romance and heterosexual love but learning to feel and to express feeling, seeing beyond the surface. Conversation between women and nurturing future generations are shown to matter more than male/female attractions. Ultimately Jane is alone, for Maudie dies and Richard moves to America. Left only are the legacy of humanity, the surrogate daughters, Jill, Kate, and Katherine, and her professional colleagues on the magazine.

In her novels, Lessing repeatedly traces a female protagonist's path to maturity. In each account, the protagonist moves from male/female pairing to a female/female pairing in which patriarchal assumptions are undercut and a new feminine community is established which somehow benefits the future. A micro version of this movement is presented by Lessing in *The Summer Before the Dark.* In a series of mirror confrontations, middle-aged protagonist Kate Brown imaginatively undergoes male/female and female/female pairings and is pulled between an internalized patriarchal voice and a subversive female voice. The familiar patriarchal voice, as in Snow White's mirror, emphasizes female objectification and female competition, dominating a woman's perception of herself, not only when she is actually looking into a mirror, but whenever her thoughts turn to appearance. The other, less familiar voice, is the voice of another woman, a nonmale-identified, nonintellectual voice that subverts woman's objectification.

In the initial mirror scene, Kate sees a many-angled self portrait within the masculinist framework of self-conscious femininity. She compares her adult shape to her remembered shape of youth, and notes an almost identical shape, "give or take an inch or so" (34). She decides her attributes now may be even better than twenty-five years earlier because of all the chemistry, medication, dieting, and attention to hair, teeth, and eyes that have gone into creating "this artifact" (34). Kate notices her general shape, her sexually valued attributes—limbs, waist, breasts, mouth, hair, neck, "the equipment with which she had attracted a dozen young men nearly a quarter of a century ago, with which she had married her husband" (34). This self appraisal is broken by the eruption of her best friend Mary Finchley's face into her thoughts, and she recalls their "eye-to-eye woman to woman collusion" which "seemed to nullify her official or daylight view of herself" and "threatened . . . to start off a roar of . . . ribald laughter at the whole damned business" (34). Kate argues within herself about whether or not even to think of Mary, dismisses the troubling unintellectual female voice, and heads off to the hairdresser where she sits "watching the world from behind a facade only very slightly different from the one she had maintained since she was sixteen" (43). She refuses to hear Mary's voice and reinscribes her own object position.

The second mirror scene in a hotel room to which Kate has gone to regain her health and reflect on her life comes after Kate has experienced physical and psychic illness, considerable weight loss, graying of her hair, and inattention to her appearance. Here, she begins with the same appraising eye as in the first mirror scene, but that appraisal quickly shifts to the act of appraising the notion of appraising her image at all. The rebellious female voice of Mary Finchley has been internalized and has changed. Instead of hearing laughter, Kate analyzes "the whole damned business" (34), and she begins to experiment with new bizarre facial expressions instead of rushing off to the hairdresser. In looking at her wrinkled and untended face in a hand mirror, she recalls the accumulated time she has spent since adolescence, looking into mirrors to "see what he is going to see." She feels humiliated that she has spent entire years of her life preoccupied with how "he" would see her, making the most important decisions of her life, including whom to marry, because "he admired that face she had so much attended to, and touched, and turned this way and that" (160-61). She begins to experiment with an entire range of facial expressions, trying out grimaces and rage after decades of limiting her expression to those considered pleasing.

In contrast to the two private mirror scenes, in the third scene Lessing portrays Kate's conflicting responses to seeing not only her own reflection but that of the self-confident beautiful younger woman, Maureen, the epitome of the patriarchal standard of female beauty and objectification. Kate vacillates between a familiar sense that she needs to alter her appearance, "get her hair done, buy a dress that fitted," because of the incredible confidence and beauty of the young girl—in other words fit herself into the image that has dominated her sense of herself since adolescence—and an opposing and quite new sense of satisfaction that for the first time in her life she need not conform to internalized notions of pleasing appearance but can experience the truth of exposure, "alone and outside a cocoon of comfort and protection" (172). Her earlier grimaces had been private. Maureen represents exposure in a public, social realm: a new moment. When Maureen sticks out her tongue "in resentment" and "self-assertion" (169) at the ungroomed, unpolished image of Kate in the mirror, Kate for the first time experiences being seen for herself without a protective image. At first reduced to tears, she later rejoices in her new-found integrity.

Kate eventually learns to heed the female voice, the voice she associates with Mary and Maureen instead of the internalized voice that usually dominates the mirror, and she begins to take care of her body in a new sense—heeding her needs for food, for rest, for exercise—without obsessing over her appearance. Kate returns home at the end of the summer with untinted gray hair and a new determination not to be defined by her ability to attract male attention. Lessing suggests the strength to be gained when woman turns to female instead of male voices for affirmation. Kate returns to her family as a conscious choice, not knowing exactly how she will differ from the Kate who left home at the beginning of the summer, but quite sure what she will not perpetuate. That band of gray roots signals her determination not to scale herself down to societal expectations of female appearance.

Lessing, like Woolf, exposes the tremendous cost to woman of the identification of heterosexualized body with self. Lessing's fiction is peopled with female characters whose beauty and biology implicate them in the marriage plot, a plot she sees as depleting but inevitable on the way to self-knowledge. Despite being depleted by the combined assumptions concerning gender roles and female beauty, her characters, unlike Woolf's Mrs. Ramsay, are able to avoid premature death and to at least face the potential of rich lives beyond the marriage plot. Martha Quest has a second chance with Lynda in which to rework her memories, to develop her powers, to contribute to global peace and healing. Kate Brown's potential is unrealized within the novel, but we have no reason to suspect an early death or recapitulation to object status. Jane Somers, unlike Mrs. Ramsay, outlives her husband, has a successful career, and develops meaningful friendships not only with Maudie, but also within several communities of women—the elderly poor, colleagues on the magazine, and the next generation of younger women. Affiliative relationships replace romance and the objectification at the heart of male/female relationships. Female characters deeply split between body and mind begin to develop a sense of wholeness once they outgrow their preoccupation with sex.

While the female communities implicit in Woolf and explicit in Lessing are appealing, and one senses relief for female characters outside the marriage plot, a disturbing implication of both writers' novels is that to survive, the thinking female must either avoid or outgrow her sexuality. In addition, she must value her mind over her body, mistrusting her body because of its capacity for reproductive sexuality. We can see why heterosexuality is portrayed as a problem. While the hand that rocks the cradle may also write the books, reproductive sexuality is a problem for women. Patriarchal objectification of women's bodies is deeply disturbing. Sexuality is dangerous. And, somehow, the female body is primarily sexual. Neither writer has created female characters who are mind/body, who celebrate health, flexibility, strength, vitality. Lessing's characters cannot walk down a street without feeling conscious of the external appearance of their eroticized body parts until they become invisible in the disguise of old age. Woolf's characters exist only by disregarding or "metaphorizing" their bodies. The female body is by definition sexual object in both writers' novels. Mind/body wholeness is possible only in a separate female realm—whether in adolescence at Bourton, old age after the death or abandonment by the men, an island after the catastrophe, or a mythic zone. Hints abound in both texts that female/female relationships are the only spaces in which modern woman can begin to heal the deep divisions between mind and body.

Even in Lessing's space fiction, in *The Marriages Between Zones Three, Four, and Five,* in spite of the necessity for the male and female zones to intermarry if there is to be generativity, the closest, most enduring bonds are between females, and the highest zone is one in which the body becomes transparent. In Woolf's *The Years,* we see a move beyond the large Victorian household with single women living active lives in flats and apartments without men and children, yet Woolf portrays them primarily through their consciousness and gives no sense of pleasure in their bodies. Both writers create wonderful scenes in which we can put together the minds of women and create maps of human experience, yet each requires that we consider the body suspect, implicated in and defined by patriarchal definition. Each requires as a rite of passage that the female protagonist who survives must lay down her body.

Neither Woolf nor Lessing imagines new social, cultural paradigms which allow for images of women's minds and bodies as coexistent: lesbianism, onanism, newly defined heterosexualism, new family/maternal plots, new configurations of community. Both begin this work, but deep within each writer's work is a lurking suspicion that woman's biology may indeed be a trap for her brain. While Woolf argues that the mind of the writer must be sexually neutral—both "woman-manly or man-womanly" (*ARO* 108), the female writer's body is not, and it poses a continual peril to textual possibility. And while Lessing documents the bodily processes and urgings of her female characters, her most wise, caring, and self-knowing characters by middle age have lost all interest in sexuality and experience their bodies primarily as containers of consciousness. In spite of Woolf's peroration in *A Room of One's Own* where she longs for the resurrection of Shakespeare's sister, ultimately both Woolf and Lessing reject woman's body, neither one ready to "put on the body which she has so often laid down" (118).

# 7
— ◆ —

## VIRGINIA WOOLF AND DORIS LESSING:
## INTRANSITIVE TURN OF MIND

### Linda E. Chown

The academic and popular book markets are currently full of studies dealing with mind or consciousness.[1] Such attention to mind reflects the effects of "several dovetailing scientific revolutions."[2] These revolutions are bringing consciousness, a hitherto subdued genie, out of the bottle and back into a critical spotlight. In the arts and the humanities, however, mind has long been taboo, and, in today's critical world, it generally has been rejected as soft and nonscientific, identified with "private consciousness," a dubious "inner." Generally rejected as culturally and critically passé, many current literary scholars passively concur that consciousness-focused study has "by contemporary critical discourse . . . been stripped of its validity" (Wang 177). A primary purpose of this study is to present the Lessing and Woolf conceptions of, and literary engagements with, mind as deliberate challenges to those concepts of self and of mind based primarily in theories that have ossified in models of an inner existence divorced from life.

Literarily, such models have led in turn to interpretations founded in "character" and "personality," which in turn are read in terms of ego, id, narcissism, and so forth. Lessing and Woolf in their writing and thinking have engaged consciousness more dynamically, in a constructive view of inner life in terms closer to its actual experience. Their novels script a directly experienced inner life free in varying degrees of psychologically derived categories and their institutionally fixed and limiting ideas about what mental

living ought to be. Ironically, Lessing and Woolf go directly in their writings
to esthetically rich, promising replacements for those psychologically based
notions of inner life which in no small measure have provoked contemporary
criticism to attempt to reject entirely the notion of consciousness. This essay
explores Lessing's and Woolf's negative responses to the effects of organized
psychology. In the early twentieth century, there were, for instance, various
painters, aestheticians and artists who were similarly ambivalent about, if
not openly against, emerging psychology's influences on creativity.

Twentieth-century analytic involvements with mind and consciousness
have been virtually useless for the formation of a literary poetic appropriate to
the realities of inner life. Doris Lessing and Virginia Woolf, dissimilar in many
respects, share a fascination with mental life as an important root/route of
literature. Without ever considering mind as isolated from a "real" social world,
each has made a convincing extrafictional case in behalf of the importance of
inner life. Woolf found "flights of mind" of utmost importance in her life as well
as her novels. She conceived mental life in thoroughly physical terms and found
there was "no more delicious sensation" (Leaska 178–79). Lessing, meticulous
and data bound, conceives of "map[s] of the human mind." She has declared
that "what interests me more than anything is how our minds are changing"
(Mitgang; Raskin 66). An early Lessing critic concluded that "the common
denominator in Lessing's fictional world is . . . the mind discovering, interpreting, and ultimately shaping its own reality" (Rubenstein 7).

In spite of a virtual taboo on mind in the latter part of the twentieth
century, research abounds as to its importance in reading Lessing and Woolf.
Presuppositions about mind have, however, seriously skewed critical interpretations, and induced misinterpretations of their fictions. There are strikingly
similar antipathetic responses to organized psychology in Lessing's and Woolf's
fiction. Four general parallels in their writing reveal their alternatives to what
they consider psychology's seriously limiting, formularized, and overly objectified approaches. Not in order of importance, these characteristics of their
fiction are: (1) transparencies, (2) engagements with "dark sense," (3) ludic
playfulness, and (4) revised relations between wholeness and disorder.


## INNER LIFE


Those who have written encomiastically of the role of mind in Lessing and
Woolf have unfortunately neglected close examination of what their fiction
does in and with mind as direct, immediate experience—that is, as what we
will call "psychal" rather than as "psychological." Each novelist has overtly

challenged "the psychological," that is, the adequacy of organized psychology's models of mental action as means for dealing with natural irregularities of mental living. The novelists enter into minds as immediate experiences of psyche itself, as *psychal* experience, not as experience mediated by preconceived, *psychologized* theory. In contrast, much Lessing-Woolf criticism starts and stays within the frameworks of the dominant Western psychological constructs that these novelists do not consider valid and that they mock in their fiction. The novelists are not alone in this distrust; other critics of contemporary critical practice have indeed decidedly challenged prevailing psychological models.[3] David Miles for one has decried psychology's overly influential status; he identifies a widespread, far-reaching "psychologicalization of reality."[4] Ferdinand Savater has even irreverently declared that psychology is, ironically, "that from which innerness is totally absent precisely because it aspires only to contain that innerness" (11).

In briefly summarizing effects of the unwarranted power that has accrued to practitioners of psychology since the late seventeenth century, Elizabeth Abel has identified a rift between soul and mind which has been resolved in mind taking over the functions of both. Mind thereby has been made both a "psychic and mental organism" (x). Abel further argues that psychoanalysis creates in the late nineteenth century a world in which men were "more apt than women to be granted mental powers" (x). Clearly, neither Lessing nor Woolf accepted such gender disbalance. Many of their principal fictive personages embody deep reactions to experience of that disbalance and to a psychologized theorizing which helped produce it.

The rift between soul and mind that Abel identifies needs to be considered in its twentieth-century extensions. The twentieth century is still dominated by a nearly religious awe of science. Mind has come to be understood in this century as the province of scientific psychology. Thus, psychology, an organized body of objectively verifiable facts and theory *about* psyche, has come to be widely considered the only valid knowledge of psyche. Accordingly, mind and inner reality have come very generally, though erroneously, to be fixed in a kind of box known as "*the* psychological." The resultant substitution of orthodox theory *about* psyche for psyche *itself* has become pervasive in twentieth-century criticism. This practice has had the insalubrious effect of almost totally eclipsing any attention to the operations in psyche itself as they actually occur in people. Objective systematization and objective results are valued more than attention to immediate individual spirit and awareness. Resenting the lack of any sense of immediate inner spirit, Lessing and Woolf react against this skewed perspective and approach human psyche directly as a realm of inner perceptions. This radically different approach we shall term "psychal" to distinguish it from "the psychological" that each author mistrusted. The fictional figures presented in these psychal terms we shall term "personages," in distinction from the more conventional presentation of "characters."

In 1940, the year before her death, Woolf wrote a biography of Roger Fry, influential critic, painter, and aesthetician. Woolf found that Fry's insistent probing of relations between spirit, morals and art invested thinking with a "peculiar quality of reality" (RF 297) which impressed her as most appropriate to her sense of things.[5] She saw him holding "close together . . . two worlds," the contemplated and the lived (RF 297). Fry concluded, "We know too little of the rhythms of man's spiritual life" (293). It is the arena of Fry's "spiritual rhythms" in which Lessing and Woolf novels take place. They engage directly such "spiritual rhythms," rhythms of psyche. The novels exist in a mode neither objectively predetermined nor predeterminable, neither preformulated nor preformulatable. Consequently, the novels do not respond fully to existing psychology-based paradigms. Instead, major Lessing and Woolf novels are exploring an alternative to replace Philip Rieff's "psychologized reality." Theirs is a *depsychologized reality* that we shall term *open reality*. Quite simply, they write to develop and sustain a growing intimacy with an unpredictably ordered and disordered inner reality. They engage a more impromptu and a far richer arena of introspective living than is available via theoretical psychology's frameworks.

Principal figures in Lessing and Woolf novels find themselves troubled by "psychological" understandings. They find they can become less self-alienated by other means, that the "peculiar qualit[ies of their] reality" hold their worlds of contemplation and of living "closer together." They find their psyches to be *not* unique oddities but semichaotic constructs of common psychal phenomena. Lessing and Woolf—far from purposely exemplifying, as has been claimed, Freud, Laing, Sufism, or esthetic theory—record a more open psychal reality, which psychology's theories reduce, in the authors' view, to a banal collection of formulas.

Frequently, criticisms of inner living in these authors have achieved less than their potentials by approaching these open realities with interpretations derived from authorized psychological theories. The fictive texts and the abstract theories start with the same open reality, but, while the texts record it, the theories break it into static classifications. The novels' fictive personages *live* the open reality that psychology's objectifications merely write about. Psychological theories, as often as not, are oriented toward abnormal mentalities, but, in truth, psyches subsist together more in normal than in abnormal phenomena. The novels are accordingly richer than the theories. Recognition of some of the psychal phenomena in which these novels evolve is a principal aim of this study.

## PSYCHOLOGY IN THE NOVELS

Lessing's antipathies to organized, authorized psychology and psychiatry do not appear exclusively in her fiction.[6] She was once properly dubbed "the most eloquent voice in the growing antipsychiatry movement" (Berman 178). She has openly taken on the psychiatric establishment and lambasted what she perceives as its insufficiencies. The psychological establishment, she proposes, has not only demonstrated an appalling neglect of spirit; it has also systematically encouraged an involuted, sterile self-consciousness. Lessing's discoveries, in all likelihood, came in fiction before her nonfictional responses to their insidious effects; at any rate it is her penetrating displacement of sterile psychological models in her fiction that we are interested in. Four of her major novels uncover gaps between the psychological establishment's excessively ordered, often authoritarian, answers and the fictional personages' evolving sense of a need, present in the form of inchoate questions, for a less rigid sense of psychal identity. They sense a need for a psyche more their own than that which approved psychology allows. In Lessing's fiction, the establishment's psychology demonstrates itself to be frighteningly and smugly ignorant of what goes on in people's psyches, that is, their intimate perceptions.

For instance, in *The Four-Gated City,* impassive psychiatrists invoke rigid analyses, dole out stupefying medications, and remain sensibly "functional" (233). Dr. Lamb's power derives from his absence of feeling and his personal control of the patient in skillfully "exploding her" (233–36, 245). Martha Quest, however, instead of accepting obliteration in the doctor's terms, chooses to study on her own a library of materials which adumbrate notions of a less rigidly categorized psyche, one more accessible to her in a more open reality (513). Establishment psychology becomes the enemy on Martha's way to escape the "set . . . programmed" education, "the education of everyone of her generation (and of how many generations back?)," which had projected her into her problematic psychology-induced state (515). *The Four-Gated City* impressively depicts the mental health establishment exerting pressures to enforce normality, but Martha's growing trust in adaptive risk-taking and a more open psychal reality succeeds where formulaic solutions uselessly collapse. Of all of Lessing's novels, this one in particular depicts at a peak her direct mockery of psychiatry's immunity from risk and its compulsive, ineffective objectifying of people.

The Golden Notebook throws further light on Lessing's sense of the limitations inherent in psychological predictions. The book uncovers a patina-like control of surfaces exerted by shallow pseudopsychological wisdom. Mrs. Marks's "small wise smile . . . conducts our [therapy] sessions like a conductor's baton"; she imposes "dry" questions and routinely displays total disinterest in the answers (233, 232, 253). Anna concludes, finally, that Mother Sugar's therapy would transmute her experience into the "safety of myth" or merely an "efficient analyst-patient relationship" (469–70). By the end, Anna will refer to Mother Sugar caustically as a "witch-doctor" and the therapy process as creating an immutable landscape of inner pain (545). In contrast, a new, impromptu, and adaptive approach to treatment allows Anna to achieve relief in the richness of a chaos free of anticipations and predictions. Anna's earlier experiences obviated her control of her own mental development. Free of psychological preconceptions, she comes to appreciate and "marvel [at] the power of human beings to hold *themselves* [emphasis added] together" (633).

An interesting irony invades Lessing's dense and misinterpreted *Briefing for a Descent into Hell*. This novel, read for the most part as a clumsy predecessor to subsequent space fiction, graphically records psychiatry's violations of mental independence. A nurse dismisses Professor Charles Watkins as having no "marks of identity"; his doctor blithely "cannot place him" (4). Meanwhile, the patient, whose abnormality remains throughout the novel a moot point, is actively coping with himself in his open reality, naming himself and his situations via intense wordplay, which the doctors dismiss as merely symptomatic. The irony-flooded novel develops in the gaps between Charles's rich narrative and the doctors' flat psychological diagnoses (13). The gap between supposed psychiatrist expertise and the puzzles of normal psyche climaxes in the book's "Afterword." The experts' resounding, disinterested inconclusiveness breaks futilely against the readers' developed intimacy with Charles's essentially normal introspective world.

In addition to questioning psychology's presumed validities, Lessing's fiction decries their negative results. Abstract, extremely self-absorbed mental armor is a consequence of the limitations of preconceived psychological realities. An abstract cast of mind parasitically thrives on self-generated hyperawareness of self. Instances of Martha Quest's entrapment in such psychologized awareness abound throughout the five-volume *Children of Violence* series. Perennially haunted by a watcher in her, she suffers from "an excess of self-observation" (*PM* 336). Locked in her "lighthouse of watchfulness," Martha impotently senses that people are "hypnotized into futility by self-observation" (*LL* 14). In *The Golden Notebook,* Anna Wulf is self-consciously "sunk in [a] subjectivity" (614) so intensely and "properly" objectified that she is terrified of becoming intimate with her inner world. Self-centered, self-conscious mentalizing shuts off access to the natural, unanticipatable vitality of life's changing.

In her ironic "blueprint[s] of psychological observation," Lessing wrote her most brilliant assault on what she came to see in *The Summer Before the Dark* as "excesses of self-consciousness" (20, 93). The heroine, Kate Brown, finally concludes about self-absorption with its attendant mirrors and often stagnant psychological concerns, "It's all nonsense" (232). In subsequent writing, Lessing has neither abandoned realism nor the struggles of daily life, as those who perceive the novels as exempla of psychological theories might say. In the light of the concept of open psychal reality, Lessing may be seen, rather, to ignore conventional models of introspection and to highlight alternatives to what are to her the crippling effects of a thoroughly psychologized orthodoxy.

Like Lessing, Virginia Woolf, too, scrutinized psychology and found it personally and novelistically wanting. Elizabeth Abel concluded recently that Woolf's "fiction . . . de-authorizes psychoanalysis" (xvi). In fact, Woolf overtly did so. In a 1920 essay, she lambasted psychology's propensity for converting "character" into "cases," for gross oversimplification and crippling mechanization of fluid mental processes ("Freudian" 154). Woolf's brother, Adrian Stephen, was one of England's early psychoanalysts. Shirley Panken has found that "On Freudian Fiction" caricatures Adrian and his psychoanalytic penchants.[7] Woolf was certainly not unaware of Freud; The Hogarth Press, which she co-owned, was his first English publisher.[8] She found him not negligible, but, for her novelist's sense of open reality, "spasmodic" and "inarticulate" (*Diary* 5: 202). Evidence, too, of her distaste for emerging psychoanalytic methods appears in her response to a Lytton Strachey biography; she characterized it as a "superficial meretricious book," "feeble," "shallow," and "steeped in the spirit of psycho-analysis" (qtd. in Abel 17).

Woolf repeatedly equated psychoanalysis with an inadequate focus on detail. In a bantering, yet caustic, tone, she notes, "I am myopic rather than obtuse. I see the circumference and the outline, not the detail" (*Letters* 4: 199). She deems herself "blind and deaf psychologically" (*Letters* 4: 199); her assertion should be taken very seriously. Woolf discerned futility in what were, to her, the misleading certainties of institutionalized psychology. Rather than its mechanistic, formulaic solutions, she pursued in her writing a free-flowing mental openendedness, which she considered constructively vital.[9] Paradoxically, her personal bouts of disorientation confirmed in her that view; she found the experience "terrific," because it "shoots out of one everything shaped, final" (*Letters* 4: 180). Woolf's persistent personal resistance to psychologists' efforts to regularize, to impose models on mental illness, was the reverse side of efforts in her fiction to nurture a potential for augmenting the "circumference" and depth of recognition of people's inner experience with themselves. Her novels develop progressively toward realizing their texts in spontaneous normalities of their personages' perceptions in the flow of everyday living.

Dr. Bradshaw in *Mrs. Dalloway* is a caricature of insensitive intolerance to patients' mental exigencies: "A master of his own actions," he is a man whose eyes "lit . . . oilily for dominion, for power," and he "swooped and devoured" so as to control unapproved social impulses (99, 101, 102). Woolf's novels move directly in the psyche's perceptions and *not* in terms of psychoanalysis. They increasingly exist in immediate contacts with unpredictable realms in feeling, perception, and knowing. They aim to join reading with living in a reality open directly in the experiencer's perception, and so to allow more "intense life," an "invigorating" sense in things (*ARO* 114). The novels reveal "traces of the minds [*sic*] passage through the world" and activate in a reader a "rhythmical sense" alive in a not unlimited but self-limiting open reality (Leaska 393; qtd. in Panken 209). Woolf bridles against the crystallization of ego, the role-playing of the "damned egotistic self," which undermines the potential for knowing a less proscribed reality (*Diary* 2:102). In her words, the novels explore "dark places of psychology" so as to fully uncover the reaches of a keen mental amphitheater ("Modern Fiction" 102).

Like Lessing, whose fiction is concerned with humans experiencing their own psyches, Woolf's novels record progressively in her major fictive personages a bypassing of psychology's stultifying certainties. Her novels foreground tensions plaguing figures fixed in ruts of orthodox introspection. Major personages struggle against their own psychologizing impulses; each evolves in his or her own way through painful quagmires of sterile, self-contemplation. In *The Voyage Out,* Woolf's first novel, Rachel Vinrace becomes enveloped in chronic uncertainties, occasions in which "she was always being just too late to hear or see something which would explain it all" (340). In the same novel, a male friend of Rachel's longs to be without the "terrific self-consciousness" that "showed him his own face and words perpetually in a mirror" as though he were something other (311). He does not succeed. Rachel does not live to enjoy her developing mastery of herself. In a later novel, *Mrs. Dalloway,* unmitigated self-consciousness devastates Septimus Smith, whose war-intensified hyperawareness locks him into a self-destructing channel. In the same novel, Clarissa, in her acutely psychologized self-awareness,

Nightmare of history:
the fictions of V Woolf
+ D.H. Lawrence

Wussow, Helen

PR 888. W65 W87 1998

---

V. Woolf: A-Z
Hussey, Mark   1995
PR 6045. 072 Z729

---

V. Woolf's Renaissance
    Juliet Dusinberre
PR 6045. 72  Z 626

---

Unknown Virginia Woolf
   Roger Poole
PR 6045. 072  Z 862

PR 6045. 072 Z~~~  ~~~

Everyday Life
among the
American Ind.
Candy Moulton

Paper Trail
Michael
Dorris'

unlocks her introspective prison when, in the close of the novel, she allows herself to feel the unpsychologized reality of a woman she observes from a distance "looking out of the window, quite unconscious that she was being watched" (126).[10]

The next novel, *To the Lighthouse,* then seesaws between "stagey" self-consciousness and moments of blissful freedom of the mind such as Mrs Dalloway had only glimpsed. In the beginning, Mrs. Ramsay, awash in her self-consciousness, shuns whatever at all reminds her that she might be seen as what she fears she *should not* be—a thinking, reflecting woman (68). Meanwhile, in the same novel, Lily Briscoe, a modernistic painter, seeks to operate free of objective preconceptions, querulously repeating "What does it all mean?" about both her personal and her esthetic quandaries. Finally, less self-bound, each finds her solace in an open solitude divested of her need for personal conformity to a priori understandings. Still later, the personages in *The Waves* may be seen in contrasting sets dividing those who insist on prior elaborated psychal "certainties" from those capable of flowing psychally without preknowing.

Indeed, each of Woolf's major novels juxtaposes two kinds of personal figures, those caught in "I," that is, in psychology's analyses, and those who can break or stay free of such alien impositions. In *The Waves,* the tendencies dominate the book's structure in a weaving of the two alternate psychal tendencies. On the one hand, observing herself in a looking glass, Jinny recognizes in herself the former tendency. She notes resignedly, "I always prepare myself for the sight of myself" (165). Bernard, of the latter tendency, knows he "cannot be entirely sure what is myself" (99). A need for assurance freezes the mind in psychology's prior "certainties." In Woolf novels, doubt and self-consciousness are core impediments to inhabiting one's own open reality. Those free of need for assurance, like Bernard in *The Waves,* learn to inhabit a world "seen without a self," a world in which preestablished expectations give way to spontaneities of perception that facilitate personal discoveries (287).

## CONSTRUCTIVE CHAOS

The fields of unusual perception that pervade these authors' novels are not, then, the perceptual maelstroms they may at first seem. They are instead textual renderings of spontaneous normal perceptual experiences that depict a more open and accessible inner reality—that is, a reality essentially free of, or recognizing the limitations of, preconceptions. Each novel grows to its own conclusion through the ways of its personages' perceptions. However, there are two kinds of perception involved: the usual novelistic, so-called "normal" objective realistic perception; and the equally "normal" inner perceptions which one experiences in the field of perception itself where, for example, one object may be seen palimpsestically coexisting in the same place as another. The events in these direct replications of common realities of inner perception are—in the novels—interweavings in various degrees of complexity of strands of perceptive experience.

It is better, for this purpose, not to think of the major figures in these novels as "characters," that is, not as examples of the usual novelistic figure, but as "personages," that is, as fictive persons acting in their entirety each in his or her own perceptions. The experience of a "personage" is for the reader then markedly different from the experience of a "character." Events constituting the presences of the personages in these novels are composed of "unusual" (that is, not novelistically usual) ways of inner perceiving. Each way is for the personage a perceptual channel accessing a preconceptual open reality of his or her own. The successions of events in each novel may then be thought for critical purposes to consist of strands woven of the succession in time of the personages' various ways of perceiving. The novels are products of interweavings of those strands by the authors. Each novel is at once an interweaving of percepts experienced by the personages in their time *and* the interweavings of the author in the making of the novel. Strands are a critical concept facilitating examination of this insight.

In effect, then, in these compositions, the novelists conceive the novels themselves in an open reality, free in various ways of the usual structures of traditional novels. Simultaneously, within the novels, the major fictive personages deal in their own open realities. Thus, the perceptions of fictive persons are textualized in the unusual perceptions characteristic of more open reality, and the novels themselves create their own more open forms distinct from more familiar orthodox novelistic reality. Nonetheless, perceptions in the novels stay within recognizable types—once they are pointed out—of everyday perceptive capacity. We will identify for critical purposes strands of which the novels' texts may be thought to be woven. As will appear in the following discussion, the four here considered as strands are traced through instances discernible in the novels.

Much criticism, overlooking the novels' wider-base perceptual structures, has taken the unusual perceptions as mental malaises and sought to impose a cure for them, or to rationalize their occurrence. Thus, in supposedly ameliorating effects of irregularity, critics have, unwittingly, prescriptively limited and obfuscated the more open reality which the novels are realizing in their narrative techniques. Some recent readings of Lessing and Woolf have urged that "chaos and form are inextricably bound to one another in a dialectical process" (Draine 70); these novels so demonstrate—provided always that chaos or chaoses, as contemporary thinking is coming to see, be understood to consist in radically unusual orders. In one sense, the novels may be considered forms "impose[d] on chaos" (Draine 72), though imposed *in* chaos may be more accurate. In contrast to any enforced "impositionings," Lessing and Woolf do not regulate or tame chaos, but rather, each systematically courts a protean chaos that decisively eludes an illness-oriented psychology's preconceived hermeneutics.[11] The novelists have deftly recorded normal forms of inner perception.

Perhaps because of their focus on the "inner," Lessing and Woolf alike have been faulted for an alleged aloofness from reality. Their personal histories clearly demonstrate the contrary—both were constantly engaged in matters of social and public concern. Their central focus as writers, however, engages what can be thought of as a kind of first reality, the open reality of people's daily awareness recorded in their ways of being aware. They add to the familiar modernist "inner" a commitment to documenting artistically an inner reality that is not hermetically sealed away from life. They add verisimilitude by including a personage's inner- as well as outer-oriented percepts. Their writing develops means to temper, to attenuate the hold of the flat, logical, overly ordered mind dominated by objective realist terms whose orthodox interpretive preconceptions disenfranchise any emergence of the unpredictable. No runaway mystics estranged from a real world, their lifelong cultivation of potential chaos as a means to a wider sense of reality develops in, for instance, the four interwoven strands mentioned above: (1) visualizing in terms of *transparencies,* not mirrors, (2) activating of *dark sense* (potent but dimly discerned convictions as opposed to "logofied" certainties), (3) focusing on *dynamic evolvings,* emblemized in ludic play, and (4) engaging a reader, sometimes chaotically, with *structural novelties,* to the detriment or even exclusion of standardized novelistic wholeness.

The first strand of which the novels are woven, that of transparencies, equates to cinematic superimposition or montage. It is a conduit, or channel, creating in the novels a more open reality, and it operates psychally—not psychologically—to foreground a neglected potential for understanding.[12] Transparencies in both Lessing and Woolf provide occasions for deconstructing arbitrary, limiting distinctions. Transparencies serve as reminders of meaning's multiple contexts and deepen understanding in personages and readers alike. Most of all, transparencies significantly undermine the dominance of psychology's rigid ego, of an "I" locked in a single context such as its own skin, away from an objective reality "out there." The strand of transparencies is not mutually exclusive from other strands. They have in common an interpermeability among themselves. They are areas in literary perception which warrant further study as literary perceptions and as critical concepts. We are not here proposing precise classifications. Rather, as a recent critic of Mexican art has said, we are "risking approximations" (Herrera 23).

Transparencies, like the other strands, are events in an arena of overlapping *transitive* and *intransitive perception*. For instance, inner perception is basically intransitive, which is to say, objects visualized in our "inner eyes" may overlap with one another, intermix, pass through one another, and have no effect on one another in doing so. This is a realm of intransitive perceptions. On the other hand, transitive perceptions are those we are familiar with in the objective world of discrete objects which cannot come into contact without transmitting physical effects, one to another. In the mind's eye, one may drive one's car through a huge boulder and create no damage to car or rock. In the "out there," however, we know that terrible damage will, in fact, occur.

Inner perceptions, then, are basically intransitive. However, inner perceptions may be voluntarily limited to the kind of transitive limits that are absolutely essential in our physical actions. When we drive a car down the road and perceive in inner perception that we are about to turn a blind street corner where we know there is a big boulder in the road, we must restrict inner perception to the transitive reality "out there" or we are in serious danger. To race around the corner as though the boulder were safely permeable would be insanity. Inner perceptions, then, are always intransitive unless intentionally limited to transitive terms. Much of our daily perception we perforcedly and habitually limit to transitive terms. When we reflect, think back over events, we need not stay within transitive limits. Impelling need to understand, indeed, often provokes a relaxing of transitive limits in behalf of achieving a comprehension which frustratingly may otherwise elude us.

In Lessing's *The Golden Notebook,* the uncertainties for Anna in her sense of vulnerable openness appear in the transparent, intransitive understanding in which she "sees" herself enveloped. Persons, words, scenes, and images lose their objective distinctness for Anna. She feels permeable: that "what he was thinking got into my mind" (620). Though she ultimately becomes more able to control a crippling compartmentalizing, it is only after the projectionist's dream—when the montaging images flick by her so fast that "there was a fusion"—that she is clearly enabled to do so (635). Anna begins, finally, to abandon a need for carefully separated individuation. Consequently, she grows closer to the things and people that previously threatened her.

In *The Four-Gated City,* protagonist-narrator Martha's mind derives new light from the potential of a kind of transparency that displaces her hardminded subject-object, inner-outer psychoanalytical models. She reknows herself in coming to see that "her mind seemed to be a thin light texture through which other textures, feelings, sensations kept passing" (493). In *The Summer Before the Dark,* Kate Brown evolves in Spain into a similar dissolution of predictable surfaces which she characterizes as a "semi-transparent veil" (84). She routinely moonbathes therapeutically at night, in a curious transparent inversion of sunbathing. She conceives herself literally to soak up insights from the dark. Then, in *The Memoirs of a Survivor,* the survivor's famous "ambiguous wall" becomes a "transparent screen" (46, 77), bridging the transitive and intransitive worlds. Charles Watkins in *Briefing for a Descent into Hell* feels the inside of his skull "being washed with moonshine" (41); and in *The Marriages Between Zones Three, Four and Five,* similarly, persons and places become increasingly see-throughable (194). Later, the *Canopus in Argos* series engages with transparencies on a cosmic scale. Overall, transparencies expose and enlarge psychal experiences in understanding.

In Woolf's prose, too, a sense of transparency figures intimately—in diaries, letters and fiction. For instance, in a diary entry she lauds the fullness of transparency: "The sun is flooding the downs. The leaves of the plant in the window are transparent with light. My brain [mind] will be filling" (*Diary* 4: 56). Transparency equates in these passages to a sense of intransitive intimacy, with "the grass semi-transparent" and "space & leisure" lying "all about" (*Diary* 4: 27). Woolf's novel *The Waves* is infused with enjoyment of transparencies and of undifferentiated forms. In one intense paean to transparency, Rhoda recalls a

> momentary alleviation . . . moments when the walls of the mind grow thin; when nothing is unabsorbed and I could fancy that we might blow so vast a bubble that the sun might set and rise in it and we might take the blue of midday and the black of midnight and be cast off and escape from here and now. (224)

Another personage feels "a hole had been knocked in my mind, one of those sudden transparencies through which one sees everything" (106). In *The Years,* a personage perceives the physical world itself as transparent: "things seemed to have lost their skins; to be freed from some surface hardness; even the chair with gilt claws, at which she was looking, seemed porous" (220). Percepts, essentially transparent, figure intricately in both Woolf's and

Lessing's writing as an unsettling of fixed limits, encouraging free play in openings of psychal potential.

A second strand discernible in these two authors reveals an engagement with a constructive chaos in a disturbing interplay of dark uncertainties and positive convictions, which I have elsewhere termed "dark sense."[13] In a recent *New York Times* statement, Lessing questions controlled or preregulated readings and displayed her longstanding involvement with such a dark sense, saying, "Art—the arts generally are always unpredictable, maverick, and tend to be, at their best, uncomfortable" ("Language"). Such art emanates from a dark, unformulated, but potent sense of how one finds life. This knowing normally takes no shape until called forth by a context that demands it as a way of identifying how "things" are. In prose commentary, Lessing has clearly implied that people productively, though painfully, discover just such dark sense in "a series of shocks," in "the dark region" ("What Really" 98; "All Seething" 130). So, in *The Four-Gated City,* once solemnly reason-bound Martha Quest means to trust a "soft, dark empty space" in her mind. Therein, she learns laboriously to step "in the dark" (38, 586). Trust in a validity for dark sense's inexplicable convictions encourages in Martha an intimate respect for the open unknown, for the same unknown she previously found daunting.

The image of learning out of darkness recurs in Lessing's fiction. In *The Four-Gated City,* Linda Coldridge and Martha Quest go down into the basement with its "drawn curtains" and in a dark "great chaos of sound" enter an open reality in which Martha will develop telepathic capacities (490, 498). In *The Summer Before the Dark,* the title does not denote a finality following the summer. Darkness is not a symbol of defeat and occlusion; rather, the dark has come in the end to be a source of growth potential, much as many Eastern philosophies envision.[14] In this book's great learning adventure, a key turning point lies in Kate's self-immersion in the light-dark transparencies of her moonbathing in Spain. The famous seal dream releases her out of dark surrounding dreams into her own reality, free of the shapings of custom and surroundings. In the dream, she goes continuously into the sun's light in order to find herself finally with the sun's light before her, and she is released from the obsessive dream into a more open reality (146, 241). In yet another example of the importance of uncertainty, darkness and the unknown for learning, in *The Memoirs of a Survivor,* Emily makes an escalator excursion into learning which carries her "from the dark into the dark" (99). Lessing novels sustain a steady questioning of ritual and customs. They spotlight places "where words, patterns, order, dissolve" (*GN* 633). Out of the dark of this, uncertainty, Lessing's novelistic personages construct in self-understanding frameworks for their future; these frameworks commingle transitive and intransitive perceptions intimately. This dark sense is one with Lessing's intellectual conviction of the need for another kind of knowing: "One certainty we . . . accept is the condition of being uncertain and insecure" (*SPV* 5).

Virginia Woolf's novels also record the emergence of personalities through a similar trust in dark sense. Their important experiences in the novels grow out of what Jung called *enantiodromia,* the process by which things connect into their opposites, dim and dark relations "between things that seem incompatible yet have a mysterious affinity" (qtd. in Panken 209).[15] Things of the worlds of Woolf's novels come into new relations formerly precluded by exclusive, transitive-oriented categories and limits. So, Elizabeth, Mrs. Dalloway's daughter, brings to light "what lay slumbrous, clumsy, and shy on the mind's sandy floor to break surface" (*MD* 137).

As is possible in the direct, intransitive psychal experience prevailing in these novels, a personage's perceptions are like a commingling of superimpositioned metaphoric envisionings. More than literary figures conceived by the author to suggest a "character's" experience, the delicately perceptive complex recognitions *are* the actual occurring of the metaphors *in* a personage reflecting in its own psyche. On various occasions in *To The Lighthouse,* Lily Briscoe derives from pervasive bewilderment a positive "concentration of painting" (*TL* 158).[16] She develops a concentration *enantiodromically* bred both of artistic control and the "fluidity of life" (*TL* 158). Dark sense envelops Mrs. Ramsay at her dinner party, and, when reading, all the "odds and ends of the day stuck to this magnet," leaving her mind "swept . . . clean" (101, 121). The signally misunderstood passage in which Mrs. Ramsay authorizes solitude in herself catches the hugely serious dark-sense potential. In it, Mrs. Ramsay recognizes how, in release from her preconceived role, "one shrunk" to "a wedge-shaped cone of darkness" in which "her horizon seemed to her limitless" (62–63). For Woolf as for Lessing, dark sense plays a central role as an incomprehensible source of productive resolutions to uncertainties in orientation.

A third strand of novelistic weaving of intransitive perception may be characterized as ludic playfulness. This serious playfulness has, ironically, eluded some very serious, psychology-minded readings. A critical solemnity has shut out recognition of ludic impulses in Lessing occurring as early as *The Golden Notebook.* Anna's psychal chaos forces her to unself-conscious word play. In these nonorderly moments, she is intently, if not logically, in pursuit of understanding: "Words. Words. I play with words, hoping that some combination, even a chance combination, will say what I want" (633). Closely allied to dark sense, her ludic play encourages dark sense to shape her wording with unforeseen significance.

By *Briefing for a Descent into Hell,* one of Lessing's favorite novels, puns, mock solemnities, and tangled, juxtaposed images spin out. Charles struggles in serious play with what he knows. He plays with literary allusions: "gotta use words when I talk to you, Eliot" (147). Criticism has barely touched this more-than-whimsical play, an intricate mixture of lyric and flat-footed voices. Charles will shed his "good ship Why" (27). Merk Ury warns of the dangers of psychologicalization. Charles opines that "that was no weak, that was my wife" (5). His is a stream of playfully unconscious irony: "And the eye that would measure the pace of sand horses, as I watch the rolling gallop of sea horses would be an eye indeed. Aye Aye. I" (5). The contrast between Charles's flexible seriousness and the brittle solemnities of medical talk and pompous conferences is significant. As the "Afterword" accentuates, the "scientists" come to naught; Charles is closer to the daily unstructured inner vitality of life all along. His presence is a psyche in unselfconscious reflection, a personage—not a character type. Absence of that distinction has led to criticism in which Charles's world has been dismissed as a product of Lessing's heavyhandedness, indelicate prose, or lack of intellectual subtlety. In truth, Charles's realistic world of inner perception constitutes an intricate mockery on Lessing's part of twentieth-century psychology. In the novels following *Briefing,* the little-recognized ludic spirit turns increasingly more subtle. The books become flooded with ludic play, but always in behalf of dissolving prescriptive twentieth-century notions of psychology and of literature.[17] The entire *Canopus in Argos* series is a kind of cosmic-scale ludic play,contributing via a constructive chaos to undermining a strictly scientific psychology.

Woolf's novels likewise eschew pursuit of any hard and fast mimesis of a mind's contents as presupposed by psychological theories. The major novels are depictions of psychal experience directly in vital "shivering fragments of . . . the whole mind in action" (Leaska 393; *Diary* 4: 214). The minds of Woolf's personages are fluid, their heads "hive[s] of words that wont [*sic*] settle" (*Letters* 4: 312). The "whole pressure of the [outside] world is to make you take things seriously," Woolf recognized unhappily (Leaska 169).[18] Introspective worlds of personages dominate the best novels, and those worlds need not and do not adhere to the limits of outer perceptions. In them, too, ludic play characterizes their evolving psyches.

Their discourse is playful and their narrative voices fluctuate and shift. This ludic performance has been seen primarily rhetorically; the practice, however, taps a radical supposition growing steadily among twentieth-century artists (Caughie 19). From sculpture to painting to dance, a growing body of the century's artists find themselves taking on the fathoming of unconsciousness, or, as it is pseudo-objectively termed, "The Unconscious." Strictly transitive-oriented sciences, including psychology, impede access to unconscious routes of mind and art. It seemed to Woolf increasingly probable, as she found in her biography of Roger Fry, that in order "to create, unconsciousness was necessary" (*RF* 241). However, her unconscious, like Lessing's, is not inaccessible but is in fact accessible in the dark places of consciousness. Woolf's release from the limits imposed on art entails displacements of prevailing psychological models by more open access to those "dark places of psychology," as she termed them ("Modern Fiction" 152). These dark places are emblematized in art's ludic play, an area proverbially shared intimately by madness and creative artistry.

In *Mrs. Dalloway,* Septimus, badly shocked by his war experiences, engages in a grave free-word-play, coaxing overlapping layers of inner speech, spoken dialogue, semiotic moans (35), all interlaced with factual skywritings. Septimus is a fascinating ludic extreme in a choreography of five interlocked minds. Septimus sees himself "called forth . . . to learn the meaning" (67). In a struggle to balance his runaway inner intransitive life with the scientifically dominated "out there," he becomes in himself a veritable humanistic crisis. He writes on a postcard, "Human nature is upon you" and disjointedly spins out in reference to his war service, "I have—I have . . . committed a crime" (92, 97). His dissociations evidence themselves in a melange of inner and outer perceptions. Birds chirp his name "in Greek" (24). Septimus, like Charles Watkins in *Briefing,* foregrounds the tenuous lines dividing insanity and art. Around him, Woolf's novel becomes an undulating collage of figures cursed in varying degrees by damaging engagements with overcontrol. Later, in their structural novelty, the forms of Woolf's succeeding novels reflect their personages' inhabiting of chaos as ways of replacing predictable forms. They are psychal records of people learning to live in the uncertainties of feeling.[19] The novels mingle in varying proportions, on scales ranging from personal to historic, modernism's two often irreconcilable lines—its obsession with consciousness and its absorption with language.[20]

An understanding of the events of the novels we are considering as plays of inner and outer perceptions helps a reader grasp significance. Direct psychal experience—as explained above in the introductory paragraphs—is recorded in major personages in lieu of experience transcribed to accord with institutionalized psychologic concepts. The resultant personages in the chaos of their unalloyed experience form an open reality which is un-predigested. The novelties of form which occur are parts of their experience. Their perceptions in daily living are the shapes that the personages take as beings in a preconceptual, open reality preceding intellectualized, psychologic formulations. Each personage makes its strength in shaping a frequently chaotic open reality.

So, too, the novelistic structures take shape in an open reality. This, the fourth strand of development, most criticism flatly disallows to Woolf and Lessing novels. It involves the issues of chaos and wholeness. In grossest terms, this entails, on the one hand, the standard, expected shape of a book, whether novel or biography, as compared, on the other, with the shape of Woolf's *The Waves*—whose shape must evolve for a reader as the reading progressively takes place. The intensely constant mingling of inner perception with outer perception (to varying degrees in each of the novels we are considering) is a reality of individual human awareness. This mingling opens to each novel a vast range of material that serves to make a ground reality of the uncertainty of individual awareness. The resultant panoply of open-endedness—verbal, perceptual and actional—displaces story plots and their clear problems, crises, and resolutions with realities of psychal awareness. The novels' personages muddle through attempts to understand their intransitive inner realities in conjunction with their physical worlds.

Criticism of her writing has alienated Lessing because of its calls for clearly explicable wholeness, discernible systematic patterning.[21] Much criticism has fixated on readings of character and character development. A keynote was, it seems, sounded in an early groundbreaking book, which proposed that Lessing's characters "retreat from outer chaos to a vision of inner order."[22] Lessing has criticized such reading unequivocally as "a form of self-indulgence" (Stamberg 3). She stresses instead the real inevitability of uncertainty as opposed to the superficial calculability of character. In keeping with what is evidenced above, she has declared that in reality one must repeatedly step "in the dark" (*FGC* 586). Rather than infusing alien order, it appears Lessing's power resides in her capacity to tolerate multiplicity, to encourage and fertilize a diversity of response and counterresponse. Character in the usual sense is for her an artificial novelistic solution that obviates engagement with the fluid multiplicities of psychal reality in evolving personages. Character reading alone or commentary focused on single meanings, signals for Lessing a critical disorientation.

Certainly, the structures of Lessing's novels have accordingly over the years become more disjunctive, fluid, and unpredictable. Recently, writing of Lessing's influence, Myrtha Chabrán refers to the impermanence in which Lessing was schooled, which helped facilitate for Chabrán a "double vision, to sleep with my eyes open and to see with my eyes closed. And never to feel at home anywhere except for brief moments."[23] Chabrán's recognition is consonant with that *growing in chaos* that is characteristic of personages in these novels. The fiction calls for a "both/and" approach in which inner and outer perceptions mingle, as opposed to the "either/or" interpretations that have prevailed for years. Lessing has particular antipathy to critics who read her novels as mirrors, message-bearing stories of character, readings that miss the novels' shapes as literary compositions. Instead of being master author delivering answers to the multitudes, Lessing increasingly insists on making an experiment of both her writing and authorship.

Fictional personages in her novels confirm this movement toward an encouragement of constructive chaos as opposed to refuge in prefabricated orders of whatever ilk. Initially, Anna Wulf encloses herself in that familiar insolvable problem: "I was faced with the burden of re-creating order out of the chaos my life had become" (GN 619). By the end of the novel, however, she links herself positively and openly with chaos, disorder, and disintegration. Martha Quest also strips herself of a personalized ego and settles for existing in what is. In these, Lessing's most commented upon novels, personages visibly reject secure models for being alive. Lessing's personal "turn" to Sufism validates a movement away from a psychologically secure closure, which she detests. In 1984, she concluded, "The older you get, the more you're able to tolerate a great deal of confusion. This is being civilized, this is growing up. You have to tolerate uncertainty" (Stamberg 15).

Such an orientation dominated Lessing from *The Golden Notebook* onward until she shed personality-oriented novels and divested herself of contemporary realistic settings. As early as *The Golden Notebook*, the chaos inherent under orthodox understandings was recognized as something to "rescue" and to name (GN 470). And the famous phrase "out of the chaos, a new kind of strength" (GN 467) neatly describes Lessing's trajectory away from the dominance of psychologically oriented unifying frameworks that deny the chaos of psychal reality.[24] Appropriately, Charles Watkins, in *Briefing for a Descent into Hell,* scoffs at psychiatrists' definitions of anxiety, because he has learned to trust dark sense in himself, "that part of ourselves [which] knows things we don't know" (BDH 272). Lessing has rid herself of a need to novelize and has turned to fable, teaching stories and other nonpsychologically rooted narrative forms. However, her novels to date have demonstrated a striking ability to "survive beyond order, in the dangerous air of freedom" (Watson 37).

Woolf, like Lessing, undertook to depict the disabling effect of psychology on the open reality underlying living and writing. She forthrightly declared her sense of a need for integrated transitive and intransitive wholeness, to "relate inner and outer, self and the scene without asking that they be united" (*Letters* 5: 429). Woolf is ever fascinated with what she thinks of as "crossfertilizing" the inner and outer realities of the world. She seeks no simpleminded resolution or synthesis of polarities, but wants "to adjust the two worlds" (*Diary* 4: 202). Particularly in her later books, she weaves in and conjures up groupings, combinations, and reconstructions so as to dispel the apparent solidity of orthodox appearances. Like her sister Vanessa in painting, Woolf experimented with the physical world in order possibly thereby to "destroy the solidity of the thing" (Gillespie, *Sisters* 282). Her essay, "The Sun and the Fish," examined the earth with the color blown out of it, a foreshadowing of Bernard's asking in *The Waves,* "How then does light return to the world after the eclipse of the sun?" (286). Early in life, she and some friends participated in practical joking on a scale which provoked national displeasure. Her novels continue her experimenting with the unanticipated that underlies structures supposedly immutable.

Small wonder then that she is willing to unmake and remake expected genre conventions in the writing of biography, as in *Roger Fry* and the fictionalized biography *Orlando.* Radical rearrangings of perception and perspective are entailed in her concept of "tunnelling," in her freer architectonic rhythms of time, in her backgrounding and foregrounding, and in her balancing of transitive and intransitive, knowing and experiencing. In *Moments of Being,* she names and praises a "shock-receiving capacity" as the most open approach possible to personal awareness amid the deadweights of prior expectations (72).

Throughout her novels, Woolf's writing grows progressively into a more and more intense and complex psychal verisimilitude. This verisimilitude thrives on unexplained connections and on the absence of final frameworks. One suspects the writing of *Orlando* was for Woolf an enormous pleasure partly because in it she could coordinate her own chaotic promptings with historic realities. Certain scenes in *Orlando* spell out a contrast between order and chaos: "Now—she leant out of her window—all was light, order, and serenity. . . . All was dark; all was doubt; all was confusion. The Eighteenth century was over; the Nineteenth century had begun" (225–26). In a mock epic, fog-invaded, often cacophonous British setting, this novel puts a seal of value on disruptions at all levels. In it, Woolf plays with the rapid shifts of the "spirit of the age," as she does with that core drive that makes a sustaining history of uncertainty in the vicissitudes of Orlando's gender changes (236). The novel ceaselessly calls attention to disruption and instability, ending with "the cold breeze of the present brush[ing] her face with its little breath of fear" (328). A brain image illuminates "a back" and "a pool where things dwell in darkness so deep that what they are we scarcely know" (323). *Orlando,* a chaotic book written as a kind of lark to become free of meaningful books, was a profound exercise in historic, virtually cosmic uncertainties.

In *To The Lighthouse,* the famous "Time Passes" section is itself a measured prose/poetry ode to chaos, to time, dust, disorder, death, and, *enantiodromically,* to repair, restoration, and survival: "Listening (had there been anyone to listen) from the upper rooms of the empty house only *gigantic chaos* could have been heard tumbling and tossing" (134, emphasis added). This "gigantic chaos" underscores and infiltrates the entire novel; and it emerges in the book's many unenacted hints of violence, of swords, knives, in Lily's intransitive perceptions, in her figurative leaps "into the waters of annihilation" (181). One of the novel's central issues inhabits Lily's plaintively uncertain insecurity: "Was there no safety? No learning by heart the ways of the world? No guide, no shelter, but all was miracle, and leaping from the pinnacle of a tower into the air? Could it be, even for elderly people that this was life? a startling, unexpected unknown?" (*TL* 180). Survival through such chaos emphatically permeates Woolf's fiction. In every book from *The Voyage Out* to *Between the Acts,* personages come to appreciate that beneath the surface of things lies a psyche maintaining itself not in spite of, but by means of, learning via chaos to know anew. Major personages abide with chaos everywhere: the "wave has tumbled me over, head over heels, scattering my possessions, leaving me to collect, to assemble, to heap together" (*TW* 293).

Woolf criticism, however, has not seriously considered the pervasive acceptance of chaos that her novels present. Although Patricia Laurence in *The Reading of Silence* places Woolf's writing in an intransitive focus, a more usual orientation concludes that "Like Chekhov, Woolf sought a final harmony, a completed meaning growing out of an embodied intention" (Beattie 521). Underlying the vast majority of critical readings is a similar assumption of intentional author impositions. Critics have too often and too easily assumed that Woolf's books present a kind of coherence even in their incoherence. In truth, like Lessing's, Woolf's novels, in integrating inner and outer perceptions, undermine the false certainties of institutionalized psychology. They affirm the shadowed normalities of *irregularity* in the minds of people, a territory that has been misshapen by psychology's impositions. Each courts artistically a kind of chaos in which their major personages also court his or her chaos and shape new "strength." Out of the uncertainties of minute to minute, mingled inner and outer perceptions, they create open realities which vitally defy inert formulas of novelistic "characters" enacting exempla of psychological case studies. In their elaborations of textual and perceptual transparencies, in their evolving trust in dark sense, in their letting loose of serious ludic play, and in their willingness to experiment with novelistic structure, each contributes mightily to reassessment of the rigidity, if not the very legitimacy, of a supposed clean, irreparable break between inner and outer, intransitive and transitive worlds.

In these inner and outer territories of living central to Lessing's and Woolf's undeniably singular contributions to twentieth-century writing, they break the mold of conventional thinking and knowing. As Lessing has observed of chaos and an intransitive inner experience interwoven with a transitive outer experience, "The people who have been there, in the place in themselves where words, patterns, [and] order, dissolve, will know what I mean" (*GN* 633). What Pamela Caughie recently observed of Woolf is equally true of Lessing: "a change in narrative" technique is easily achieved; the more difficult job is "changing . . . conceptual paradigms and . . . understanding[s] of how literature and language function" (Caughie 208). Much that has been considered opaque, maladroit, or inappropriate as a result of older paradigms may be viewed more positively when studied using the approaches introduced in this study.

---

### NOTES

1.  Selected recent studies of mind or brain include Bill Moyers, *Healing and the Mind;* R. Joseph, *The Right Brain and the Unconscious: Discovering the Stranger Within;* Nicholas Humphrey, *A History of the Mind;* Daniel Dennett, *Consciousness Explained;* and John Searle, *The Rediscovery of the Mind.* The debates between what is considered mind or brain provide an interpretive key to shifting currents of thinking about inner, dominant theoretical systems and the nature of creativity.
2.  This recognition appears in Hofstadter 347.
3.  Current theoretical writing has highlighted various Western fascinations with center points—single self, a privileged knower, and so forth. In a pertinent turn of orientation, Sufi sayings illuminate feasible alternates to predictable models of inner life. For instance, Jalalludin Rumi observes, "Concentrate upon spirituality as you will—it will shun you if you are unworthy. Write about it, boast of it, comment upon it—it will decline to benefit you; it will flee. But, if it sees your concentration, it may come to your hand, like a trained bird" (Shah, *The Sufis* 125).
4.  Miles 989; Philip Rieff explicitly lambasts the "science of self concern" (355), chiding "the tyranny of [a] psychology legitimating self-concern as the highest science" (355). Rieff questions the thoroughly psycholog-

ical man who has "withdrawn into a world always at war . . . intent upon the conquest of his inner life" (357).

5. Fry keenly differentiated between the psychic or *spiritual* and the behavioral or *moral*, saying, "I should be inclined to deny to morals (proper) any spiritual quality—they are rather the mechanism of civil life—the rules by which life in groups can be rendered tolerable." These "rules" he contrasts with "states of mind" which are to him "'spiritual' functions that are not moral" (Woolf, *RF* 230).

6. Lessing has devoted considerable attention in nonfictional forms to psychology's limitations and to affirming the emerging tenure of a kind of chaos. See in particular *Prisons We Choose to Live Inside, A Small Personal Voice,* and *African Laughter.*

7. Panken, 5, 299; Woolf, "On Freudian Fiction" 153–54. Woolf bitingly observes in this review of Beresford's *An Imperfect Mother* that "in the ardours of discovery, Mr. Beresford has unduly stinted his people of flesh and blood. In becoming cases, they have ceased to be individuals" (154).

8. Hogarth Press first published Freud in 1924. Woolf's justification for reading Freud in 1939 was explicitly, if perhaps ironically, to "enlarge the circumference" (*Diary* 5: 255).

9. *Letters* 4, August 15, 1930, 199; at this time, Woolf praises Ethel Smyth's "magnificent" lack of self-consciousness (*Letters* 4: 302).

10. Clarissa and Septimus are complex mirrors of each other; both often obsessively read into their environments uncanny inverted parallels and distorted reflections. At the dressing table, before its mirror, Clarissa assembles herself again and again. Similarly, Septimus reads pain in the glassy surface of the sky (*MD* 68–70). At Lady Bruton's party, equations between the soul and mirror-like terms recur, such as "prismatic," "half looking glass" (109). At the end, when Clarissa opens the curtains, the old woman mirror-like "in the room opposite . . . stared straight at her" (186).

11. In a turn of attention much like Woolf's, Wallace Stevens has developed an alternate kind of concentration: "a meditative state of consciousness that was itself selfless . . ." (Bevis 5).

12. Caws's *Women of Bloomsbury* includes some useful examples of Woolf's images of transparency. See in particular 162.

13. Chown, 114–26; in a different historical context, Roy Pascal did much to develop the idea of the riskiness of the autobiographical endeavor, of its unpredictable foundations (Pascal 182). Such understanding explores the arena of dark sense.

14. Sufi thinking posits the "luminous blackness" of the "black-and-white checker effect" or "light-understanding comes from darkness" (Corbin 2; Shah, *The Sufis* 419).

15. Carl Jung says of *enantiodromia*, "the view that everything that exists turns into its opposite" (6: 425–26).

16. Abel figures the mind in Woolf's *A Room of One's Own* as both stomach and womb, writing as digestion and birth (Abel 95). The model remains

enclosed and, as such, made perhaps questionable by Lessing's and Woolf's transparency-rich, unpredictably shaped structures.

17. Hugo, half dog, half cat in *The Memoirs of a Survivor,* is one such unforegrounded instance of the far-fetched ludic in Lessing. Lessing has observed that Hugo is an impossibility, "a thought that was genetically impossible" (Wilson 92).

18. Virginia Woolf's wholly irreverent participation in the Dreadnought Hoax, something in which she participated over Vanessa's objections, reveals her readiness to invent elaborately, wildly, illogically. See Quentin Bell's narrative of the Hoax in his *Virginia Woolf: A Biography,* 157–61.

19. In her conceptual writing on art, stasis, and "significant form," Woolf persistently allies form and feeling. In a letter to Roger Fry in 1924, she observes, "form in fiction . . . is emotion put into the right relations" (*Letters* 3: 133).

20. Two directions of attention in modernism are today becoming apparent. In addition to Gilbert and Gubar's *No Man's Land,* for a comprehensive description suggesting differences between men's and women's modernism, see Sydney Janet Kaplan, *Katherine Mansfield and the Origins of Modernist Fiction,* especially 6–10; see also Michael Levenson, *A Genealogy of Modernism* for extended analyses of differences between a Joycean/Ford and a Yeatsian/Proustian focus.

21. Alvin Seltzer openly writes of Virginia Woolf's "technique for controlling chaos" and the "necessity for metaphor to control chaos" (133, 140). For a similar privileging of the achievement of wholeness over chaos in Lessing, see Mary Cohen, "Out of Chaos, a New Kind of Strength: Doris Lessing's *The Golden Notebook.*"

22. Rubenstein, 247; other studies speak of "the need for integration as being one of Lessing's major themes" (Draine 33). Many 1960s and 1970s readings of Lessing mine her books for internal coherence and order in the face of social or personal breakdowns and of compartmentalization.

23. Chabrán 29; in a parallel recognition, Spanish novelist Carmen Martín Gaite feels as though she were "in the crest of a wave that still hasn't broken, able to look toward the two perspectives" (Tola 219).

24. Beattie 521; there is increasing attention paid to chaos in Woolf criticism. Chaos and closure often operate as an abstract, objective seesaw: "The novel's closure invites a return to the chaos it recuperates, and it displaces its own center" (Emery 232). Chaos as presented in my analysis occurs not as a spatial or linguistic abstraction but as a vital element of inner activity.

# 8

— ◆ —

## ON CREATIVITY:
## WOOLF'S *THE WAVES* AND
## LESSING'S *THE GOLDEN NOTEBOOK*

### Jean Tobin

In "Sojourner," an essay from *Teaching a Stone to Talk,* Annie Dillard uses the metaphor of mangrove islands, clusters of trees that attract and create their own soil, and thus are enabled to float and to live on the salty, inhospitable sea. A mangrove island may begin with a single seed, she writes: "The germinated embryo can drop anywhere—say, onto a dab of floating muck. The heavy root end sinks; a leafy plumule unfurls . . . Soon aerial roots, shooting out in all directions trap debris. . . . The soil thickens . . ." (149). It is a fine metaphor for the creation of human culture, which is how Annie Dillard uses it. But I would like to appropriate her figure of speech momentarily and suggest it is also an apt metaphor for the individual consciousness in the act of creating—writing a novel, for instance, or elaborating upon a self.

This metaphor for the gradual accumulation of materials necessary in creative work is opposed to the popular and still pervasive view of creativity based solely upon inspiration. The view is a legacy of the Romantic age, and its proponents frequently cite as prototypes Coleridge at the moment of creating "Kubla Khan," as well as Mozart anytime.[1] Coleridge, it will be remembered, composed his poetic fragment after falling into a "profound sleep" during which, by his own account, he "could not have composed less than from two to three hundred lines." Upon awakening and seizing pen, paper, and inkpot, he scribbled the fragmentary poem we know, but being interrupted by the famously anonymous "person on business from Porlock," Coleridge forgot almost all the rest of his lines (296).[2] At its most extreme and as a major component of what Robert W. Weisberg has recently termed the "genius theory," this popular and romantic view sees creativity as mere passive receptivity, during which a work appears suddenly and whole in a moment of inspiration.[3] In opposition to this popularized Romantic view of creativity, I would suggest there may or may not be a single "moment of inspiration," resulting in the equivalent of the germinated embryo or seed; more often there may be many such moments. Certainly, however, a complex work does not emerge complete and whole. Usually even the most minor work is the result of a gradual accumulation of necessary materials.

I would like to appropriate a second controlling metaphor for discussing creativity in this essay, one from the opening lines of "A Lesson in Floating," in which poet Hilda Morley advises:

> Leap out into the air to begin
> with,
>            you'll find more of a footing
> there than you thought possible
> (12)

Her image of launching oneself into an unfamiliar element suggests my view of creativity as active, dynamic, deliberate—requiring courage. It is opposed not only to the popularized Romantic view of creativity as passive receptivity, but also to several aspects of the Freudian view of creativity as founded in unfulfilled wishes welling up from the unconscious. Freud's view, popularized in the public's idea of the artist as neurotic or sick, has been dominant during much of the twentieth century, and certainly from 1925 to 1962, years of importance to this essay.[4] Showing a somewhat different relationship with the unconscious than Freud suggests, my view is that creativity requires a decision that allows oneself deliberately to move into the unknown, not knowing what will happen—an act of courage, but an exhilarating one.

Such creativity requires the engendering of the materials on which one will walk. One makes the solid footing that is originally there only as faith; in this, one resembles the mangrove tree creating the muck of its own island. Obviously this process has to do with growth, at times unconscious growth, rather than true passivity. An active, healthy process, it is about choice and requires courage. The growth of the self during this process may be prodigious.

This process we can observe in the writings of Virginia Woolf, where we can see with extraordinary clarity how her mind worked, how it gathered materials, how it wrote. We can, for example, trace with delight Woolf's development of *The Waves* between 1926 and 1931, following its progress from the journals and letters and essays, through the various drafts of the manuscripts, to the published novel (1932). The sheer accumulation of material is useful for the study of creativity; all those pages in which we can watch what happened are in themselves a magnificent gift.

We have no comparable mass of material from Doris Lessing in which to trace the development of *The Golden Notebook* (1962). In 1994, no early drafts and manuscripts have been given to academic libraries; no notes or diaries have been published, not even excerpts in little magazines. It is part of the argument of this essay, however, that in a single work, in *The Golden Notebook* itself, Lessing provides us with journals, essays, manuscripts, novels—and more—dated from 1946 to 1957 and all of them intricately related, so that to read that textually dense novel is to be presented with an experience somewhat akin to reading the collected Woolf papers, say, from 1925 to 1931.

— ◆ —

Before examining the context of Woolf's *The Waves* and the text of Lessing's *The Golden Notebook,* in a fruitful comparison of apple and orange, it is well to ask why one might wish to look at these two writers together. To be sure, in many ways they are similar. Both are British women novelists, each a major writer by any standard and, if not prolific, each nonetheless with a substantial body of work accomplished, complementary in that they have neatly divided up the twentieth century between them. Both have lived in London and have written novels permeated with the sights and smells of that city, its omnibuses and furled umbrellas, its violet sellers and businessmen. As young women, neither received much formal education and in truth educated themselves, Woolf wandering purposefully into her father's library, Lessing reading voraciously after leaving school at fourteen. Both loved fiction, particularly thick, nineteenth-century novels, and both were influenced by the Russian novelists. Both have been outsiders; both have been critical toward society. Both have written books of great value to women, in part because each has had a fierce determination to write from her own—and thus a woman's—point of view, yet each has disliked being called a feminist. Each has been vitally interested in madness, and in the workings of the mind, at times fearlessly recording the intricacies of her own. Each, in part because of her stance as outsider, has been able to break free—even after becoming an established writer—to go on adventuring, to change styles and to experiment with her life and art.

Yet there are many major differences, and a few might be listed here. Woolf expressed her political views primarily from a "feminist" stance, as in *A Room of One's Own, Three Guineas,* and *The Years;* Lessing felt her "feminism" was incidental to her strong early political stance. There is a class difference of sorts: Woolf's father was part of the London literary establishment of his day, literary critic, historian, and editor of the *Dictionary of National Biography;* Lessing's father was a near-failed farmer in the colonies. Woolf grew up crammed into a Victorian household of siblings, half sisters and half brothers, parents and maids, allowed merely the respite of summers in Wales; Lessing lived with her parents and a single brother in a much-loved mud house with a clear view to the horizon. Their childhoods thus differed greatly, and Woolf was ever after haunted by memories of waves breaking on a northern shore, Lessing by memories of the hot African sun on the veld. Sexually abused in childhood and adolescence by her half brothers, Woolf was unable to write directly about sex; for example, she needed to speak metaphorically—about a girl fishing—even to make the point in "Professions for Women" that she was unable to tell "the truth" about her "own experiences as a body" (*CE* 2: 288). In contrast, Lessing was one of the first to write frankly and matter-of-factly about menstruation, women's sexual pleasure and passion, and childbirth.

Moreover, there is little direct evidence of Woolf's influence on Lessing. In 1962, around the time of *The Golden Notebook,* Lessing indicated Woolf's experience was "too limited" and that Woolf was "too much of a lady," but even that much reference to the older novelist was rare (qtd. in Joyner 204–5). Almost thirty years later, on January 31, 1991, at New York's 92nd Street Y, Lessing gave a "warm, extended . . . appreciation of Woolf and her novels" (see Sprague in Chapter 1 of this volume), but her remarks stood in notable contrast to her earlier lack of comment. Lessing's near total silence about Woolf is in itself interesting. How could a young woman novelist, newly come to London at midcentury, have escaped awareness of Woolf? In 1953, Leonard Woolf published his own selection from his wife's journals, called *A Writer's Diary.* How could Virginia Woolf not have been a presence with which to reckon?

Textual evidence, however, shows Lessing was influenced by Woolf in a major way. If Lessing ever took *A Writer's Diary* in hand,[5] she may have read passages such as the following, recorded by Woolf on September 10, 1928:

> I have entered into a sanctuary; a nunnery; had a religious retreat; . . .
> That is one of the experiences I have had here in some Augusts: and got
> then to a consciousness of what I call "reality": a thing I see before me;

something abstract; but residing in the downs or sky; beside which nothing matters; in which I shall rest and continue to exist. Reality I call it. (*AWD* 130)

In *The Golden Notebook,* an invented "lady author of early middle-age who . . . was afflicted with sensibility," after entering the Russian Orthodox Church in Kensington, gushes,

> This was reality. I was aware of reality. . . . I went home, nearer to reality I think than ever in my life. And, in silence, to my fresh narrow bed. (*GN* 437–38)

Certainly there seems to be some intended similarity between this parodic diary entry of the black notebook devised by Anna and her young American friend James Schafter and such passages from Woolf's journal. Lessing's ironic scorn for such a sensibility can be seen in her creating a "lady author" who burbles about the "grave, harmonious, *masculine*" priests and "thundering rich *virile* waves of the Russian singing." And the "fresh narrow bed" may remind many of the bed given by Woolf to Clarissa Dalloway. Of course, the "lady author" is of necessity also vaguely associated with Anna and even with Lessing herself by having experienced an invented stay of several years in an African colony.

Parody is usually a conscious act. However, influence can also be seen in passages in which images or rhythms or patterns of speech are repeated unconsciously—the influence absorbed unaware. As will be shown later, Woolf in this manner experienced the influence of Melville, expressed unconsciously in echoes from Ahab's final speech within the final speech of Bernard. Similarly, there is clear evidence within *The Golden Notebook* of Lessing's having read and been influenced by Woolf's novels. Two brief examples of influence will probably suffice to make this point; one might use Woolf's *The Years,* as it, like *The Golden Notebook,* is a London novel.

For the first example, here are two brief passages, one from Woolf's novel, the other from Lessing's. In one, Sara and Martin, having lunched together, walk through crowded streets from Fleet Street to Charing Cross. In the other, Anna and Reginald Tarbrucke, having lunched together, walk through unnamed, but similarly crowded London streets:

> They passed the woman selling violets. . . . She had no nose; her face was seamed with white patches; there were red rims for nostrils. She had no nose—she had pulled her hat down to hide that fact. (*TY* 235)

> We are at the underground entrance. Crowds of people. The man selling
> newspapers has no face. No nose, rather, his mouth is a rabbit-toothed
> hole, and his eyes are sunk in scar tissue. (GN 287)

The similarity of the passages is increased by context, as after Anna next
records a mocking screen scenario for *Frontiers of War* of which both Woolf
and Sara—neither a stranger to mockery of the military—might have
approved, she concludes: "The newsman with the rabbity face and no nose
is shouting: 'War in Quemoy. War in Quemoy'" (GN 287). This moment is
also reminiscent of Woolf, as shortly after Martin and Sara see the noseless
woman selling violets, "[t]hey had to stop. Newspaper boys held placards
against their legs. Men were buying papers: some loitered; others snatched
them" (TY 235). Throughout Woolf's novel, based as it is upon "fact," the
news of an era—the death of Parnell, the death of the King, the end of World
War I—is announced by those hawking newspapers and shouting in the
midst of traffic. Is it coincidence that in *The Golden Notebook* newspapers
and a noseless vendor are juxtaposed on the London streets?

For the second example, here are two additional passages, one from
Woolf in which Peggy listens to the pale young man at the party, and the
other from Lessing in which Anna listens to Saul Green:

> Her attention wandered. She had heard it all before. I, I, I—he went on.
> It was like a vulture's beak pecking, or a vacuum-cleaner sucking, or a
> telephone bell ringing. I, I, I. (TY 361)
> He talked—I found myself absent-minded, then with my attention half
> on what he said, realised I was listening for the word *I* in what he said.
> I, I, I, I, I—I began to feel as if the word I was being shot at me like bullets
> from a machine gun. (GN 556)

Far from being an incidental detail, the phrase "I, I, I," recurs again and again
as a significant refrain in *The Years*. During the same walk mentioned above,
for example, Sara and Martin discuss the fat man on his platform at the
Speakers' Corner; "'Oi, oi, oi!' [Sara] exclaimed, imitating his cockney accent"
(241).[6] And earlier in Woolf's work, Mrs. Ramsay uses the same words in
regard to Charles Tansley: "'I-I-I.' He was thinking of himself and the
impression he was making, as she could tell by the sound of his voice, and
his emphasis and his uneasiness" (TL 160). It is difficult not to hear Woolf
in the passage written by Lessing.

If evidence in *The Golden Notebook* suggests the influence of Woolf on
Lessing—including even at times the unconscious adaptation of the rhythm

and pattern of Woolf's speech—one is encouraged to look more closely at Lessing's novel with Woolf in mind. Is there any real significance to the influence of Woolf upon Lessing's writing and specifically upon *The Golden Notebook?* Yes, from this perspective, one immediately sees that Lessing has here created a writer called Anna Wulf/Woolf, a novelist who keeps an extensive diary in a series of notebooks, lives in London, and at the heart of her writing is suicidal.

Undoubtedly, the suicidal lady novelist is not a figure with which Lessing—or almost anyone else—would wish to identify, and it is a thoroughly superficial, inaccurate, and unfair characterization of Woolf. However, it is a figure to come to terms with and discard. It is interesting that at this time Lessing had published three volumes of her *Children of Violence* series and was at work on a fourth. *Children of Violence* is generally seen to be autobiographical; the close correspondence of Martha Quest, the major character, to Doris Lessing has often been noted. But Martha Quest is not an author. If this is in any way an autobiographical series, there is no room in it for a record of Lessing's writing self. Such is the material that is destined for *The Golden Notebook.* Part of that material may well be Lessing's fear of becoming like, and identified with, a stereotypical view of Virginia Woolf.

Lessing, however, in effect conceals this material so that the obvious correspondence of Woolf and Wulf, both surnames and authors, has been little commented upon. In addition to the many other things *The Golden Notebook* is, it is also a novel about madness and suicidal impulses as intricately connected to the artist and her work. Lessing writes a novel about Anna, who in the yellow notebook writes a novel about Ella, who writes a novel about a young man who is making preparations for suicide without his own conscious knowledge. As will be discussed at greater length later, *The Golden Notebook* is shot through with suicide. Not only Ella writes about suicide; Anna writes of it in both the yellow notebook and in *Free Women,* as her character Tommy attempts to commit it. However, when one briefly compares *The Golden Notebook* with Sylvia Plath's *The Bell Jar* (1971), one can see how convoluted Lessing is. Lessing hides the idea of suicide in the heart of her novel, and makes the way to it a maze. In contrast, in her autobiographical novel, Plath foregrounds the suicide attempt of her major character.

When one looks at the breakdown of Plath's character, Esther, one has no doubt about the seriousness of the experience Lessing's Anna undergoes. Notably, Plath satirizes her writing self, momentarily creating a novel within her novel, and thus briefly using the same device earlier employed at length by Lessing. Sitting down at her typewriter, Sylvia's major character Esther decides to write a novel about Elaine, counts on her fingers, discovers the name has six letters just like her own, and decides it is a lucky omen. Truly blocked, unable to get her heroine beyond sitting at a typewriter, Esther next decides she will instead "spend the summer reading *Finnegans Wake*" for her thesis (100). What happens then is an indication of the breakdown that puts Esther into a mental institution and leads to her taking a nearly fatal overdose of pills:

> Words, dimly familiar but twisted all awry, like faces in a funhouse mirror, fled past, leaving no impression on the glassy surface of my brain. . . . The letters grew barbs and rams' horns. I watched them separate, each from the other, and jiggle up and down in a silly way. (102)

The similarity of Anna's experience is evident:

> I am in a mood that gets more and more familiar: words lose their meaning suddenly. I find myself listening to a sentence, a phrase, a group of words, as if they are in a foreign language—the gap between what they are supposed to mean, and what in fact they say seems unbridgeable. I have been thinking of the novels about the breakdown of language, like *Finnegans Wake*. (GN 300)

However, Anna, unlike Esther, tries out suicide only in her fiction, not her life; her writing makes her stronger by the end of the novel. By 1971, Lessing discusses "breakdown" positively as a means of growth: "sometimes when people 'crack up' it is a way of self-healing, of the inner self's dismissing false dichotomies and divisions" (*GN* viii). By 1991, in her lecture at the 92nd Street Y, Lessing strikingly praised Woolf's "ability to bracket . . . depression" and contrasted Woolf's stance "to the 'victim' posture of writers such as . . . Plath" (Sprague in Chapter 1 of this volume).

— ◆ —

Mangrove islands become "thickets of lapped mysteries," according to Annie Dillard; they are "interlocked in a tangle of dependencies." After the "soil thickens," she writes, "[m]ore seeds and more muck yield more trees," and sometimes an island may even "stave into another mangrove island in a crash of clacking roots, and mesh" (148–50). Dillard's appropriated metaphor may be applied easily to the creation of *The Waves,* for Woolf's novel—in refutation of the popularized Romantic view of creativity—can be traced back not to one germinated embryo or one seed, but to many, each of which gathers the muck of its individual island, slowly developing on its own until it joins with the larger mass. The origins of *The Waves* have been discussed extensively and often, thus the following remarks will aim not at a comprehensive treatment of the matter, but rather at summary and presentation of new material. Three "germinated embryos" will be examined here: first, at some length, Woolf's remark that she was haunted by the "life of a woman"; second, briefly, her decision to "find some theory about fiction"; third, her famous observation of a "fin passing far out." These three distinct starting points for *The Waves* all occurred within a year, as the date for her theory is December 7, 1925, that for the fin, September 30, 1926; and that for the woman, November 23, 1926 (*AWD* 86, 103).

Certainly there are many additional starting points from which to choose. Among them are Woolf's determination to solve the stylistic problem of the "purple patch"[7] and her early intention to discover a new kind of novel to express the new emotions of the modern age, a poetic novel that would have "something of the exaltation of poetry, but much of the ordinariness of prose" (*CE* 2: 224). Mentioned below only in passing, moths are another starting point; the image can be traced from letters to and from Vanessa Bell after the publication of *To the Lighthouse,* to Woolf's diary (*AWD* 109), through the essay "The Death of the Moth"—an essay Carl Woodring earlier considered to belong "in point and idea to *The Waves*" (30) and A. D. Moody thought to be a "blueprint" for the novel (47)—to the original title of the manuscript in which the image of the moths decisively gives way to the waves themselves. We could even go back to Woolf's study of Greek poetic drama. The point to be made here is that the origins of *The Waves* are "interlocked in a tangle of dependencies."

Woolf's November 1926 comment that she was "now and then haunted by some semi-mystic very profound life of a woman, which shall all be told on one occasion . . ." (*AWD* 103–4) reminds us that in its origins *The Waves* resembled *The Golden Notebook* by being the presentation—in some aspects autobiographical[8]—of the consciousness of a single female writer and storyteller. "I am not trying to tell a story," Woolf wrote on May 28, 1929, "Yet perhaps it might be done in that way. A mind thinking. . . . Autobiography, it might be called. . . . But who is she?" (*AWD* 139). As often noted, when a month later Woolf's new work began to sound like the novel eventually published ("dawn; the shells on the beach . . . and then all the children at a long table—lessons"), the "life of a woman" became a collection of stories "she" would tell: "Then the person who is at the table can call out any [character] at any moment and . . . tell a story. . . ." Indeed, the solitary narrator became not only story-teller, but writer: "She might have a book…to write in" (*AWD* 140).

At the Berg Collection in the New York Public Library and now on microfilm, scholars can follow the published text of *The Waves* back through manuscript to Woolf's first handwritten pages, where an old woman tells over to herself the story of the world, the same woman Bernard later apprehends in his authentic Elvedonian vision of his own origins.[9] Just as Lessing in writing *The Golden Notebook* created the consciousness of a writer, probably female, who writes stories including those of Anna and Ella, who write stories of their own, so too Virginia Woolf in the manuscript and text of *The Waves* created a vast and lonely mind, embodied as a solitary narrator, probably female, who tells stories including those of Bernard, who eventually picks up the stories in his long concluding summary and tells them over again about himself and the others. In each novel we thus have, as Woolf wrote, "many characters and yet only one" (*AWD* 167). In truth, however, both the story-telling old woman and the writer "Anna" have been left decisively outside the published novels.[10] (Within both novels, alternative selves are given, and the fluidity of characters, as they remain themselves yet become indistinguishable from each other, is remarkable.)

   To trace the growth of this particular "germinated embryo" is to reveal the extent to which Woolf's original inspiration for the "life of a woman" was tentative and incomplete. Long after Woolf has begun her manuscript, her writing is marked by dogged persistence; "I am not reeling it off; but sticking it down," she writes on October 11, 1929, speaking of the novel's "vague yet elaborate design." At that date she doesn't know how to write her novel: "In particular is there some radical fault in my scheme?" she asks; "I am not quite satisfied with this method of picking out things in the room and being reminded by them of other things" (*AWD* 142). On November 2, 1929, four days after she has finished the first long volume of manuscript, she writes in terms which both recall Hilda Morley's metaphor and suggest a divided purpose: "There is *something* there . . . but I can't get at it, squarely; . . . Is there some falsity of method, somewhere? Something tricky?—so that the interesting things aren't firmly based? I am in an odd state; feel a cleavage; here's my interesting thing; and there's no quite solid table on which to put it" (*AWD* 145). Clearly Woolf, in her "leap out into the air," has yet to find firm base and solid footing.

   Woolf is able to create solid ground for herself, solving her problem in her second volume of manuscript, when she at last abandons her solitary narrator, moving from the outside of the characters which the narrator had created, to the inside. This happens very quickly and is fascinating to watch. On December 30, Woolf writes a long description of the gasometers and factories of London and the effect of a train arriving in the heart of the city. The ensuing narration is matter-of-fact and told in the third person: "It was an ordinary day; blue/fine perhaps in the country; here neither one thing nor the other; . . . Henry Mitchell started off, on foot/to walk. Mrs. Clay had to consider the best way of reaching Oxford Circus" (qtd. in Tobin 138). On January 3, titling the page "Conversation" and still using a somewhat traditional narrative form, Woolf begins the conversation with Bernard: "Unfortunately one cannot trust these moments of illumination, said Bernard; these moments he continued, as he . . . handed his coat to the waiter, when life has no more mysteries . . ." (qtd. in Tobin 139).

In the course of the conversation which follows, as the characters talk about the meaning of life, Bernard and the others gain their proper voices, with only tags—"said Bernard"—for identification. The conversation develops into the good-by party for Percival, and is closely similar to the first two pages of the fourth chapter of *The Waves*; the description of the gasometers and the factories is eventually given over to Bernard. Woolf's difficulty with the novel at this point is noted in her diary: "I incline now to try violent shots—at London—at talk—shouldering my way ruthlessly—" she writes, "But . . . I don't have it in my head all day . . ." (*AWD* 146). Her breakthrough is recorded in the next diary entry:

> *Sunday, January 12th*
> Sunday it is. And I have just exclaimed: "and now I can think of nothing else." Thanks to my pertinacity and industry, I can now hardly stop making up *The Waves*. The sense of this came acutely about a week ago on beginning to write the *Phantom Party*: now I feel that I can rush on, after 6 months' hacking, and finish: but without the least certainty how it's to achieve any form. (*AWD* 147)

At this point, more than three years have passed between the original "inspiration" of November 1926 and the breakthrough of January 1930; Woolf has been at work on the manuscript itself for six months. The idea for the work scarcely emerged whole at the "moment of inspiration"; rather, Woolf's continued uncertainty—now about form—is still apparent. Clearly, too, this breakthrough, and its ensuing energy, comes as a result of conscious choice and active work, Woolf's self-acknowledged "pertinacity and industry."

In all likelihood, Woolf's shift from the storytelling of the solitary narrator to the soliloquies of Bernard, Susan, Rhoda, Neville, Jinny, and Louis, marks the point at which she shifted from writing one kind of novel to writing another.[11] This brings us to the second "germinated embryo" mentioned above, Woolf's decision on December 7, 1925, to devise the "theory about fiction" particularly important to her work between 1925 and 1937: "I think I will find some theory about fiction; I shall read six novels and start some hares." The two extremes of her critical theory, the novel of fact and the novel of vision, are established in her further remarks: "I don't think it is a matter of 'development' but something to do with prose and poetry, in novels. For instance Defoe at one end; E. Brontë at the other" (*AWD* 86). The growth of this "germinated embryo" has been traced extensively, first through Woolf's journal, and next through sixteen and more essays[12] before it finds fulfillment in *The Waves*. The seed had its own individual fulfillment in "The Phases of Fiction," a long, three-part essay meant to have been a book on its own until E. M. Forster published a similar volume, *Aspects of the Novel*.[13] But this is a case of mangrove islands colliding. Woolf places Proust about midway in the continuum of her "theory about fiction," among the psychologists (*CE* 2: 85–89). Earlier, she had talked of Proust as a poet, and clearly in her original "method of picking out things in the room and being reminded by them of other things" (*AWD* 142), Proust served as a model. (Her method was also a direct continuation of her "tunneling" experiments in *Mrs. Dalloway* and *To the Lighthouse*.) When six months into her manuscript she abandons her method, therefore, her novel shifts from that of a psychologist-poet to a true poetic "novel of vision." Her model is no longer Proust, but Emily Brontë—and, interestingly enough, Melville.[14]

The "germinated seed" Woolf herself most consciously associated with the creation of *The Waves* is the often-noted visionary moment she experienced toward the end of finishing *To the Lighthouse* in 1926:

> I wished to add some remarks to this, on the mystical side of this solicitude; how it is not oneself but something in the universe that one's left with. . . . One sees a fin passing far out. What image can I reach to convey what I mean? . . . But by writing I don't reach anything. All I mean to make is a note of a curious state of mind. I hazard the guess that it may be the impulse behind another book. (*AWD* 103)

Woolf alludes to her visionary moment after the completion of every stage of the novel, as on February 7, for example, when she writes "I have netted that fin in the waste of water."[15] But Woolf was long uncertain as to the image she could "reach to convey" her vision. The "fin passing far out" became associated in the first moments with a puddle she could not cross in childhood (*AWD* 103), and the grey waters of both puddle and the waste of waters linked with grey waves suggested by a grey napkin in the first pages of her manuscript, upon which babies toss, one per wave. The fin—alive in those indifferent waters—resembles both the living babies and a stream of moths showing light/life through; the single fin is like the single moth. In the manuscripts of the Berg Collection are Woolf's further attempts to embody her vision in an image. One such experiment similarly showing a living being against a vast impersonal landscape can be seen, for example, in the following excerpt from the manuscript of *The Waves*:

> Indeed you have brought back the inexplicable marvel of existence: . . . as if tired after a long march, being dazed with snowstorms, the whirling blackness had vanished & in the snow peeping out, there had been, some extraordinary humble but valiant bud, say a rose, say a imagine a little little creature, say a mouse, say a squirrel say something as I see you now, sitting up on its haunches in the midst of the appalling desolation, actually alive: And, this little beast makes me weep. (qtd. in Tobin 187)

In this passage, bud, rose, little creature, mouse, and squirrel are akin to the emblematic "fin," all of them astonishingly alive, but vulnerable, surrounded by and subject to nonliving, enormous, indifferent forces: "whirling blackness," "snowstorms," "the waste of water," "appalling desolation."

It is clear from Woolf's extensive work with these images what attracted her to Melville. The same vision is expressed in *Moby Dick,* as here in a passage after little Pip has fallen overboard and been abandoned: "Now, in calm weather, to swim in the open ocean is as easy to the practiced swimmer as to ride in a spring carriage ashore. But the awful lonesomeness is intolerable. The intense concentration of self in the middle of such a heartless immensity, my God! who can tell it?" (529).

Thus when we come to Bernard's final soliloquy in *The Waves,* we understand why Woolf consciously and unconsciously gathered materials from *Moby Dick* and why Bernard's last words echo the last words of Melville's equally defiant Ahab:

> Oh, lonely death on lonely life! Oh, now I feel my topmost greatness lies in my topmost grief. Ho, ho! from all your furthest bounds, pour ye now in, ye bold billows of my whole foregone life, and top this one piled comber of my death! Towards thee I roll, thou all-destroying but unconquering whale; to the last I grapple with thee . . . *Thus,* I give up the spear! (Melville 721)

> And in me too the wave rises. It swells; it arches its back. I am aware once more of a new desire, something rising beneath me like the proud horse whose rider first spurs and then pulls him back. What enemy do we now perceive advancing against us, you whom I ride now, as we stand pawing this stretch of pavement? It is death. Death is the enemy. It is

> death against whom I ride with my spear couched . . . Against you I will
> fling myself, unvanquished and unyielding, O Death! (*TW* 383)

Not only are the wave, the spear, and defiance at an identical pitch of emotion
present in both passages, so too is the manner in which both men become
one with the waves. In this final permutation of Woolf's original image, fin
merges with wave, as in combatting the waste of waters, the living Bernard
feels the wave rise within him.[16] Once again, the "moment of inspiration"
did not yield even the central image of Woolf's novel complete and whole.
Four-and-a-half years passed between the original vision of "a fin passing far
out" (*AWD* 103) and the last permutation of that image on February 7, 1931,
as Woolf completed her manuscript and recorded in her journal how she sat
"in a state of glory, and calm, and some tears" (*AWD* 161).

Disconcertingly, Woolf is given to announcing moments of inspiration
completely in keeping with the popularized Romantic view, as in this journal
entry from 1931: "I have this moment, while having my bath, conceived an
entire new book . . . Lord how exciting!" (*AWD* 158–9). Her work on *The
Waves,* however, belies the Romantic view by demonstrating the extent to
which she indeed leapt "out into the air to begin with," knowing there was
"*something* there," but not knowing how to go about creating it. Further, by
continuing to write under such circumstances month after month, Woolf
demonstrated daily courage and conscious tenacity, not traits—to move
ahead in the argument for a moment—attributed by Freud to the writer
creating from unfulfilled wishes welling up unbidden from the unconscious.

—◆—

When we look at *The Waves* and *The Golden Notebook* together, we see that
in each, the novelist deliberately—in Woolf's words—broke "the mould" of
the novel (*AWD* 206). Nothing like either of these novels had been seen
before; each was a unique and extraordinary achievement. This, rather than
a supposition of influence between the two books, is the reason for choosing
these novels to discuss in an essay on Woolf, Lessing, and creativity. In the
*context* of Woolf's novel, however, it is possible that some influence on *The
Golden Notebook* may be discerned. If so, in turning from the context and text
of *The Waves* to the text of *The Golden Notebook,* we are not surprised to find
Lessing carefully includes within Anna's notebooks and novels unabashed
moments of inspiration. In its five notebooks or five volumes of a journal,
*The Golden Notebook* certainly may be called a writer's diary, one Anna, like
Woolf, uses "in a very individual way as a writer and artist" (*AWD* viii). The
format for dates differs slightly (Lessing's left margin "15th Sept., 1951"
versus Woolf's right margin "Thursday, September 30th") but the look of the

page is often much the same. Material is sliced differently (thematically in the notebooks versus chronologically in Woolf's journals), but nonetheless it is interesting to look at *The Golden Notebook* in terms of the criteria Leonard Woolf established for *A Writer's Diary*.[17] As is the case with Woolf's journals, much within Anna's notebooks is of use in the study of creativity, although additional care is needed here, for the material is fictionalized and also may at times be slightly derivative.

If we take Lessing's hint that *Free Women* may be read as a separate novel (*GN* vii), we find it is a novel which dwindles markedly in quality as it progresses, almost as if its writer had lost interest by the end. For a realistic novel, the plot thins alarmingly, the Ronnie-Ivor story seems out of proportion to the whole, and characters begin to act without sufficient motivation. It seems charitable to consider it a draft for a novel, and there is perhaps no reason to believe it is anything more. In *The Golden Notebook,* we have then, as if laid on a trestle table, five notebooks plus the draft of a novel, all (as is stylistically apparent) written by one person, whoever she or he may be. As we have only the evidence of the writing itself, it is convenient to follow the convention that "I" within a diary refers to the author of that diary, in this case "Anna," even though fictionalized diaries and "autobiographies" have existed for a very long time ("I was born in the year 1632," begins Defoe's classic; ". . . we call ourselves, and write our name, Crusoe"). Placing "Anna" outside the notebooks and draft of the novel doesn't make Anna indistinguishable from Lessing; Anna remains a fiction, just as Rhoda is a fiction in spite of having experienced Woolf's own inability to cross a puddle.

In the black notebook, Anna twice recalls the inception of her novel *Frontiers of War,* writing of it immediately before and after she writes down the lengthy Mashopi hotel narrative. The moment of inspiration is instantaneous and dramatic: "I remember very clearly the moment in which that novel was born. The pulse beat, violently; afterwards, when I knew I would write, I worked out what I could write" (*GN* 63). Her imagery is similar to that in Morley's phrase, "Leap out into the air to begin/with," when she recalls again "very clearly the moment" as she stood on the steps of the Mashopi hotel in the moonlight: "I was filled with such a dangerous delicious intoxication that I could have walked straight off the steps into the air . . ." (*GN* 152–53). A similarly instantaneous experience is also given to Ella as created by Anna in the yellow notebook: "The idea for this novel had come to Ella at a moment when she found herself getting dressed to go out to dine with people after she had told herself she did not want to go out" (*GN* 173–74).

However, this plethora of Romantic moments of inspiration is undercut by other material related to writing in the novel. Interestingly, Ella later remembers her experience differently when she finds herself thinking, "I shall write another novel. But the trouble is, with the last one there was never a point when I said: I shall write a novel. I found I was writing a novel." Using a Woolfian phrase, "state of mind," Ella deliberately chooses to use a particular mental state to engender another novel: "Well, I must put myself in the same state of mind—a kind of open readiness, a passive waiting. Then perhaps one day I'll find myself writing" (*GN* 314). Later in Anna's novel, "Ella decides to write again, searches herself for the book which is already written inside her, and waiting to be written down. She spends a great deal of time alone, waiting to discern the outlines of this book inside her" (*GN* 459). In these decisions, she sounds like Woolf, as for example when on November 28, 1928, Woolf similarly chose to wait: "As for my next book [*The Waves*], I am going to hold myself from writing till I have it impending in me: grown heavy in my mind like a ripe pear; pendant, gravid, asking to be cut or it will fall" (*AWD* 135–36). In deciding to wait "passively," both Woolf and Ella make active choices, consciously directing their unconscious minds to mull over a possible new novel.

Just as Woolf's and Ella's waiting represents more than the passive receptivity of the popularized Romantic view of creativity, so too does it belie the Freudian view of creative work as based upon unfulfilled desires, spontaneously welling up from the unconscious. Clearly Woolf and Ella are consciously employing the unconscious to aid in their writing; their practical attitude toward it is that of an artisan toward a tool traditionally used in a skilled and practiced way. This is akin to Lessing's own view of the "unconscious as a helpful force" as expressed in a 1969 interview: "The Freudians describe the conscious as a small lit area, all white, and the unconscious as a great dark marsh full of monsters. In their view, the monsters reach up, grab you by the ankles, and try to drag you down. But the unconscious can be what you make it, good or bad, helpful or unhelpful" (qtd. in Raskin, *SPV* 67). Indeed, in writing *The Golden Notebook,* Lessing newly made use of a technique for manipulating the unconscious long familiar to sonneteers, who habitually express intense emotion within 140 syllables and a rigid rhyme scheme: "Perhaps giving oneself a tight structure, making limitations for oneself, squeezes out new substance where you least expect it," she wrote in the 1971 introduction to the novel. "All sorts of ideas and experiences I didn't recognise as mine emerged when writing" (*GN* x). Fifteen years later, indicating to an interviewer the novel resulted from a "concentration of psychological pressure and events," Lessing said, "I said I want this tight structure, so I did the structure. But what came out in between was something else, and not always foreseen" (qtd. in Gray 336). In 1971, Lessing asserted "It was under control"; in 1986 she conceded, "It was almost out of control" (qtd. in Gray 336).

After the moment of inspiration at the Mashopi hotel steps, we are told, Anna consciously acted upon her new knowledge, working out what she would write. Readers never see Anna writing this first novel, and its publication is a given within *The Golden Notebook*. We do see, however, Anna reworking this material over and over again until she gets it right. For example, the Mashopi hotel material, apparently first written about in Anna's *The Frontiers of War,* continues to be presented in her black notebook, as in the biting synopsis of *Forbidden Love* (56–59), the reviews of the novel written as if in 1951 and 1954 (59–60), and the comic parodies of *Frontiers of War* as a filmed "comedy about useless heroism" (282–88) and as a musical comedy for television of black U.S. GI's in England (288–96). A serious attempt at reworking the material occurs in the Mashopi hotel story, which begins with a Woolfian phrase—"I will try to put down the facts merely" (65) and is summed up as the "material that made *Frontiers of War*" (152). Further reworking occurs in Anna's remembrance of the Mashopi hotel pigeon shoot (412–33) and in her record of a "dream of total sterility," which changes the Mashopi hotel material through a "choice of shots or of timing" by black technicians using cameras as machine guns (524–25); as the dream clearly comes in part from Anna's revulsion at various film and television projects for her novel, it fittingly appears not in the blue notebook, but in the black notebook used as a sort of record for *Frontiers of War*. A final reworking can be seen in Anna's recording of other dreams in her new golden notebook, as the "invisible projectionist" shows different versions of "the Mashopi film" (619). She revisits the group at the Mashopi hotel (616–17), rewrites a portion of her material in June Boothby's style (620), and becomes aware of previously unnoticed details such as Willi's "desperately lonely humming" and Mr. Lattimer's bending down, "shaky with drunkenness, to stroke the feathery red dog" when listening to "his beautiful red-haired wife's laughter" (634–35). Anna finally gets it right, knows "what was really important," when she switches off the film and is able to "read the words off a page [she] had written: That was about . . . a small painful sort of courage which is at the root of every life, because injustice and cruelty is at the root of life" (634–36).

In *The Golden Notebook,* Lessing does show us Anna actively gathering the material from which she will write the draft of a third novel, *Free Women* (her abortive second, in draft in the yellow notebook, is *The Shadow of the Third*). Like Woolf, Anna amasses this material, rewriting things over and over, using material in significantly different ways. Thus, just as we see Woolf in her writing describe the eclipse of the sun once in her diary, use the visual impression the incident made upon her in a developing "theory about fiction," describe the eclipse again in the essay "The Sun and the Fish," and for a third time in Bernard's long soliloquy in *The Waves,* so can we similarly follow within *The Golden Notebook* the evolution of Anna's idea of joy in destruction in her recorded dreams of spiteful malice in the blue notebook (476–77), in her recognition of the living principle in Nelson (495) and de Silva (501), in her account of the principle dreamed positively (594–95), and finally in its embodiment within *Free Women* in the character of Tommy, who suddenly is portrayed as "calmly but triumphantly malicious," giggling with spite (*GN* 260, 270, 276).

In reading in this way, of course, we are reading *The Golden Notebook* not in order as the published novel, but as the compilation of Anna's dated manuscripts, rearranging them chronologically to follow the development of her thought. We are assuming that the so-named "diary" and blue notebook (*GN* 229) is closest to an account of her "real" life, that the fictionalized life written for herself found in Anna's yellow notebook is fiction, but for that reason may contain some emotional truths she cannot fully face consciously, and that the draft of *Free Women* in being written last and for the public is furthest away from the self and the least "raw" treatment of some of the same experiences. We are, in effect, reading *The Golden Notebook* as we read, for example, the collected papers of Virginia Woolf from 1925 to 1932.

— ◆ —

"We laymen have always been intensely curious to know," wrote Freud in 1908, ". . . from what sources that strange being, the creative writer, draws his material." In a self-deprecatory remark placing writers in a special category and presenting creativity as a mystery rather than as a normal and natural human activity, he then added that "not even the clearest insight into the determinants of [the writer's] choice of material and into the nature of the art of creating imaginative form will ever help to make creative writers of *us*" (143). Freud, as Gary Morson and Caryl Emerson point out, notably "partakes of the romantic tendency to regard creativity and inspiration as exceptional" (187).[18] But it is Freud's view of creativity, popularized in a view of the artist as neurotic, which has dominated much of the twentieth century.

This view can be traced to the 1907 lecture and 1908 publication of "Creative Writers and Daydreaming" ("Der Dichter und Das Phantasieren"), where Freud links the writer's creations with daydreams (fantasy) and play, opposing all three to "what is real" and declaring that all three originate in "unsatisfied wishes." Although Freud states that "most people construct fantasies," his examples unfortunately serve to link the child at play, "victims of nervous illness" telling over their fantasies, and the creative writer.

Moreover, Freud proclaims, without immediate justification, that "a happy person never phantasies, only an unsatisfied one" (144–46).

Describing in her 1971 introduction to *The Golden Notebook* how she had made "an artist, but with a 'block'" a major theme in the novel, Doris Lessing speaks slightingly of the Romantic model of the artist, "a creator all excesses of sensibility and suffering and a towering egotism" (xii), but it is the Freudian model of the artist that Anna most loathes:

> I am interested only in stretching myself, in living as fully as I can. When I said that to Mother Sugar she replied with the small nod of satisfaction people use for these resounding truths, that the artist writes out of an incapacity to live. I remember the nausea I felt when she said it; I feel the reluctance of disgust now when I write it: it is because this business about art and the artist has become so debased, the property of every sloppy-minded amateur that any person with a real connection with the arts wants to run a hundred miles at the sight of the small satisfied nod, the complacent smile. (*GN* 62)

In Lessing's desire to give "the intellectual and moral climate" and "ideological 'feel' of our mid-century," *The Golden Notebook* is necessarily permeated with the beliefs of Freudian-Jungian ideology as well as Marxist ideology. A punning conflation hinting at relationships between the two is seen in the naming of Anna's analyst, Mrs. Marks, and the two belief structures are similarly questioned—including the Freudian theory of creativity, especially as popularized.

Instead of viewing creativity as evidence of psychological disability, Lessing's Anna—like Plath's Esther—associates a failure of words with mental breakdown, recording in her blue notebook, "I am increasingly afflicted by vertigo where words mean nothing. . . . It occurs to me that what is happening is a breakdown of me, Anna, and this is how I am becoming aware of it" (*GN* 476). Creativity, Anna implies, occurs during periods of relative energy and health. That Woolf not so incidentally also believed the ability to create denoted psychological well-being is shown by her recording a five-day "whole . . . breakdown in miniature," during which she "[t]hought of [her] own power of writing with veneration, as of something incredible, belonging to someone else; never again to be enjoyed by [her]" (*AWD* 97). She soon asserted that "*Returning health* . . . is shown by the power to make images," and placed herself midway between Shakespeare and "poor Mrs. Bartholomew," an afflicted woman as "blind, dead, dumb, stone-stockish and fish-blooded" compared to Woolf as Woolf saw herself compared to

Shakespeare (*AWD* 99). Clearly Woolf, in opposition to Freud, associated creativity with wholeness, energy, and good health and pitied those who were lacking. Indeed, upon a return from Italy, unable to get back to writing that day and experiencing a "cold slab of a brain," she suggested that as what Freud terms the "creative writer," she lived more fully than many others: "It occurs to me that this state, my depressed state, is the state in which most people usually are" (*AWD* 195).

In *The Golden Notebook,* Lessing creates a writer, unable to meet her own standards for writing, who is in a very "depressed state." As mentioned earlier, the novel is, among many other things, about madness and suicidal impulses as intricately connected to the artist and her work. Indicating that she wrote about the "theme of 'breakdown'" for the first time in *The Golden Notebook,* Lessing disclosed that "[h]ere it is rougher, more close to experience, before experience has shaped itself into thought and pattern—more valuable perhaps because it is rawer material" (*GN* viii). In the configuration of writers like Chinese boxes Lessing creates—Lessing, Anna, Ella, the young man—psychological sophistication and awareness dwindle. Ella finds herself writing a novel unaware about a young man who, thoroughly unaware, is preparing for suicide. In her blue notebook, a more cognizant Anna questions what she herself is doing in her writing: "It struck me that my doing this—turning everything into fiction—must be an evasion. Why not write down, simply, what happened . . ." (*GN* 228–29). She writes in her black notebook, "I am simply asking myself: Why a story at all—not that it was a bad story, or untrue, or that it debased anything. Why not, simply, the truth?" (*GN* 63). In her questions, Anna hints at her acceptance of what Howard Gardner in *Creating Minds* (1993) considers Freud's "focal idea": "*repression,* the process (more technically, the defense mechanism) whereby certain potentially upsetting notions are withheld from consciousness" (65).[19]

Lessing does two things which are of interest here, neither of which—despite Mrs. Brown—have an analogue in Woolf. First, as will be discussed later, she provides authorial commentary about the relationship between a writer and the fictional character she creates. Second, by giving us as it were a novel of practice writing—of diaries and drafts—she provides us with a compendium of five techniques by which writers of fiction choose to alter "the truth." Clearly in many cases, to answer Freud, writers draw some of their material from life and, in a decision which may be an act of courage resulting in personal growth, they may choose one or more of the following techniques—shifting pronoun, shifting gender, transposing, shuffling, and generalizing—to allow difficult material to flow more freely.

## Shift in Pronoun

One of the easiest ways to distance oneself from material that is both personal and painful is to shift pronouns from "I" to "she." The moment one does that, someone else is created to bear the pain. Thus it is significant that the material Anna fictionalizes in *The Golden Notebook* is her emotional life, her deep love for the man she calls Michael/Paul. For readers of *The Golden Notebook,* the yellow notebook, given over to Anna's novel *The Shadow of the Third,* is where we come to expect transposed details of Anna's emotional life, fictionalized and written in the third person; it is the notebook, she says, "in which I make stories out of my experience" (*GN* 475).

## Shift in Gender

A second, more drastic, way to distance oneself from painful material is to shift gender. Such transpositions at times can be ridden right out of the confines of the novel; a simple example is the writing by Lessing, a novelist then living with her son Peter, about the writing by Anna, a novelist then living with her small daughter Janet, about the writing by Ella, a novelist then living with her small son Michael. Clearly Lessing herself is fully conscious of what she is doing in showing us this technique. Within *The Golden Notebook,* a significant use of the device is seen in the yellow notebook in Ella's choice of a young man as protagonist to explore the theme of suicide in her novel. (Woolf similarly chose Septimus Smith to explore themes of madness and suicide in *Mrs. Dalloway.*) Ella's novel about suicide surfaces with obvious importance five pages into Anna's novel and then occupies almost three pages.

Anna (and here she is shifting pronouns) makes Ella aware enough to be "surprised and ashamed of [her novel's] subject . . . and sometimes frightened," as Ella wonders, "Perhaps I've made a secret decision to commit suicide that I know nothing about? (But she did not believe this to be true)" (*GN* 174). Later in *The Shadow of the Third,* however, Anna is able to show Ella fully prepared for passive suicide on the flight from France to England and to allow her a moment of realization:

> As for Ella, she had climbed into the aircraft as she would have climbed into a death-chamber. . . . As the aeroplane began to vibrate, she thought: I'm going to die, very likely, and I'm pleased.

> This discovery was not, after the first moment, a shock. She had
> known it all the time: I'm so enormously exhausted, so utterly, basically
> tired, and in every fibre of myself, that to know I haven't got to go through
> with living is like a reprieve. (*GN* 316–17)

Lessing thus creates an Anna eventually able to depict a female consciously
longing for passive suicide, but when Anna again writes of an active attempt
at suicide, making it central to her novel *Free Women,* it is again a male,
Tommy, who will pull a trigger. Interestingly, Tommy's motivation for the
act is little understood, although some conventional reasons are given, and
the Anna character is seen in the role of arguing against suicide with a Tommy
intent on killing himself in spite of what he has seen in her notebooks, or
perhaps because of it. His action makes more emotional sense in light of the
Anna creating him than in his own volition as a character.


### The "Psychological Game"

As Lessing shows, authors play what she calls the "psychological game,"
hiding from readers and at times themselves correlations between art and
life, character and human being, plot and event (*GN* 63). As author, Anna
knowingly writes of Willi/Max, Michael/Paul, Anna/Ella, Molly/Julia, and so
on, as for example, when she notes:

> And so now, looking back at my relationship with Michael (I used the
> name of my real lover for Ella's fictitious son with the small over-eager
> smile with which a patient offers an analyst evidence he has been waiting
> for but which the patient is convinced is irrelevant), I see above all my
> naivety. . . . I, Anna, like Ella with Paul, refused to see it [the end of the
> affair]. (*GN* 211)

Anna here gains in self-knowledge; further, the passage shows not only her
awareness she's playing the writer's "psychological game"—that "this relationship was the psychological twin of that" (*GN* 63)—but also the emotionally meaningful transposition of names. In just such a way, Anna significantly
used the name Paul, the young lover of her 1954 Mashopi hotel narrative—
about being with whom she once wrote, "I have never, in all my life, been
so desperately and wildly and painfully happy as I was then" (*GN* 150)—to
stand in for her lover Michael.

## Shuffling

An additional way to conceal painful knowledge from both readers and the self is to place vital information in unexpected places. In *The Golden Notebook,* the black, red, blue, and yellow notebooks are assigned topics and titles, and readers are given to expect certain kinds of information in each. Moreover, until she finally joins the fragmented parts of her life in the single golden notebook, Anna seems scrupulous in maintaining her assigned order: "(but this kind of observation belongs to the blue notebook, not this one)," she writes in the black notebook and stops her thought (*GN* 137). In fact, however, the most significant personal moments are not recorded in the blue notebook's "diary." Anna's realization of imminent mental breakdown, for example, is recorded in the red notebook about her involvement with the Communist Party, a notebook that seems deceptively of importance equal to the other three notebooks, but that comprises surprisingly few pages.

Another example of the shuffling of expected material occurs when Anna examines her novel about Ella and Paul at the end of the first section of the yellow notebook: "Supposing I were to write it like this: two full days, in every detail, one at the beginning of the affair, and one towards the end?" she muses. She further decides that "to show a woman loving a man one should show her cooking a meal for him . . . while she waits for his ring at the door. Or waking in the morning before he does to see his face change from the calm of sleep into a smile of welcome" (*GN* 228). At this point Anna has already written the day "at the beginning of the affair" into the yellow notebook, but the three other passages, all given within *The Golden Notebook,* aren't likewise placed within *The Shadow of the Third.* Instead, the second full day, "towards the end," is the September 17, 1954, entry in the blue notebook (331–68). The moment of "cooking for Michael" occurs within it, but the phrase "while she waits" ironically shifts in meaning from pleasurable anticipation to watchful despair as Anna waits for a man who will not arrive: "All the kitchen is full of good cooking smells; and all at once I am happy, so happy I can feel the warmth of it through my whole body. Then there is a cold feeling in my stomach, and I think: Being happy is a lie, it's a habit of happiness from moments like these during the last four years" (364). The intimate moment of "waking in the morning" is recorded just three weeks earlier on August 28, 1954, in the red, political notebook Anna titles *The British Communist Party* (153). The passage begins, "But this morning when Michael woke in my arms he opened his eyes and smiled at me," and poignantly contains Anna's most joyous writing: ". . . now when happiness floods right through me like being flooded over with warm glittering blue water, I can't believe it" (299). The essential moments showing Anna's love for Michael thus are placed within three different notebooks—yellow, blue, red. Part of what is hidden within complex form is the cruel factor of time: less than three weeks before the end of the affair, Anna had written of her happiness, "The truth is I don't care a damn about politics or philosophy or anything else, all I care about is that Michael should turn in the dark and put his face against my breasts" (299). The emotional center of this novel about "breakdown" is the devastating effect of a sudden breakup between two lovers upon the woman. Anna says of her novel about Paul and Ella, "the form is a kind of pain" (*GN* 228); the same is true of the larger novel about Anna.

### "Making the Personal General"

A final technique for concealing the self is to place it within the context of larger humanity, in a sense, to hide in the crowd. As Anna is aware, many create for themselves alone; ashamed of her novel on suicide, Ella "could not see what good it would do anyone to read a novel of this kind. Yet she . . . continued to write the novel, making excuses such as: 'Well, there's no need to get it published, I'll just write it for myself'" (*GN* 174). Yet writing in that way may be cowardice, Tommy harshly suggests to the Anna character in *Free Women* (*GN* 39). Moreover, one can get over that shame by seeing the self from a new perspective, as Lessing noted in her 1971 preface to *The Golden Notebook:* "At last I understood that the way over, or through this dilemma, the unease at writing about 'petty personal problems' was to recognise that nothing is personal, in the sense that it is uniquely one's own. . . . The way to deal with the problem of 'subjectivity,' that shocking business of being preoccupied with the tiny individual . . . is to see him as a microcosm and in this way to break through the personal, the subjective, making the personal general . . ." (xiii).

Anna knows more after writing than she has allowed herself to know before, we might note before turning from this compendium of techniques for altering "the truth" to Lessing's commentary on the author-character relationship. But her painful discoveries scarcely seem to be the wish fulfillment described by Freud. Instead they seem to be a means—deliberately undertaken and courageously pursued—to continue writing, a means resulting also in personal understanding and growth.

When Lessing discusses the relationship between writer and fictional character, she frequently is talking about a more immediate kinship than that implied in Woolf's writing. Woolf obviously drew upon her own life, but when she remembered Thoby upon the completion of *The Waves* it was 1931, a quarter-century after his death. Lessing's Anna allows a shorter lapse of time between experience and word: "I came upstairs from the scene between Tommy and Molly," she writes, "and instantly began to turn it into a short story" (*GN* 228). For Anna, the self serves as an immediate starting point for creation. Showing herself to be aware of pronoun shifting, Anna nonetheless insists upon a separation between herself and her arguably autobiographical fictional character: "I Anna, see Ella. Who is, of course, Anna. But that is the point, for she is not" (*GN* 459). Name change may itself engender character, as indicated when Anna focuses directly on creation: "The moment I, Anna, write: Ella rings up Julia to announce, etc., then Ella floats away from me and becomes someone else. I don't understand what happens at the moment Ella separates herself from me and becomes Ella. No one does. It's enough to call her Ella, instead of Anna" (459). Anna explores the elaboration of character and choice of fictional name, seemingly without being aware of similarities in the words *Anna* and *Ella,* recalling how she observed a party guest who was "small, thin, dark—the same physical type" as herself. The party guest named Ella set an exact limit to her level of intoxication, a boundary Anna, on the edge of breakdown and all too aware of chaos, might desire. Again insisting on difference, Anna remarks, "Well I would never do that. That's not Anna at all" (*GN* 460).

Lessing considers not only the self as a starting point for creation, but also the creation of an alternative self, at times highly idealized, as a writer's means of growing stronger. She shares this view with Anna, who late in the novel thinks about a new story and wonders, "How, for instance, would it change if I used Ella instead of myself?" Anna begins to apply her fictional character to her own life, "imagining how she would be with Saul—much more intelligent . . . cooler," and eventually realizes she is devising a character "altogether better" than herself:

> For I could positively mark the point where Ella left reality, left how she would, in fact, behave because of her nature; and move into a large generosity of personality impossible to her. But I didn't dislike this new person I was creating; I was thinking that quite possibly these marvellous generous things we walk side by side with in our imaginations could come in existence, simply because we need them, because we imagine them. (*GN* 637)

In an interview given in London, April 23, 1980, Lessing talked about her experience of being "very broken down in various ways" in the years immediately before the publication of *The Golden Notebook:* "When I was in my late thirties and early forties my love life was in a state of chaos and disarray and . . . I was, in fact, and I knew it, in a pretty bad way. Unconsciously I used a certain therapeutic technique which just emerged from my unconscious." Later, from reading, she was able to label her discovery a "Jungian technique": ". . . you take some part of you which is weak and *deliberately* fantasize it strong . . . make it as you would like it to be . . . "(qtd. in Ziegler 203–4, my emphasis).

It is reasonable to assume that the act of creating characters, especially autobiographical characters, among other things allows the author to finalize various versions of the self, as well as to create images of alternate versions of the self, and thereafter to examine them. Here I am building on ideas about human relationships from Mikhail Bakhtin: "What I can see about you that you cannot see about yourself constitutes my surplus with respect to you . . . The surplus allows me to finalize and complete an image of you, to create a finalizing environment in which you are located for me. Whereas my own totality is open and 'my position must change every moment'" (Morson 185). The finalized character may yield new information to the living, mutable self. Lessing's Anna asserts, "Literature is analysis after the event" (*GN* 228), and Anna describes Ella's attitude toward her novel about the suicidal young man as "a passion . . . indulged in solitude . . . like acting out scenes with an invisible alter ego, or carrying on conversation with one's image in the looking glass" (*GN* 175). Such analytical dialogue is to be prized; Bakhtin believes the "essentially aesthetic act of creating such an image of another is most valuable when we seek not to merge with or duplicate each other, but rather to supplement each other, to take full advantage of our special fields of vision" (Morson 185). Lessing's *The Golden Notebook* exploded the form of her novels into a shower of fragments, splinters of the original stuff, and led to her own "prophetic novel," *The Four-Gated City,* and beyond. But *The Golden Notebook* also changed Lessing, who stated in the 1971 introduction, ". . . I was learning as I wrote. . . . The actual time of writing . . . and not only the experiences that had gone into the writing, was really traumatic: it changed me" (*GN* x).

In writing *The Golden Notebook,* Lessing apparently came to terms with sensibility, breakdown, suicidal impulses, and madness—those stereotypical "suicidal lady novelist" characteristics frequently attributed to Woolf. Clearly Lessing did not become visionary on Woolf's terms; *The Four-Gated City* is not a Woolfian visionary novel, for example, and would not fit Woolf's "theory about fiction." But by the time she was writing *The Four-Gated City,* Lessing had newly become—on her own terms—visionary and prophetic.

Following *The Golden Notebook,* Lessing wrote frequently of madness, a theme that had not entered her earlier, realistic novels.[20] After Anna came a stream of characters who are "mad"; Lynda Coldridge in *The Four-Gated City* is among the most interesting, particularly as Lessing includes her in *Shikasta,* thus connecting the ten novels of her two great cycles, *Children of Violence* and *Canopus in Argos.* Lynda characteristically hears "voices"; it is natural to speculate on their kinship to the voices heard by Woolf. Woolf feared them, as after she had concluded *The Waves:* "I wrote the words O Death fifteen minutes ago, having reeled across the last ten pages with some moments of such intensity and intoxication that I seemed only to stumble after my own voice or, almost, after some sort of speaker (as when I was mad); I was almost afraid, remembering the voices that used to fly ahead" (*AWD* 161). For Woolf, the voices signalled madness, and her fear of them was great enough to have been instrumental in her choosing death: "I feel certain I am going mad again. . . . I begin to hear voices, and I can't concentrate. So I am doing what seems the best thing to do" (qtd. in Bell 226).

Lessing, however, after decades of writing about madness, takes an experimental, even practical point of view of such "voices." Her characters matter-of-factly discuss the technical difficulties of hearing voices, as Lynda Coldridge does when she describes the accidental first telepathic contact with George Sherban: "I thought it was my own mind talking to me. . . . I know that one's own mind can say all kinds of things. You think it is someone else but it isn't, it is you" (*S* 351).[21] And significantly in Lessing, characters who hear voices are valued. Johor, for example, places this sympathetic assessment of Lynda Coldridge in the Canopean archives; the passage interestingly calls to mind the early death of Julia Stephen when Woolf was thirteen:

> She undertook to risk her sanity—in a time when more and more people become mad, or live on the edges of madness, or . . . can expect to "break down" several times in a life—in order to explore those areas calmly and chart them, for the benefit of others. This was more than she was able to sustain. She had to undergo more and worse pressures than we expected, due to the early death of her mother. Some individuals near her have learned from her as to the possibilities and risks and lessons of mental imbalance. . . (*S* 178).

Significantly, Lynda Coldridge does not contemplate suicide because she hears voices. After *The Golden Notebook,* "madness" is largely disassociated from suicidal impulses in Lessing's work.

Similar in their disinclination to follow Freud in his thinking about creativity, Virginia Woolf and Doris Lessing explore and chart the topography of the mind not from the point of view of illness, but from practical professionalism and intellectual curiosity. "At forty I am beginning to learn the mechanism of my own brain—how to get the greatest amount of pleasure and work out of it," Woolf wrote in 1922 (*AWD* 58). Sounding like Woolf in "The Narrow Bridge of Art" (1927), Lessing stated in a 1969 interview: "What interests me more than anything is how our minds are changing, how our ways of perceiving reality are changing. . . . Inevitably the mind changes" (qtd. in Raskin, *SPV* 66).

— ♦ —

Virginia Woolf and Doris Lessing resemble each other in their abundant creativity, a prolific energy seen in artists such as Picasso and Stravinsky.[22] Just as we watch, for example, Picasso move through his blue and rose periods, in and out of various classic periods, through analytic and synthetic cubism and so on, so too we watch Woolf and Lessing move through successive identifiable periods, radically changing the form of their art. They do this while fully intending to experiment and explore. The "leap into the air" and into the unknown for each of them is made consciously and, I believe, courageously.

As Woolf wrote in the summer of 1934, her experimentation was deliberate: "I have to some extent *forced myself* to break every mould and find a fresh form of being, that is, or expression, for everything I feel or think" (*AWD* 206, emphasis mine). After her experimentation in *Jacob's Room,* she delighted in her discovery of psychological "tunnelling" in *Mrs. Dalloway.* She refined her new techniques in *To the Lighthouse,* and experimented further by giving in "Time Passes" an "empty house, no people's characters, the passage of time, all eyeless and featureless with nothing to cling to" (*AWD* 91). Deliberately gathering material for the form of a new kind of novel, she listed in "The Narrow Bridge of Art" characteristics of "this book . . . we see on the horizon" and later embodied them in *The Waves* (*CE* 2: 224), a "novel of vision" I believe to represent a major creative breakthrough of the sort discussed by Howard Gardner in *Creating Minds* (1993). Woolf's work on her aborted but remarkable experimental "Essay-Novel" originally titled *The Pargiters* (published as *The Years* and *Three Guineas*) should be mentioned in this list, as well as her experiments with various levels of being in *Between the Acts.* Further, neither *Flush* nor *Orlando* can be considered staidly ordinary. As Woolf declared in her journal, "it's useless to repeat my old experiments; they must be new to be experiments" (*AWD* 263).[23]

Although Lessing began conservatively, writing novels to fit the mold of the realistic nineteenth-century bildungsroman, she has been energetic in her experimentation since publication of *The Golden Notebook*. Lacking a writer's diary or anything resembling Woolf's journal for Lessing herself, we find she has presented similar kinds of information in her interviews. "I've had *Children of Violence* set up for twenty years," she remarked in 1969; "By the time I wrote the last volume [*The Four-Gated City*] I'd put myself into a damned cage, but it's probably better now that I've heaved the rules out. I'm very proud of the form of *The Golden Notebook*" (qtd. in Raskin, *SPV* 65). In 1982, she was ruefully proud of *Shikasta,* her most recent novel: "*Shikasta* is a mess, but at any rate it is a new mess." Asked whether art wasn't always reductive, Lessing responded, "Yes it is, but that is why we are all breaking the form, we have to break it" (qtd. in Ziegler 204). Woolf, of course, used similar language in her journals: "Here in *Here and Now* [*The Years*] I am breaking the mould made by *The Waves*" (*AWD* 206).

In 1986, Lessing was even more ambitious, stating, "But what I'm interested in, you see, is breaking down these forms that we set up for ourselves—you know, you have to have a novel, and there's a poem there, and a short story there, and there's an essay there. . . . I would like to have another shot at a work—I'm thinking about it now as a novel—which would have all these different things in it" (qtd. in Gray 335). In Lessing's desire for inclusiveness, for a poem-novel-essay containing "all these different things," her words may recall for some readers both Woolf's remarks about her "Essay-Novel, called *The Pargiters*" that "it's to take in everything" (*AWD* 179) and her comment about *The Waves:* "Why admit anything to literature that is not poetry—by which I mean saturated? . . . I want to put practically everything in . . ." (*AWD* 136). Here I am suggesting not influence—although there may be a little of that too—but a similarity in the marked boldness of the creative impulse in both Woolf and Lessing.

Such creativity has its dangers, isolation among them. "What it means I myself shan't know till I write another book," Woolf declared after completing *The Waves*. "And I'm the hare, a long way ahead of the hounds my critics" (166). Lessing too at times has left all but the most dogged critics behind; few in recent years, for example, have managed comfortably both her move back to the social realism of *The Diaries of Jane Somers* and the move into the future of her "space fiction" in *Canopus in Argos*.

Both novelists were aware that their respective novels, *The Waves* and *The Golden Notebook,* were beyond the immediate comprehension of reviewers and literary critics. On October 5, 1931, just after reviews of *The Waves* had appeared, Woolf wrote in her journal: ". . . if the W. is anything it is an adventure which I go on alone; . . . but Lord, how far away I become from all this; . . . I wonder if it is good to feel this remoteness—that is, that *The Waves* is not what they say" (*AWD* 167). Eight years after publication, in her preface to the 1971 edition, Lessing still felt it necessary to explain the structure and major ideas of *The Golden Notebook*. Asserting the novel was about "breakdown," she remarked, "But nobody so much as noticed this central theme . . ." (*GN* viii). Like Woolf, she too expressed a momentary acceptance of being alone: "why should there be anyone else who comprehends what [the writer] is trying to do? After all, there is only one person spinning that particular cocoon, only one person whose business it is to spin it" (*GN* xv).

But isolation is not the only danger, especially when the experiment proves successful. As Lessing dryly observed in 1984, "the main problem of some writers is that most reviewers and readers want you to go on writing the same book" (*DJS* xi). Giving them some of what they wished, "preferably *The Golden Notebook* over again," Lessing tested the entire publishing establishment by bringing out two realistic novels, first *The Diary of a Good Neighbour* and then *If the Old Could* . . . under the pseudonym Jane Somers, in effect publishing anonymously. She wished, she said, to "get free of that cage of associations and labels that every established writer has to learn to live inside" (*DJS* vii). Less publicly, Woolf at fifty took up her own defiant stance of anonymity in a personal manifesto: "I will not be 'famous,' 'great.' I will go on adventuring, changing, opening my mind and my eyes, refusing to be stamped and stereotyped. The thing is to free one's self: to let it find its dimensions, not be impeded" (*AWD* 200). She wished, she said, "to adventure and discover and allow no rigid poses: to be supple and naked to the truth" (*AWD* 214), and she fashioned a "philosophy of anonymity" often signaled by a tag refrain she quoted to remind herself to be heedless of critics and to bolster her courage: "What care I for my goosefeather bed. I'm off to join the raggle taggle gipsies, oh!" (*AWD* 180, 257). The "philosophy" is variously identified by references to "last winter's revelation" (*AWD* 200), "my revelation two years ago" (*AWD* 214), and "that spiritual conversion . . . in the autumn of 1933 or 4" (*AWD* 271), and it concerns her relationship to both her public and the critics. In October 1933, she sent off an angry letter inviting fellow writers to "take an oath not to . . . give interviews; not to give autographs; not to attend public dinners; not to speak in public; not to see unknown admirers provided with letters of introduction from friends—and so on, and so on" ("The Protection of Privacy" 511); the day after the letter was published in *The New Statesman and Nation,* Woolf called it "the crude public statement of a part of [the 'philosophy of anonymity']" (*AWD* 200). By 1938, her lightheartedly defiant imagery of herself as "the hare" pursued by "the hounds my critics" (*AWD* 166) had become harsher as, reminding herself of the "spiritual conversion," she again proclaimed her philosophy: "I can take my way: *experiment with my own imagination in my own way.* The pack may howl, but it shall never catch me. And even if the pack—reviewers, friends, enemies—pays me no attention or sneers, still I'm free" (*AWD* 271, emphasis mine).

What is important here is that Woolf's philosophical stance and Lessing's experiment in publishing express the novelists' own tough independence at a point in their lives when they might have settled back into cultivating their growing literary reputations, meeting critics' expectations for repetitive "masterpieces," and enjoying the intellectual quietude of fame. In their energetic refusal to rest unchanged, both novelists fit Ella's description of "people who deliberately try to be something else, try to break their own form as it were" (*GN* 466). Clearly, in both Woolf and Lessing, a willingness to "break the mould" of the novel is linked to a willingness to experiment boldly within their own lives. In each case, what is required is creativity and courage.

—◆—

"A mangrove island turns drift to dance," Annie Dillard writes at the end of "Sojourner" (152). Her metaphor, appropriated to our use, suggests a view of creativity as both dynamic and joyous.

In opposition both to the popularized Romantic view, still pervasive today, of creativity as passive reception of a "moment of inspiration" and also in opposition to the Freudian view, dominant in this century, of an inherently passive creativity based on unfulfilled wishes welling up unbidden from the unconscious, this essay has asserted that creativity is dynamic. It has also opposed the Freudian view as popularized of creativity as "sick," as neurotic, asserting instead that creativity is a normal, healthy human activity requiring deliberate choice and courage.

In "A Lesson in Floating," Morley urges:

> But try it:
>> learn to
> immerse yourself in strangeness
> (13)

Interestingly, the "strangeness" or unfamiliar element in writing *The Waves* and *The Golden Notebook* differed. In writing *The Waves,* Woolf sought a form by which to contain her vision, while for *The Golden Notebook* Lessing early constructed a fixed form and later expressed her sense of strangeness in her novel's content. In *The Golden Notebook*, Lessing provides valuable informa-tion about the relationship between the writer and her work, demonstrating techniques by which Anna can alter "the truth" enough to use painful personal material within her writing, and showing us how by (re)creating earlier and alternate selves the writer is able to "finalize" those selves and learn from them. What emerges is a view of Anna—the writer—deliberately gaining painful self-knowledge while she continues to write. Creativity is about choice and courage—is, in a word, dynamic.

It may seem perverse to present a view of creativity as joyous in an essay that has had so much to do with breakdown, madness and suicidal impulses. Particularly it may seem odd to talk about creativity as a joy when using Woolf and Lessing as examples. People might grudgingly accept Lessing, noting she at least is a survivor. Although she seemingly is a sober, responsible creator, often serious to a fault, it is not that surprising to find her matter-of-factly remarking about her *Canopus in Argos* novels, "I really enjoy writing them" (qtd. in Gray 338). But Woolf, the same people might object, suffered fearsome difficulties—while writing *The Years,* for exam-ple—in her work; she long had a reputation for illness and eventually committed suicide. Clearly, these people might say, Woolf can offer no support for the view of creativity as joyous.

To this I would respond, with the smallest of samplings, that Woolf's journal is filled with excitement and exuberance and sheer pleasure in creating novels. "I am now galloping over *Mrs. Dalloway* . . . ," she exclaimed; "I can write and write and write now; the happiest feeling in the world" (*AWD* 74). Of *To the Lighthouse* she mused, "I believe I could spin it off with infinite relish" (*AWD* 85), and later wrote in anticipation of the following work: "I shall be off again, feeling that extraordinary exhilaration, that ardour and lust of creation . . ." (*AWD* 106). "I want to kick up my heels and be off," she wrote at the start of *Orlando;* "I think this will be great fun to write" (*AWD* 106). After recording a "state of glory, and calm, and some tears" at the completion of *The Waves,* she exclaimed, "How physical the sense of triumph and relief is!" (*AWD* 161–62). She noted "a queer very happy free feeling" in completing a draft of *The Years* (*AWD* 242), and even at the worst point in writing that novel, when she had not written for two months and had experienced "almost catastrophic illness," she returned to her 600 pages with pleasure: "Oh but the divine joy of being mistress of my mind again! . . . I think I can—I think I can—but must have immense courage" (250). That writers create because they often take joy in it is little remarked, yet not surprising. Mihaly Csikszentmihalyi, known for his research on optimal experience and a state of consciousness he terms "flow," in *The Evolving Self*

(1993) mentions artists with those other adults who "participate in sports, grow gardens, learn to play the guitar, read novels, go to parties, walk through woods" and concludes: "In fact, everyone devotes large chunks of time doing things that are inexplicable unless we assume that the doing is enjoyed for its own sake" (xii).

In presenting a view of dynamic and joyous creativity, this essay has used Virginia Woolf and Doris Lessing for examples, and thus has necessarily looked at these two writers together. Apparently Lessing was directly influenced by Woolf, just as Woolf was directly influenced by Melville. In that *The Waves* originally began as a presentation of the consciousness of a solitary narrator and writer—probably female—it usefully resembles *The Golden Notebook*, and in that *The Golden Notebook* consists of diaries and drafts, it is reminiscent of *A Writer's Diary* and the context of *The Waves*. The two novels are most comparable, however, in being unique and extraordinary achievements; nothing like either of them had ever been published before. Together, Woolf and Lessing may be seen as writers and women possessed of abundant creativity and courage, unusually eager to experiment, and equally determined to "break the mould" of the novel and to "break the form" of their lives.

---

NOTES

1. See Briggs 82, 274, 286; Ghiselin 44–45, 84–85; Perkins 9–10. Mozart allegedly wrote a letter stating of his own musical ideas, "*Whence* and *how* they come, I know not; nor can I force them. . . . the whole, though it be long, stands almost complete and finished in my mind, so that I can survey it . . . at a glance." The authorship of the famous letter is now disputed (Weisberg 46).
2. As early as 1953, the strict accuracy of Coleridge's account was disputed by E. Schneider in *Coleridge, Opium, and Kubla Khan* (Chicago: University of Chicago Press, 1953). Even earlier, in a classic study, *The Road to Xanadu* (Boston: Houghton Mifflin, 1927), J. L. Lowes showed how images for both "Kubla Khan" and "The Ancient Mariner" had originated in Coleridge's extensive reading.
3. Passive receptivity is characteristically apparent in the quintessential image for Romantic inspiration, the eolian harp, an instrument of delicate strings within a wooden frame, hung in a tree or—as in Coleridge's poem "The Eolian Harp"—under the casement to be played upon by the wind.
4. Among those opposed to Freud on this matter is Bakhtin, who believed creativity to be a normal, healthy human characteristic, as shown in this summary of his ideas by Gary Morson and Caryl Emerson:

> To see creativity only as a kind of redirected unhappiness or a
> healthful use of a potential pathology, Bakhtin intimates, is to
> misunderstand the very nature of human experience and daily
> activity.
>     Of course, some creativity may indeed be "Freudian." But
> according to Bakhtin, creativity is as a rule positive, conscious,
> and the result of work undertaken by the whole personality.
> (187)

5. I have deliberately chosen in this essay to use only materials from
   Woolf's journals available from 1953 onward, thus all references are to
   Leonard Woolf's edition of *A Writer's Diary*, rather than to Anne Olivier
   Bell's edition of *The Diary of Virginia Woolf*, the first volume of which
   appeared much later (New York and London: Harcourt, 1977).

6. The phrase "Oi, oi, oi!" is associated with a fat man gesticulating in this
   scene, as Martin thinks, "There wouldn't be much justice or liberty for
   the likes of him if the fat man had his way—or beauty either" (*TY* 241),
   and thus with Mussolini, for there is the "usual evening paper's picture
   of a fat man gesticulating" in the "Present Day" of 1937: "'Damned—'
   Eleanor shot out suddenly, 'bully!' She tore the paper across with one
   sweep of her hand and flung it on the floor" (*TY* 330). Lessing similarly
   associates the phrase with the origins of war, and her machine-gun
   imagery becomes more and more deadly, as Anna "knew, but really
   knew, how war waited"; see *GN* 628–29.

7. Woolf's examination of the problem of the "purple patch" can be seen
   most clearly in "Impassioned Prose," an essay on de Quincey first
   published in *Times Literary Supplement* on September 16, 1926 (and
   thus closely coinciding in time with Woolf's vision of the "fin passing
   far out"), and in "The Narrow Bridge of Art," first published in the *New
   York Herald Tribune* on August 14, 1927, where she noted that "the
   objection to the purple patch . . . is not that it is purple but that it is a
   patch" (*CE* 2: 226).

8. Autobiographical elements exist in each novel, more obviously in *The
   Waves*; for example, Woolf gives over to Rhoda her own childhood
   experience, significantly recalled when recording her vision of the "fin
   passing far out," of not being able to cross a puddle (*AWD* 103; *TW* 219,
   285). But Lessing similarly uses selected experiences from her own life
   in *The Golden Notebook*, suggesting that Mrs. Marks/Mother Sugar
   resembles her own psychotherapist (qtd. in Raskin 68), that the
   Mashopi hotel and the Boothbys have their origins in real life (*AL* 76),
   and that her own "love life" was difficult close to the time she was
   recording the difficulties of Anna and Ella (qtd. in Ziegler 203). Writers
   do this, of course, and I am not here attempting to argue that *The Waves*
   and *The Golden Notebook* are autobiographical novels.

9. There is an elusive, even haunting correspondence between Bernard's
   "lady [who] sits between the two long windows, writing" (*TW* 186), the
   female writer at the start of the manuscript of *The Waves*, the "I" of "The

Death of the Moth" who sits looking out of the window, pencil in hand (CE 1: 360–61), and Woolf herself, writing near the long windows of Rodmell. The images of the lady writing and the gardeners who inexorably "sweep the lawn with giant brooms" together, with their intimations of creation/origin and death, seem Woolf's personal evocation of the fates, and when Bernard remembers them as an old man, they direct his thoughts toward what is "beyond and outside," "symbolic, and thus perhaps permanent" (TW 349). They have been interpreted differently, and recently Jane Marcus has suggested the lady is a "Britannia figure" ("Britannia" 230–31); however, the lady writing seems rather the author of Bernard's origins, the gardeners sweeping a grim reminder that human life is as fleeting as that of grass. With childish prescience, Bernard warns Susan, "if the gardeners saw us they would shoot us" (TW 186).

10. Just as the solitary narrator, the old woman telling over to herself the story of the world, has disappeared (except for Bernard's Elvedonian "vision") from the published text of The Waves and now remains outside it, so too the "Anna" who wrote the various manuscripts which appear in Lessing's The Golden Notebook is outside the novel. She may or may not have edited the compilation of manuscripts that make up the novel; the uncertainty of the tone of the objective remarks suggest not, but we can't know for sure: "then a title appeared, as if Anna had, almost automatically, divided herself into four . . ." (55); "The yellow notebook looked like the manuscript of a novel, for it was called The Shadow of the Third. It certainly began like a novel" (169). See Rubenstein (103–7) and Hite (Other 97–99).

11. It is worth noting that this radical shift from one kind of novel to another is foreshadowed by Woolf's statement in November 1929 that she "[felt] a cleavage" although she believed also there was "something there" (AWD 145).

12. The essays most valuable for this purpose are "Defoe," "Jane Eyre and Wuthering Heights," "On Not Knowing Greek," "Notes on an Elizabethan Play," "Robinson Crusoe," "On Being Ill," "Impassioned Prose," "How Should One Read a Book?" "The Narrow Bridge of Art," "Is Fiction an Art?" "Life and the Novelist," "The Novels of E. M. Forster," "Thomas Hardy's Novels," "The Novels of George Meredith," "The Sun and the Fish," and "Phases of Fiction." For a thorough discussion of the origins of Woolf's "theory about fiction" and its relationship to the origin of The Waves, see Tobin 22–125.

13. Woolf published a review of E. M. Forster's Aspects of the Novel on October 16, 1927, called "Is Fiction an Art?" and a revised version called "The Art of Fiction" on November 12, 1927. An interesting exchange of letters between E. M. Forster and Woolf resulted (Bell, 2: 134); see also Tobin 65–68.

14. After discussing Emily Brontë in the last section of "Phases of Fiction" as a poet capable of a "master stroke of vision" in Wuthering Heights, Woolf suggests the "same thing happens . . . in Moby Dick" and explains,

In both books we get a vision of presence outside the human beings, of a meaning that they stand for, without ceasing to be themselves. But it is notable that both Emily Brontë and Herman Melville ignore the greater part of those spoils of the modern spirit which Proust grasps so tenaciously and transforms so triumphantly. (CE 2: 96)

15. See Woolf's journal entries for April 29, 1930 (AWD 153); February 2, 1931 (AWD 159–60); February 7, 1931 (AWD 161–62); July 17, 1931 (AWD 165); October 5, 1931 (AWD 167).

16. "The Death of the Moth" helps to explain this complex image. In this essay, Woolf indicates that the same "enormous energy of the world" (CE 1: 360) is present alike in fields, in the "lean bare-backed downs," in rooks, horses, and ploughmen, in the many "narrow and intricate corridors in [her] own brain and in those of other human beings," and in the moth (CE 1: 359–60). During the death struggles of the moth, the narrator looks "as if for the enemy" (emphasis mine), but apprehends that the "power was there all the same, massed outside indifferent, impersonal, not attending to anything in particular" (CE 1: 361). In death, the energy that links all living things is withdrawn from the individual; the individual dies. The analogy with the individual wave sinking anonymously back into the sea is clear. Rhoda says, "This is life then to which I am committed. . . . life emerges heaving its dark crest from the sea. It is to this we are attached; it is to this we are bound, as bodies to wild horses" (TW 219).

17. In his introduction to The Writer's Diary, Leonard Woolf stated Woolf "used her diary partly . . . to record what she did and what she thought about people, life, and the universe. But she also . . . communed with herself about the books she was writing or about future books which she intended to write. She discusses the day-to-day problems of plot or form, of character or exposition . . . I have included also . . . other kinds of extract. The first consists of a certain number of passages in which she is obviously using the diary as a method of practising or trying out the art of writing. The second consists of a few passages which, though not directly or indirectly concerned with her writings, . . . give the reader an idea of the direct impact upon her mind of scenes and persons, i.e., of the raw material of her art" (AWD viii–ix).

18. For an early discussion of Freud, romanticism, and creativity, see Lionel Trilling's "Freud and Literature" and "Art and Neurosis" in The Liberal Imagination: Essays on Literature and Society, 1940 (New York: Viking, 1968).

19. Gardner states that "Freud himself confirmed the centrality of this idea in saying, 'The doctrine of repression is the foundation-stone on which the whole structure of psychoanalysis rests'" (65). The next section of this essay assumes the validity of Freud's doctrine of repression.

20. Although outside the scope of this essay, other influences, such as the ideas of R. D. Laing, are also important here.

21.  In Lynda Coldridge's report, Lessing presents the hearing of voices in
     childhood as nothing to be feared (*Shikasta* 181–89).

22.  In *Creating Minds: An Anatomy of Creativity Seen Through the Lives of
     Freud, Einstein, Picasso, Stravinsky, Eliot, Graham, and Gandhi,* Howard
     Gardner recently suggested that each of these great creators experienced
     a "breakthrough" about ten years after they first began to practice their
     art, and a second breakthrough about ten years later. Gardner noted his
     "short list of individuals" is "notable for its absences: Why T. S. Eliot,
     rather than . . . Virginia Woolf?" (5–6). Nonetheless, his theory seems
     to be roughly applicable to the shifts in Woolf, who published her
     psychological "tunnelling" novel *Mrs. Dalloway* nine years after her first
     novel, and her radically new visionary novel *The Waves* eight years later.
     Less true to Gardner's theory, Lessing published *The Golden Notebook* in
     1962, thirteen years after she arrived in London with her first novel.
     *Shikasta*, if for the sake of comparison we take the *Canopus in Argos* series
     as an equivalent breakthrough, was published in 1979.

23.  Compare Picasso's attitude as expressed in these comments: "Don't expect
     me to repeat myself. My past does not interest me any more. . . . I like
     discovery too much" (qtd. in Gardner, 170–71). Gardner notes the "con-
     tinuous evolution" of Picasso's art (180).

# WORKS CITED

## Works By Virginia Woolf

*Between the Acts.* New York: Harcourt, 1941.

*Collected Essays.* 4 vols. New York: Harcourt, 1967.

*Diary of Virginia Woolf.* Ed. Anne Olivier Bell. 5 vols. New York: Harcourt, 1977–1984.

*Jacob's Room and The Waves.* New York: Harcourt, 1959.

*The Letters of Virginia Woolf.* Ed. Nigel Nicolson and Joanne Trautmann. 6 vols. New York: Harcourt, 1975–80.

*To the Lighthouse* (1927). Rpt. New York: Harcourt, 1955, 1989.

"Modern Fiction." *The Common Reader.* First Series. 1925. New York: Harcourt, 1984, 146–54.

*Moments of Being.* Ed. Jeanne Schulkind. New York: Harcourt, 1976. 2nd ed. New York: Harcourt, 1985.

"Mr. Bennett and Mrs. Brown" (1924). Rpt. *The Hogarth Essays.* Ed. Leonard and Virginia Woolf. Freeport: Books for Libraries, 1970, 3–29.

*Mrs. Dalloway* (1925). New York: Harcourt, 1953, 1981, 1990.

"On Freudian Fiction." Review of *An Imperfect Mother* by J. D. Beresford. *Contemporary Writers.* Rpt. London: Hogarth Press, 1965, 152–54.

*Orlando: A Biography* (1928). Rpt. New York: Harcourt, 1956.

"The Protection of Privacy," *The New Statesman and Nation,* October 28, 1933: 511.

*Roger Fry: A Biography* (1940). Rpt. New York: Harcourt, 1968.

*A Room of One's Own* (1929). Rpt. New York: Harcourt, 1957, 1981, 1989.

*The Voyage Out* (1915). Rpt. New York: Harcourt, 1948.

*The Waves* (1931). Rpt. New York: Harcourt, 1977.

*A Writer's Diary: Being Extracts from the Diary of Virginia Woolf.* Ed. Leonard Woolf (1953). Rpt. New York: Signet, 1968.

*The Years* (1937). Rpt. New York: Harcourt, 1965; rpt. London: Panther Books, 1985.


## Works By Doris Lessing

*African Laughter: Four Visits to Zimbabwe.* New York: HarperCollins, 1992.

"All Seething Underneath." *Vogue* (February 15, 1964): 80–81, 132–33.

"Among the Roses." *The Real Thing: Stories and Sketches.* New York: HarperCollins, 1992, 117–24.

*Briefing for a Descent into Hell.* New York: Knopf, 1971; rpt. New York: Bantam, 1972; rpt. New York: Vintage, 1981.

"The De Wets Come to Kloof Grange." *African Stories.* New York: Random House, 1964, 103–28.

*The Diaries of Jane Somers.* New York: Vintage, 1984.

"Flavours of Exile." *African Stories.* New York: Random House, 1964, 547–54.

*The Four-Gated City* (1969). (Vol. 5 of *Children of Violence.*) Rpt. New York: Bantam, 1970.

*Going Home* (1957). New York: Ballantine, 1968.

*The Golden Notebook* (1962). Rpt. New York: Ballantine, 1972; rpt. New York: Bantam, 1973.

"Impertinent Daughters." *Granta,* Vol. 14 (Winter 1984): 51–68.

*Landlocked* (1965). (Vol. 4 of *Children of Violence.*) New York: NAL, 1970.

"Language and the Lunatic Fringe." *The New York Times,* June 26, 1992, A19.

*The Marriages Between Zones Three, Four, and Five.* New York: Knopf 1980. Rpt. Vintage, 1981.

*Martha Quest.* (Vol. 1 of *Children of Violence.*) New York: Simon and Schuster, 1964.

*The Memoirs of a Survivor* (1975). Rpt. New York: Bantam, 1979.

"My Mother's Life." *Granta,* Vol. 17 (Fall 1985): 227–38.

*A Proper Marriage* (1951). Rpt. in *Children of Violence,* Vol. 1. New York: Simon and Schuster, 1964. Rpt. in *Children of Violence,* Vol. 2. New York: NAL, 1970.

*Re: Colonised Planet 5: Shikasta.* New York: Alfred A. Knopf, 1979.

*A Small Personal Voice: Essays, Reviews, Interviews.* Ed. and intro. Paul Schlueter. New York: Vintage, 1975.

*The Summer Before the Dark* (1973). New York: Bantam, 1974.

"What Really Matters" (with David Storey). *Twentieth Century* 172 (Autumn 1963): 96–98.

## General Critical Works

Abel, Elizabeth. *Virginia Woolf and the Fictions of Psychoanalysis.* Chicago: University of Chicago Press, 1989.

Allen, Orphia Jane. "Interpreting 'Flavours of Exile.'" *Doris Lessing Newsletter* 7, no. 1 (Summer 1983): 8, 12.

Apter, T. E. *Virginia Woolf: A Study of Her Novels.* New York: New York University Press, 1979.

Arthur, Marilyn. "Politics and Pomegranates: An Interpretation of the Homeric Hymn to Demeter." *Arethusa* 10 (1977): 7–47.

Athanassakis, Apostolos N. *The Homeric Hymns.* Baltimore: Johns Hopkins University Press, 1976.

Auerbach, Erich. "The Brown Stocking." In *Mimesis: The Representation of Reality in Western Literature,* trans. Willard R. Trask (Princeton: Princeton University Press, 1953). Rpt. in Claire Sprague, ed. *Virginia Woolf: A Collection of Critical Essays.* Englewood Cliffs, N.J.: Prentice-Hall, 1971, 70–89.

Bakhtin, M. M. *The Dialogic Imagination,* ed. Michael Holquist. Austin: University of Texas Press, 1981.

————.*Problems of Dostoevsky's Poetics,* ed. and trans. Caryl Emerson. Minneapolis: University of Minnesota Press, 1984.

Barrett, Eileen. "Matriarchal Myth on a Patriarchal Stage: Virginia Woolf's *Between the Acts.*" *Twentieth Century Literature* 33, no. 1 (Spring 1987): 18–37.

Bassoff, Evelyn Silten. *Mothering Ourselves: Help and Healing for Adult Daughters.* New York: Dutton, 1991.

Bauer, Dale M., and S. Jaret McKinstry, eds. *Feminism, Bakhtin, and the Dialogic.* Albany: State University of New York Press, 1991.

Bazin, Nancy Topping. *Virginia Woolf and the Androgynous Vision.* New Brunswick, N.J.: Rutgers University Press, 1973.

Beattie, Thomas C. "Moments of Meaning Dearly Achieved: Virginia Woolf's Sense of an Ending." *Modern Fiction Studies* 32, no. 4 (1984): 521–41.

Bell, Quentin. *Virginia Woolf: A Biography.* New York: Harcourt, 1972.

Berman, Jeffrey. *The Talking Cure: Literary Representations of Psychoanalysis.* New York: New York University Press, 1985.

Bertelsen, Eve. "Interview with Doris Lessing." In *Doris Lessing,* ed. Eve Bertelsen. Johannesburg: McGraw-Hill, 1985, 93–118.

Bevis, William. *Mind of Winter.* Pittsburgh: University of Pittsburgh Press, 1988.

Blotner, Joseph L. "Mythic Patterns in *To the Lighthouse.*" *PMLA* 71 (1956): 547–62. Rpt. in *Myth and Literature: Contemporary Theory and Practice,* ed. John B. Vickery. Lincoln: University of Nebraska Press, 1966. 243–55.

Briggs, John. *Fire in the Crucible: The Self-Creation of Creativity and Genius.* Los Angeles: Tarcher, 1990.

Brownstein, Marilyn L. "Postmodern Language and the Perpetuation of Desire." *Twentieth Century Literature* 31 (1985): 73–88.

Budhos, Shirley. *The Theme of Enclosure in Selected Works of Doris Lessing.* Troy, N.Y.: Whitston, 1987.

Caramagno, Thomas C. *The Flight of the Mind: Virginia Woolf's Art and Manic-Depressive Illness.* Berkeley: University of California Press, 1992.

Caughie, Pamela. *Virginia Woolf and Postmodernism: Literature in Quest and Question of Itself.* Chicago: University of Illinois Press, 1991.

Caws, Mary Ann. *Women of Bloomsbury: Virginia, Vanessa and Carrington.* New York: Routledge, 1991.

Chabran, Myrtha. "Puerto Rican Poet: Julia de Burgos: A Bridge to My Mother and a Prism on My Past." *MS* 12 (1984): 22–24, 29.

Chodorow, Nancy. *The Reproduction of Mothering: Psychoanalysis and the Sociology of Gender.* Berkeley: University of California Press, 1978.

Chown, Linda. *Narrative Authority and Homeostasis in the Novels of Doris Lessing and Carmen Martin Gaite.* New York: Garland, 1990.

Cohen, Mary. "Out of the Chaos, a New Kind of Strength: Doris Lessing's *The Golden Notebook.*" *The Authority of Experience,* ed. Arlyn Diamond and Lee R. Edwards. Amherst, Mass.: University of Massachusetts Press, 1977, 178–93.

Coleridge, Samuel. *The Poems of Samuel Taylor Coleridge,* ed. Ernest Hartley Coleridge (1912). Rpt. London: Oxford University Press, 1961.

Collins, Patricia Hill. *Black Feminist Thought: Knowledge, Consciousness and the Politics of Empowerment.* New York: Routledge, 1990.

Cook, Blanche Wiesen. "'Women Alone Stir My Imagination': Lesbianism and the Cultural Tradition." *Signs* 4, no. 4 (1979): 718–39.

Coover, Robert. "The End of Books," *New York Times Book Review,* June 21, 1991, 1, 23–25.

Corbin, Henry. *The Man of Light in Iranian Sufism,* trans. Nancy Pearson. Boulder, Colo.: Shambhala, 1978.

Cramer, Patricia. "Notes from Underground: Lesbian Ritual in the Writings of Virginia Woolf." *Virginia Woolf Miscellanies: Proceedings of the First Annual Conference on Virginia Woolf,* ed. Mark Hussey and Vara Neverow-Turk. Lanham, Md.: University Press of America, 1992.

Csikszentmihalyi, Mihaly. *The Evolving Self: A Psychology for the Third Millennium.* New York: HarperCollins, 1993.

Derrida, Jacques. "Structure, Sign, and Play in the Discourse of the Human Sciences." *The Structuralist Controversy,* ed. Richard Macksey and Eugenio Donato. Baltimore: Johns Hopkins University Press, 1972, 247–72.

DeSalvo, Louise A. *Virginia Woolf: The Impact of Childhood Sexual Abuse on Her Life and Work.* Boston: Beacon Press, 1989; New York: Ballantine, 1990.

———. *Virginia Woolf's First Voyage: A Novel in the Making.* Totowa, N.J.: Rowman and Littlefield, 1980.

Dillard, Annie. "Sojourner." In *Teaching a Stone to Talk: Expeditions and Encounters.* New York: Harper, 1982.

Donovan, Josephine. "Style and Power." In *Feminism, Bakhtin, and the Dialogic.* Albany: State University of New York Press, 1991, 85–94.

Drabble, Margaret. "Mimesis: The Representation of Reality in the Post-War British Novel." *Mosaic* 20, no. 1 (Winter 1987): 1–14.

Draine, Betsy. *Substance Under Pressure: Artistic Coherence and Evolving Form in the Novels of Doris Lessing.* Madison: University of Wisconsin Press, 1983.

Driver, C. J. "Profile 8: Doris Lessing." *The New Review* 1, no. 8 (November 1984): 17–23.

DuPlessis, Rachel Blau. *Writing Beyond the Ending: Narrative Strategies of Twentieth-Century Women Writers.* Bloomington: Indiana University Press, 1985.

Emery, Mary Lou. "'Robbed of Meaning': The Work at the Center of *To the Lighthouse.*" *Modern Fiction Studies* 38, no. 1 (1992): 217–33. Virginia Woolf Special Issue.

Ezergailis, Inta. *Women Writers: The Divided Self.* Bonn: Bouvier Verlag Herbert Grundmann, 1982.

Fishburn, Katherine. "The Nightmare Repetition: The Mother-Daughter Conflict in Doris Lessing's *Children of Violence.*" In *The Lost Tradition: Mothers and*

*Daughters in Literature,* ed. Cathy N. Davidson and E. M. Broner. New York: Ungar, 1980, 207–16.

Fleishman, Avrom. *Virginia Woolf: A Critical Reading.* Baltimore: Johns Hopkins University Press, 1975.

Foley, Helene P., ed. *The Homeric Hymn to Demeter: Translation, Commentary, and Interpretive Essays.* Princeton: Princeton University Press, 1994.

Freud, Sigmund. "Creative Writers and Daydreaming" (Der Dichter und Das Phantasieren). *The Standard Edition of the Complete Psychological Works of Sigmund Freud,* vol. 9, trans. James Strachey and Anna Freud (1959). Rpt. London: Hogarth, 1968, 142–53.

Friedman, Susan Stanford. "Lyric Subversion of Narrative in Women's Writing: Virginia Woolf and the Tyranny of Plot." *Reading Narrative: Form, Ethics, Ideology,* ed. James Phelan. Columbus: Ohio State University Press, 1989, 162–85.

Froula, Christine. "Out of the Chrysalis: Female Initiation and Female Authority in Virginia Woolf's *The Voyage Out.*" *Tulsa Studies in Women's Literature* 5, no. 1 (Spring 1986): 63–90.

Gardiner, Judith Kegan. "The Exhilaration of Exile: Rhys, Stead, and Lessing." *Women's Writing in Exile,* ed. Mary Lynn Broe and Angela Ingram. Chapel Hill: University of North Carolina Press, 1989, 133–50.

———. *Rhys, Stead, Lessing and the Politics of Empathy.* Bloomington: Indiana University Press, 1989.

Gardner, Howard. *Creating Minds: An Anatomy of Creativity Seen Through the Lives of Freud, Einstein, Picasso, Stravinsky, Eliot, Graham, and Gandhi.* New York: Basic Books, 1993.

Garvey, Johanna X. K. "Difference and Continuity: The Voices of *Mrs. Dalloway.*" *College English* 53, no. 1 (January 1991): 59–76.

Gelfant, Blanche. *The American City Novel.* Norman: University of Oklahoma Press, 1954.

Ghiselin, Brewster, ed. *The Creative Process.* New York: New American (Mentor), 1952.

Gillespie, Diane Filby. *The Sisters' Arts: The Writing and Painting of Virginia Woolf and Vanessa Bell.* Syracuse: Syracuse University Press, 1988, 1991.

———, ed. *The Multiple Muses of Virginia Woolf.* Columbia: University of Missouri Press, 1993.

Gray, Stephen. "An Interview with Doris Lessing." *Research in African Literature* 17 (1986): 329–40.

Greene, Gayle. "Feminist Fiction and the Uses of Memory." *Signs: Journal of Women in Culture and Society* 16, no. 1 (Winter 1991): 290–321.

Gubar, Susan. "Mother, Maiden and the Marriage of Death: Women Writers and an Ancient Myth." *Women's Studies* 6 (1979): 301–15.

Guiguet, Jean. *Virginia Woolf and Her Works,* trans. Jean Stewart. New York: Harcourt, 1966.

Heilbrun, Carolyn G. *Hamlet's Mother and Other Women.* New York: Columbia University Press, 1990.

Herman, Judith Lewis. *Trauma and Recovery.* New York: Basic Books, 1992.

Herman, William. "Virginia Woolf and the Classics: Every Englishman's Prerogative Transmuted into Fictional Art." *Virginia Woolf: Centennial Essays,* ed. Elaine K. Ginsberg and Laura Moss Gottlieb. Troy, N.Y.: Whitston, 1983, 257–68.

Herrera, Hayden. "Surrounding Art with Language." (Review of Octavio Paz's *Essays on Mexican Art,* trans. Helen Lane. New York: Harcourt, 1993) *The New York Times Book Review,* May 30, 1993, 23.

Hirsch, Marianne. *The Mother/Daughter Plot: Narrative, Psychoanalysis, Feminism.* Bloomington: Indiana University Press, 1989.

Hite, Molly. "(En)Gendering Metafiction: Doris Lessing's Rehearsals for *The Golden Notebook.*" *Modern Fiction Studies* 34 (1988): 483–500.

———. *The Other Side of the Story: Structures and Strategies of Contemporary Feminist Narrative.* Ithaca, N.Y.: Cornell University Press, 1989.

Hoffman, Anne Golomb. "Demeter and Poseidon: Fusion and Distance in *To the Lighthouse.*" *Studies in the Novel* 16, no. 2 (Summer 1984): 182–96.

Hoffman, Charles G. "From Short Story to Novel: The Manuscript Revisions of Virginia Woolf's *Mrs. Dalloway.*" *Modern Fiction Studies* 14 (Summer 1968): 171–86.

Hofstadter, Douglas R. Cited in *Science News* 142, no. 21 (1992): 347.

Hooks, Susan Luck. "Woman as Spiritual Force: *To the Lighthouse.*" Paper presented at Western Kentucky University Women's Studies Conference, Bowling Green, Kentucky, September 24, 1992.

Hutcheon, Linda. *A Poetics of Postmodernism: History, Theory, Fiction.* New York: Routledge, 1988.

Huyssen, Andreas. "Mapping the Postmodern" (1984). In *After the Great Divide: Modernism, Mass Culture, Postmodernism.* Bloomington: Indiana University Press, 1986, 179–221.

Jacoby, Mario. *The Longing for Paradise: Psychological Perspectives on an Archetype,* trans. Myron B. Gubitz. Boston: Sigo Press, 1985.

Johnston, John. "Ideology, Representation, Schizophrenia: Toward a Theory of the Postmodern Subject." In *After the Future: Postmodern Times and Places*, ed. Gary Shapiro. New York: State University of New York Press, 1990, 67–95.

Joplin, Patricia Klindienst. "The Authority of Illusion: Feminism and Fascism in Virginia Woolf's Between the Acts." In *Virginia Woolf: A Collection of Critical Essays*, ed. Margaret Homans. Englewood Cliffs, N.J.: Prentice-Hall, 1993, 210–26.

Jouve, Nicole Ward. "Of Mud and Other Matter—*The Children of Violence*." In *Notebooks/Memoirs/Archives: Reading and Rereading Doris Lessing*, ed. Jenny Taylor. Boston: Routledge and Kegan Paul, 1982, 75–134.

Joyner, Nancy. "The Underside of a Butterfly: Lessing's Debt to Woolf." *Journal of Narrative Technique* 4, no. 3 (September 1974): 204–11.

Jung, Carl G. *The Collected Works of C. G. Jung*. 20 vols. New York: Pantheon, 1953-[1979]. Bollingen Series 20.

Kaivola, Karen. *All Contraries Confounded: The Lyrical Fiction of Virginia Woolf, Djuna Barnes, and Marguerite Duras*. Iowa City: University of Iowa Press, 1991.

Kaplan, E. Ann. "Feminism/Oedipus/Postmodernism: The Case of MTV." In *Postmodernism and Its Discontents*, ed. E. Ann Kaplan. New York: Verso, 1988, 30–44.

Kaplan, Sidney Janet. *Katherine Mansfield and the Origins of Modernist Fiction*. New York: Cornell University Press, 1991.

Keller, Mara Lynn. "The Eleusinian Mysteries of Demeter and Persephone: Fertility, Sexuality, and Rebirth." *Journal of Feminist Studies in Religion* 4, no. 1 (Spring 1988): 27–54.

Kerenyi, C. *Eleusis: Archetypal Image of Mother and Daughter*, trans. Ralph Manheim. New York: Schocken, 1977.

———. "Kore." In C. G. Jung and C. Kerenyi, *Essays on a Science of Mythology*, trans. R. F. C. Hull. Princeton: Princeton University Press, 1969, 101–55.

Kristeva, Julia. "Women's Times," trans. Alice Jardine and Harry Blake. In *Feminist Theory: A Critique of Ideology*, ed. N. Keohane, M. Rosaldo, and B. Gelpi. Chicago: University of Chicago Press, 1981, 31–53.

Laurence, Patricia Ondek. *The Reading of Silence: Virginia Woolf in the English Tradition*. Stanford: Stanford University Press, 1991.

Leaska, Mitchell A., ed. *A Passionate Apprentice: The Early Journals. 1907–1909/Virginia Woolf*. New York: Harcourt, 1990.

Lilienfeld, Jane. "The Deceptiveness of Beauty: Mother Love and Mother Hate in *To the Lighthouse*." *Twentieth Century Literature* 23 (October 1977): 345–76.

—————. "'Like a Lion Seeking Whom He Could Devour': Domestic Violence in *To the Lighthouse.*" In *Virginia Woolf Miscellanies: Proceedings of the First Annual Conference on Virginia Woolf,* ed. Mark Hussey and Vara Neverow-Turk. Lanham, Md.: Pace University Press, 1992, 154–64.

Little, Judy. "Festive Comedy in Woolf's *Between the Acts.*" *Women and Literature* (Spring 1977): 26–37.

Lukens, Rebecca J. "Inevitable Ambivalence: Mother and Daughter in Doris Lessing's *Martha Quest.*" *Doris Lessing Newsletter* 2 (Winter 1978): 13–14.

Lynch, Kevin. *The Image of the City.* Cambridge, Mass.: MIT Press, 1960.

—————. *What Time is This Place.* Cambridge, Mass.: MIT Press, 1972.

Lyon, George Ella. "Virginia Woolf and the Problem of the Body." In *Virginia Woolf: Centennial Essays,* ed. Elaine K. Ginsberg and Laura Moss Gottlieb. New York: Whitston, 1983, 111–25.

Maika, Patricia. *Virginia Woolf's* Between the Acts *and Jane Harrison's Conspiracy.* Ann Arbor: UMI Research Press, 1987.

Marcus, Jane. "Britannia Rules The Waves." In *Virginia Woolf: A Collection of Critical Essays,* ed. Margaret Homans. Englewood Cliffs, N.J.: Prentice-Hall, 1993, 227–48.

—————. "Pargeting 'The Pargiters': Notes of an Apprentice Plasterer." *Bulletin of the New York Public Library* (Spring 1977): 416–35.

—————. "Pathographies: The Virginia Woolf Soap Operas." *Signs* 17, no. 4 (Summer 1992): 806–19.

—————. "Taking the Bull by the Udders: Sexual Difference in Virginia Woolf—A Conspiracy Theory." In *Virginia Woolf and Bloomsbury,* ed. Jane Marcus. Bloomington: Indiana University Press, 1987, 146–69.

—————. "Thinking Back Through Our Mothers." In *New Feminist Essays on Virginia Woolf,* ed. Jane Marcus. Lincoln: University of Nebraska Press, 1981, 1–30.

—————. "Virginia Woolf and Her Violin: Mothering, Madness, and Music." In *Virginia Woolf: Centennial Essays,* ed. Elaine K. Ginsberg and Laura Moss Gottlieb. Troy, N.Y.: Whitston, 1983, 27–49.

Melville, Herman. *Moby Dick, or The Whale* (1851). Rpt. New York: Bobbs-Merrill, 1964.

Miles, David H. "The Picaro's Journey to the Confessional: The Changing Image of the Hero in the German *Bildungsroman.*" *PMLA* 89 (1973): 980–92.

Minow-Pinkney, Makiko. *Virginia Woolf and the Problem of the Subject.* New Brunswick, N.J.: Rutgers University Press, 1987.

Mitgang, Herbert. "Mrs. Lessing Addresses Some of Life's Puzzles." *New York Times,* April 22, 1984, 16.

Moi, Toril. *Sexual/Textual Politics: Feminist Literary Theory.* New York: Methuen, 1985.

Moody, Anthony David. *Virginia Woolf.* New York: Grove, 1963.

Moore, Madeline. *The Short Season Between Two Silences: The Mystical and the Political in the Novels of Virginia Woolf.* Boston: George Allen & Unwin, 1984.

Morley, Hilda. "A Lesson in Floating." In *A Blessing Outside Us.* Providence, R.I.: Pourboire, 1979, 12–14.

Morson, Gary Saul, and Caryl Emerson. *Mikhail Bakhtin: Creation of a Prosaics.* Stanford, Calif.: Stanford University Press, 1990.

Naremore, James. *The World without a Self: Virginia Woolf and the Novel.* New Haven: Yale University Press, 1973.

Olano, Pamela J. "'Women alone stir my imagination': Reading Virginia Woolf as a Lesbian." In *Virginia Woolf: Themes and Variations, Selected Papers from the Second Annual Conference on Virginia Woolf,* ed. Vara Neverow-Turk and Mark Hussey. New York: Pace University Press, 1993, 158–71.

Panken, Shirley. *Virginia Woolf and the 'Lust of Creation': A Psychoanalytical Exploration.* Albany: State University of New York Press, 1987.

Pascal, Roy. *Design and Truth in Autobiography.* Cambridge, MA: Harvard University Press, 1960.

Perkins, D. N. *The Mind's Best Work.* Cambridge, MA: Harvard University Press, 1981.

Plath, Sylvia. *The Bell Jar.* New York: Bantam, 1971.

Ragland-Sullivan, Ellie. *Jacques Lacan and the Philosophy of Psychoanalysis.* Urbana: University of Illinois Press, 1986.

Raitt, Suzanne. *Virginia Woolf's To the Lighthouse.* New York: St. Martin's Press, 1990.

Raskin, Jonah. "Doris Lessing at Stony Brook: An Interview." *New American Review* (1969), 166–179. Rpt. in *A Small Personal Voice,* ed. Paul Schlueter. New York: Vintage, 1975, 61–76.

Rich, Adrienne. "Compulsory Heterosexuality and the Lesbian Existence." In *Blood, Bread, and Poetry: Selected Prose 1979–1985.* New York: Norton, 1986, 23–75.

———. *Of Woman Born: Motherhood as Experience and Institution.* 10th anniversary ed. New York: Norton, 1986.

Rieff, Philip. *Freud: The Mind of the Moralist.* New York: Viking, 1959.

Rigney, Barbara Hill. *Madness and Sexual Policitics in the Feminist Novel.* Madison: University of Wisconsin Press, 1978.

Risolo, Donna. "Outing Mrs. Ramsay: Reading the Lesbian Subtext in Virginia Woolf's *To the Lighthouse.*" In *Virginia Woolf: Themes and Variations, Selected Papers from the Second Annual Conference on Virginia Woolf,* ed. Vara Neverow-Turk and Mark Hussey. New York: Pace University Press, 1993, 238–48.

Robinson, Annabel. "Something Odd at Work: The Influence of Jane Harrison on *A Room of One's Own.*" *Wascana Review* 22, no. 1 (Spring 1987): 82–88.

Rose, Ellen Cronan. "Doris Lessing's *Citta Felice.*" *The Massachusetts Review* 24 (Summer 1983): 369–86. Rpt. in *Critical Essays on Doris Lessing,* ed. Claire Sprague and Virginia Tiger. Boston: G.K. Hall, 1986, 141–53.

Rosenman, Ellen Bayuk. *The Invisible Presence: Virginia Woolf and the Mother-Daughter Relationship.* Baton Rouge: Louisiana State University Press, 1986.

Rubenstein, Roberta. *The Novelistic Vision of Doris Lessing: Breaking the Forms of Consciousness.* Urbana: University of Illinois Press, 1979.

Savater, Ferdinand. *Childhood Regained: The Art of the Story Teller,* trans. Frances M. Lopez Morillas. New York: Columbia University Press, 1982.

Schulkind, Jeanne. Introduction to Virginia Woolf, *Moments of Being.* New York: Harcourt, 1976, 11–27.

Seltzer, Alvin J. *Chaos in the Novel: The Novel in Chaos.* New York: Schocken Books, 1974.

Shah, Idries. *The Sufis.* Garden City, N.J.: Anchor-Doubleday, 1971.

———. *The Way of the Sufi.* New York: E. P. Dutton & Co., Inc., 1969.

Shattuck, Sandra D. "The Stage of Scholarship: Crossing the Bridge from Harrison to Woolf." In *Virginia Woolf and Bloomsbury: A Centenary Celebration,* ed. Jane Marcus. Bloomington: Indiana University Press, 1987, 278–98.

Shaw, Christopher, and Malcolm Chase. *The Imagined Past: History and Nostalgia.* Manchester and New York: Manchester University Press, 1989.

Showalter, Elaine. *The Female Malady.* New York: Pantheon, 1985.

Singleton, Mary Ann. *The City and the Veld: The Fiction of Doris Lessing.* Lewisburg, Penn.: Bucknell University Press, 1977.

Sizemore, Christine W. *A Female Vision of the City: London in the Novels of Five British Women.* Knoxville: University of Tennessee Press, 1989.

Spilka, Mark. *Virginia Woolf's Quarrel with Grieving.* Lincoln and London: University of Nebraska Press, 1980.

Sprague, Claire. "Doubles Talk in *The Golden Notebook*" (1982). In *Critical Essays on Doris Lessing,* ed. Claire Sprague and Virginia Tiger. Boston: G. K. Hall, 1986, 44–60.

————. *Rereading Doris Lessing.* Chapel Hill: University of North Carolina Press, 1987.

Squier, Susan Merrill. *Virginia Woolf and London: The Sexual Politics of the City.* Chapel Hill: University of North Carolina Press, 1985.

Stamberg, Susan. "An Interview with Doris Lessing." *Doris Lessing Newsletter* 8, no. 2 (1984): 3, 4, 15.

Stemerick, Martine. "Virginia Woolf and Julia Stephen: The Distaff Side of History." *Virginia Woolf: Centennial Essays,* ed. Elaine K. Ginsberg and Laura Moss Gottlieb. Troy, N.Y.: Whitston, 1983, 51–80.

Stevenson, Sheryl. "Language and Gender in Transit: Feminist Extensions of Bakhtin." In *Feminism, Bakhtin, and the Dialogic.* Albany: State University of New York Press, 1991.

Stewart, Grace. *The New Mythos: The Novel of the Artist as Heroine 1877–1977.* St. Alban's, Vt.: Eden Press, 1977.

Sukenick, Lynn. "Feeling and Reason in Doris Lessing's Fiction." *Contemporary Literature* 14, no. 4 (Autumn 1973): 515–35.

Suleri, Sara. "Woman Skin Deep: Feminism and the Postcolonial Condition." *Critical Inquiry* 18, no. 4 (Summer 1992): 756–59.

Taylor, Jenny. "Memory and Desire on Going Home: The Deconstruction of a Colonial Radical." In *Doris Lessing,* ed. Eve Bertelsen. Johannesburg: McGraw-Hill, 1985, 55–63.

Tiger, Virginia. Review of Doris Lessing, "Impertinent Daughters" and "Autobiography (Part Two): My Mother's Life." *Doris Lessing Newsletter* 10, no. 2 (Fall 1986): 7, 14.

Tobin, Jean. "Virginia Woolf's *The Waves* and *The Years* as Novel of Vision and Novel of Fact," Ph.D. diss. University of Wisconsin, 1973. Ann Arbor: UMI, 1973, DDJ74-10271.

Todorov, Tzvetan. *Mikhail Bakhtin: The Dialogical Principle,* trans. Wlad Godzich. Minneapolis: University of Minnesota Press, 1984.

Tola de Habich, Fernando, and Patricia Grieve, eds. *Los Espanoles y el Boom.* Caracas, Venezuela: Editorial Teimpo Nuevo, 1971, 213–21.

Tuan, Yi-Fu. *Space and Place: The Perspectives of Experience.* Minneapolis: University of Minnesota Press, 1977.

Tvordi, Jessica. "*The Voyage Out:* Virginia Woolf's First Lesbian Novel." In *Virginia Woolf: Themes and Variations, Selected Papers from the Second Annual Conference on Virginia Woolf,* ed. Vara Neverow-Turk and Mark Hussey. New York: Pace University Press, 1993, 226–37.

Tyler, Lisa. "Classical, Biblical, and Modernist Myth: Doris Lessing's 'Flavours of Exile.'" *Doris Lessing Newsletter* 15, no. 2 (Summer 1993): 3, 10–11, 13.

————. "Our Mothers' Gardens: Mother-Daughter Relationships and Myth in Twentieth Century British Women's Literature." Ph.D. diss. Ohio State University, 1991.

Walker, Alice. *In Search of Our Mothers' Gardens: Womanist Prose.* New York: Harcourt, 1983.

Wang, Ban. " 'I' on the Run: Crisis of Identity in Mrs. Dalloway." *Modern Fiction Studies* 38, no. 1 (1992): 177–91. Virginia Woolf Special Issue.

Watson, Barbara Bellow. "Leaving the Safety of Myth: Doris Lessing's *The Golden Notebook* (1962)." In *Old Lines, New Forces: Essays on the Contemporary British Novel 1960–1970,* ed. Robert K. Morris. Rutherford, N.J.: Fairleigh Dickinson University Press, 1976, 12–37.

Waugh, Patricia. *Feminine Fictions: Revisiting the Postmodern.* New York: Routledge, 1989.

Weedon, Chris. *Feminist Practice and Poststructuralist Theory.* New York: Basil Blackwell, 1987.

Weisberg, Robert W. *Creativity: Beyond the Myth of Genius.* New York: Freeman, 1993.

Wilde, Alan. "Touching Earth: Virginia Woolf and the Prose of the World." In *Philosophical Approaches to Literature,* ed. William E. Cain. Cranbury: Bucknell University Press, 1984, 140–64.

Wilson, Robert Anton. "Doris Lessing: The Unpredictable Novelist's Mystical Leanings Are Tempered by Down-To-Earth Skepticism." *New Age Journal,* January 1984, 30–34, 89–92.

Wirth-Nesher, Hannah. "The Modern Jewish Novel and the City: Franz Kafka, Henry Roth and Amos Oz." *Modern Fiction Studies* 24, no. 1 (Spring 1978): 91–109.

Woodring, Carl. *Virginia Woolf.* New York: Columbia University Press, 1966.

Wussow, Helen. "War and Conflict in *The Voyage Out.*" In *Virginia Woolf and War: Fiction, Reality, and Myth,* ed. Mark Hussey. Syracuse, N.Y.: Syracuse University Press, 1991, 101–9.

Wyatt, Jean. "Avoiding Self-Definition: In Defense of Women's Right to Merge (Julia Kristeva and *Mrs. Dalloway*)." *Women's Studies* 13 (1986): 115–26.

Ziegler, Heide, and Christopher Bigsby, eds. "Doris Lessing." In *The Radical Imagination and the Liberal Tradition: Interviews with English and American Novelists.* London: Junction, 1982, 190–208.

Zwerdling, Alex. *Virginia Woolf and the Real World.* Berkeley: University of California Press, 1986.

# INDEX